THE
WEALTH
OF
RACES

Recent Titles in
Contributions in Afro-American and African Studies

THE WEALTH OF RACES

The Present Value of Benefits from Past Injustices

Edited by RICHARD F. AMERICA

Contributions in Afro-American and African Studies, Number 132

BLOOMSBURY ACADEMIC
NEW YORK · LONDON · OXFORD · NEW DELHI · SYDNEY

BLOOMSBURY ACADEMIC
Bloomsbury Publishing Inc
1385 Broadway, New York, NY 10018, USA
50 Bedford Square, London, WC1B 3DP, UK
29 Earlsfort Terrace, Dublin 2, Ireland

BLOOMSBURY, BLOOMSBURY ACADEMIC and the Diana logo
are trademarks of Bloomsbury Publishing Plc

First published in the United States of America by ABC-CLIO 1990
Paperback edition published by Bloomsbury Academic 2024

A catalog record for this book is available from the Library of Congress.

ISBN: HB: 978-0-3132-5753-7
PB: 979-8-7651-2374-4

Series: Contributions in Afro-American and African Studies: Contemporary Black Poets

To find out more about our authors and books visit www.bloomsbury.com
and sign up for our newsletters.

Virginia Gazette, No. 779, April 25, 1766

Warwick County, April 8, 1766

Run away from the subscriber, on or about the 20th of February last, a Virginia born Negro man named George America, about 5 feet 8 or 9 inches high, about 30 years old, of a yellow complexion. Is a tolerable good shoemaker and can do something of the house carpenter's work. Walks quick and upright, and has a scar on the back of his left hand; had on a cotton waistcoat and breeches, osnabrug shirt, and yarn stockings. As the said slave is outlawed, I do hereby offer a reward of 5 L to any person that will kill and destroy him, and 40 s if taken alive.

Thomas Watkins

Dedicated to George America and to all the descendants of his and of Thomas Watkins, direct and indirect. Let justice roll down like a mighty stream.

Contents

Figures

Tables

Acknowledgments

This project evolved over many years. At Stanford Research Institute in the late 1960s, two colleagues, Robert K. Arnold and Ben Lefkowitz, stimulated my thinking about social policy. Then at the University of California, Berkeley, Edwin Epstein and Dean Richard Holton, made possible three productive years where I could pursue this and other ideas.

I also had an opportunity to discuss some of the ideas in their early form at the Rand Corporation, thanks to an invitation from Anthony Pascale.

I appreciate the forum provided annually by the National Economic Association. The support of the members allows concepts like these to develop. That is one reason the NEA was formed, and it is fulfilling that function well.

Michael R. Winston, over the years, has been a source of insight and encouragement.

At Greenwood Press, Cynthia Harris, Arlene Belzer, Maureen Melino, and Betty Pessagno nursed the project along through delays and diversions.

I thank the contributors for being willing to venture and stretch and an anonymous reviewer for helpful suggestions.

I thank my wife Dino and daughter Amy for general support and good humor.

I, of course, accept responsibility for weaknesses and defects in the book. I trust that, despite shortcomings, it will further investigation, and, ultimately, a wide range of fruitful results in both domestic and international policy.

Introduction

Past interracial relations in labor and capital markets, and in education and training, have continuing effects. Through intergenerational transfers and carryovers, they significantly influence current shares of income and wealth by class and race. Until recently, however, few people had any curiosity about these effects or any sense of their magnitudes. Moreover, only a small number had any idea about who benefited or by how much. As in other areas of policy analysis and social science, we are now beginning to be able to measure what had previously been unmeasured. The results are likely to make enormous differences in how we view the world and how we behave.

This volume sheds light on the extent of benefits that large numbers of Americans are currently realizing from past economic relationships which to this day continue to damage large numbers of others. It is both useful and enlightening to know how the current absolute and relative economic standing of large social groups, such as races, have been affected by past policies and practices, especially those that are currently illegal or considered wrongful and immoral, but that were once acceptable. Understanding such unjust enrichments may have public policy implications. The primary focus of several of the chapters in this volume is on systematic remedy in the form of targeted redistributive investment in housing, education, small business, and capital development through the progressive tax structure.

The central public policy issues affecting housing, employment training, health, family planning, education, business development, and capital formation, through set asides and affirmative action, that are race related, all involve redistributing scarce resources, thereby changing the relative economic (and social and political) standing of major social groups. Those issues obviously remain controversial, and it might help if we better understood how classes and races derive their income and wealth in the first place.

We may have not been able to conceive of more effective policy options because we lack information on how income and wealth distributions have been influenced by past practices that have now been rejected as unacceptable. Of course, any proposed income and wealth redistribution tends to meet resistance, in part, because we believe we are entitled to keep what we have, having earned it fairly and received it justly. But if income and wealth distributions derive, in part, from past injustices and transactions that violate current norms, we need to understand how that happened. Economic injustice, in this case, racial discrimination, exclusion and exploitation in employment, education, housing, and business development, produces benefits for some people. The primary beneficiaries are investors and higher skilled craft specialists, merchants, administrators, managers, and professionals earning, or likely to earn, incomes in the top 30 percent of the distribution. They benefit by having a stream of income and investment in their human capital diverted to them, which in the presence of fair competition and fair educational and training expenditures instead of racially exclusionary practices would have flowed to others.

If the present value of the flow of benefits can be measured from these past transactions, it may be a useful measure no matter how crude our initial attempts. Techniques can be refined and data improved. In 1983, for example, blacks represented roughly 12 percent of the U.S. population. Had they received 12 percent of total income instead of the 7.2 percent they actually received, that year they would have earned $264 billion instead of $159 billion. Half of the $105 billion gap may be explained by unjust distortions, such as discrimination in employment decisions. If so, that $52 billion may not have merely been lost. Instead, it may have been diverted interracially to others, who thereby received a kind of unjust enrichment. If this annual injustice accumulates, and is carried over and compounded, it may contribute significantly to the current income and wealth shares of the classes that benefit. By one estimate, the value of the benefits that accrued from labor market discrimination alone for the 1929–1969 period, measured in current dollars, was over $600 billion.

Discriminatory practices based on religion, ethnicity, and gender as well as race— all have incurred official sanction over the past decades. In this book we consider one important type, racial discrimination, and examine some of the benefits. The approach might later be replicated with other forms of injustice.

But probably the greatest benefit from past discrimination is not directly addressed in this volume. Human capital endowments of those in the top 30 percent of the income distribution have been enhanced relative to the human capital of those in the bottom 30 percent. Racially, whites in general benefited at the expense of blacks. That is, over 350 years, decision makers, legislators, governors, mayors, education superintendents, boards of education, and others have consistently and systematically allocated scarce educational funds that could have been distributed more equitably in a manner that grossly favored whites. On-the-job training opportunities have likewise been skewed. As a result, it is likely that several trillion dollars of expected lifetime earnings that can be anticipated by whites today should instead have been capitalized in the black labor force. In this important sense, this aspect of the wealth of races probably overshadows those factors that have so far been estimated.

From 1981 through 1985 these issues were addressed in a series of panels held at the annual meetings of the National Economic Association, the professional organization of black economists that meets concurrently with the American Economic Association. In creating these panels and inviting papers, it was assumed that there might be a kind of social debt arising out of past discriminatory practices. This volume includes several of the papers presented at those sessions along with several others invited separately.

There is no final consensus as to whether real unjust enrichments have currently resulted from past discriminatory practices. Several of the chapters do not reach that conclusion. The point of the volume is to begin the exploration, not to settle the questions finally. Clearly, opportunity costs to the economy as a whole, as well as to specific classes, arose from slavery and discrimination. Several chapters stress those costs. Others caution about the emphasis on quantification, "going for the numbers." There are numerous cautionary flags and caveats. The results shed new light on troubling questions of race, class, and distributive justice, and serve as a point of departure for future analysis and debate.

This book has a straightforward organization intended to create an integrated discussion. William Darity's overview chapter sets the project in historical context, offers a summary and critique of each chapter, and provides a point of departure for future research. In Part II, Stanley L. Engerman; Roger L. Ransom and Richard Sutch; and Sheryl Bailey-Williams establish the need to proceed with caution when we attempt the kind of estimation and policy creativity that unavoidably rests on models that can be disputed and on assumptions that can be challenged. The third part explores the economic impact of slavery and discrimination on labor market functioning and includes chapters by Warren C. Whatley and Gavin Wright; Larry Neal; James Marketti; Richard Vedder, Lowell Gallaway, and David C. Klingaman; and Susan F. Feiner, and Bruce B. Roberts. In Part IV David H. Swinton; The Berkeley Working Paper; Sheldon Danziger and Peter Gottschalk; Stanley H. Masters; and Lynn C. Burbridge bring the discussion up to the present and examine some of the redistributive policy implications of the various approaches to analysis of the costs and benefits of slavery and discrimination. Finally, Robert S. Browne's chapter capsulizes the broad policy setting in which the work can be carried forward.

PART I

Overview and Summary

Is it possible to measure the costs and benefits to entire social classes from past practices that involved their collective ancestors? How do we proceed when we rely on historical analyses to guide our thinking about current public policy in these matters? What do we need to keep in mind about the state of scholarly controversies regarding the effects of slavery on blacks and whites? What are the assumptions, historical and technical, that analysts need to make in order to make use of incomplete and ambiguous data and imperfect theory?

1.

Forty Acres and a Mule: Placing a Price Tag on Oppression

The late 1960s and early 1970s—a period of great social activism and ferment in the United States—witnessed a surge in calls from black Americans for reparations. Writing in 1974, Robert S. Browne, then director and founder of the Black Economic Research Center, interpreted the demand for reparations as a case for "a massive capital transfer of a sizeable chunk of America's wealth to the black community."[1] Data from the Survey of Economic Opportunity indicated that black families held no more than 2 percent of the nation's wealth.[2] Antipoverty programs and social welfare programs that left untouched what Browne viewed as the fundamental disparity in American society, the racial gap in ownership of the nation's wealth, were palliatives at best.

For Browne, racial differences in economic status and political influence found their origins in racial differences in capital asset ownership. Hence, reparations as a remedy meant a substantial redistribution of wealth. The rationale was twofold. First was a "moral justification deriving . . . from the debt owed to Blacks for the centuries of unpaid slave labor which built so much of the early American economy, and from the discriminatory wage and employment patterns to which Blacks were subjected after emancipation." Second was a justification based on "national self-interest"—Browne's perception that such "gross inequities" in the distribution of wealth would only further aggravate social tensions between blacks and whites.[3]

Apparently, neither justification subsequently has proved compelling for American legislators. No scheme of reparations of the type Browne advocated ever has been adopted in the United States. However, by 1988 the U.S. Congress had approved legislation mandating an official national apology and payment of $20,000 in reparations to living Japanese Americans who had been subjected to the notorious World War II "internment."[4] Also in 1988, the giant West German industrial firm, Daimler-Benz, agreed to pay 20 million marks (or $11.7 million) to victims of Nazi forced labor policies during the same war, as well as their families.[5] In fact, under the conditions of an agreement signed in Luxembourg in 1952 between West Germany and the World Jewish Congress, the West German government now has paid up to $48 billion in reparations to Holocaust survivors.[6]

In the early 1980s a settlement finally was reached out of court that mediated the claims to land of the Passamaquoddy Indian tribe in Maine in a lawsuit they brought against the U.S. secretary of the Interior. The agreement established that "present members of the tribe are to receive money and some undeveloped lands—the money for the Indian plaintiffs and the cash compensation to those giving up land coming from [the] U.S. Treasury."[7]

There is clear evidence that a certain class of events and policies lie so far beyond the realm of contemporary standards of human decency that a consensus can be reached that the victims—and even their descendants—merit compensation. In the case of Japanese Americans "relocated" from their homes to such camps as Manzanar, the monetary compensation is to be paid to the direct victims. In the case of the victims of Nazi policies, monetary compensation has been paid not only to surviving victims but also to their relatives. In the case of the Passamaquoddy Indians, while the full expanse of their one-time tribal territories was not restored, the compensation goes to tribal members several generations removed from the period when tribal lands were expropriated by Euro-Americans.

In all these cases an implicit or explicit price tag has been attached to acts of human oppression. Monetary compensation often is intended as a settling of accounts, eliminating, in principle, the basis for further claims of a pecuniary and/or moral nature. For instance, with respect to the Japanese-American recipients of the $20,000 reparations payment, they must "forswear any other legal claim against the [U.S.] government."[8] Similarly, the Passamaquoddy Indians de facto have foregone all further claims on lands, now held by private individuals, state and local governments, and large timber companies, that had been the domain of their tribal ancestors some 150 years ago.

It is this legal obligation to relinquish an ethical claim upon acceptance of reparations that disturbs even some of the victims. While her own archival research was instrumental in the success of the Japanese-American reparations campaign, Aiko Herzig Yoshinaga says she will not accept the money. She wants to continue to pursue a class-action suit against the U.S. government to get the Supreme Court to reconsider its 1944 opinion that the internment was a legal government action. Says Yoshinaga, "It'll hurt to say no to $20,000, but I want the Supreme Court to look at this. . . . Because no matter how nice money is, it cannot pay you for the loss of your liberty."[9] Paradoxically, a Republican senator from Wyoming, Malcolm Wallop, made a related observation when he described Congress' action in passing the law as "an 'astonishing act of materialism' [trying] to 'buy a clean conscience' with a mere $20,000 per head.'"[10]

Wallop also expressed concern that a Pandora's box of potential claimants now would be opened. The potential for compensation of American Indian "victims of the 'Trail of Tears' forced evacuation" in the nineteenth century—or, presumably, their descendants—would be a case of at least equal merit, according to Wallop.[11] Other congressional opponents of the bill argued that black Americans also had a meritorious case, once the precedent for such reparations was established in U.S. law—as it already had been in West German law.

The obvious basis for reparations for black Americans stems from slavery times. Of course, there are ample precedents for compensation associated with slavery in the New World, but in all cases it was the *owners* of slaves who received compensation, rather than the slaves themselves or their descendants. One instance—the *Zong* tragedy—was reported by Eric Williams in his study of the role of the Atlantic slave system in British industrial development, in an appropriately sarcastic passage:

In 1781 the case of the ship "Zong" was argued in the Court of King's Bench. Short of water, the captain had thrown 132 slaves over board, and now brought an action for insurance, alleging that the loss of slaves fell within the clause of the policy which insured against "perils of the sea." Not only did the Court find for the plaintiff, awarding damages of £30 for each slave, but there was not the slightest attempt to instigate criminal proceedings against the captain and crew for wholesale homicide. It was no more, said [Lord] Mansfield, than throwing horses overboard. But the society for the prevention of cruelty to animals did not yet exist.[12]

Later, with the emancipation of the slaves in the British West Indies, the British government paid the planters £2 for every slave set free—a sum coming to £20 million.[13] Thus, those who disposed of the Africans as they saw fit, given the necessities and conveniences of commerce, and those who made use of the labor of the Africans were the recipients of compensation. But no compensation ever has been paid to the relatives or descendants of those slaves who died during the drive from the interior of Africa to the western coast, of those who died in the Middle Passage, or those who died during the "seasoning" period in the West Indies, or of those who lived to labor from sunup to sundown, under a regime of inherently forced labor, on New World plantations. Nor did emancipation bring reparations for the newly freed slaves, neither in the West Indies nor in the United States of America.

Presumably only the fact that slavery in the United States came to an end via civil war precluded serious congressional discussion of compensation for Southern planters for the loss of their slaves in the 1860s. Roger L. Ransom and Richard Sutch, in their contribution to this volume, estimate that slaves as property constituted roughly 15 percent of the total private assets in the U.S. economy in the two decades prior to the onset of the Civil War. If the proponents of emancipation had purchased an end to slavery by buying the slaves' freedom from their owners, the price would have been extremely high. By 1860 Ransom and Sutch estimate that the wealth held by Southern planters in the form of human property amounted to more than $3 billion. They suggest that the expense of conducting the Civil War for the North was even greater—$2 billion in direct costs coupled with the loss of 360,000 lives. Combined with Southern mortality and war expenditures, the total expense of the Civil War was 600,000 lives and $7 billion.

One is led to conclude, if rationality played any part in these proceedings, that considerations other than emancipation of the slaves must have been at stake. Still, even after the war, the freedmen never received their vaunted forty acres and a mule. But, if in the spirit of reparations, compensation was to be paid to the victims of slavery, rather than the slaveowners, what should have been the magnitude? What is the price tag that should have been assigned to three centuries of oppression?

Norman Girvan, in an interesting essay, has argued that Western exploitation of the Third World in general led to Western economic development, and, therefore, all Third World peoples should receive compensation. Girvan's estimates of the value of the exploitation attributable to the use of black slave labor during the period 1790–1860 alone, compounded to the present, range from $448 to $995 billion.[14] Critical to Girvan's claim is the argument that, in fact, exploitation of Third World peoples was instrumental to the emergence of a pattern of divergent economic development between the West and the rest of the world. Girvan, in effect, extends Eric Williams' hypothesis concerning the fundamental role of slavery and slave trading in the process of British industrialization to the entire run of relations between the West and the Third World since, presumably, the late fifteenth century.[15] From this standpoint compensation to the descendants of slaves must be linked to the evolution of the entire wealth of the Western nations.

This line of reasoning requires that some precision be given to the concept of "exploitation." The notion that emerges from neoclassical economics is payment to labor of a wage less than its marginal product, a notion advanced, ironically, by one of the great critics of neoclassical economics, Joan Robinson as well as her more orthodox Cambridge predecessor, A. C. Pigou. But the validity of the marginal product benchmark for what a "proper" wage possesses is contingent on laborers and employers arriving at contractual arrangements voluntarily on a "free" labor market. Indeed, if in fact slaves had received the equivalent of the value of their marginal products in the form of food, clothing, and shelter from the masters, would the conclusion then be that the slave system was nonexploitative? Is it feasible to assign a price that accounts for the intrinsic involuntariness of slavery? Sheryl Bailey-Williams resoundingly answers these questions in the negative in her chapter in this volume.

The case for compensation of any victims of oppression—whether economic or otherwise—rests on the ethical proposition that a community has stepped outside of certain acceptable boundaries in its treatment of particular groups. What is acceptable, of course, is relative to each historical time and place. Slavery had been an acceptable institution for many centuries throughout the world, but by the close of the nineteenth century, it no longer was in the West. Furthermore, slavery as it was practiced in the Atlantic slave system was not identical with the practice of slavery in other times and places. Nonetheless, the idea that laborers should be "free men," rather than slaves, indentures, or serfs for that matter, certainly gained prevalence throughout the nineteenth century.[16]

As Susan F. Feiner and Bruce B. Roberts point out in Chapter 9, Karl Marx would have argued that the freedom of the wage laborer is also illusory. For Marx, wage labor was no more than wage slavery. Wage laborers are also subjected to exploitation, but in the particular sense that they are compelled to work beyond the time required to produce their means of subsistence under capitalism. In fact, from a Marxist perspective in any social system where some perform surplus labor and others expropriate the products of such labor, exploitation occurs.

This means, in turn, that from the perspective of Marxist theory it is not useful to draw the line between free laborers and slave laborers as a means of distinguishing between nonexploitative and exploitative social arrangements. From the standpoint of Marx's substantive notion of exploitation, two possible conclusions follow: Either African slaves merit no special consideration since wage laborers also are exploited, or, since both groups have been exploited, compensation should be forthcoming not only to the descendants of African slaves but also to the descendants of members of Europe's eighteenth- and nineteenth-century proletariats.

Neoclassical-minded economists would not countenance or comprehend Marx's concept of wage slavery. Bound by a method of analysis that focuses solely on the sphere of exchange or commodity circulation, the neoclassical economist sees that sphere "within whose boundaries the sale and purchase of labour-power goes on . . . [as] the exclusive realm of Freedom, Equality, Property and Bentham."[17] Thus, neoclassical economists are led to rely on market prices for their estimates of exploitation and to calculate losses to blacks from slavery in terms of the gap between the slave's marginal product and the maintenance provided to the slaves.

This approach involves numerous technical problems; moreover, it is utterly devoid of the class-analytical concerns raised by Feiner and Roberts. Nevertheless, all the authors in this volume who construct estimates of the size of the reparations bill from a neoclassical perspective arrive at spectacular numbers.

The chapters by James Marketti, Richard Vedder, and his coauthors, and Larry Neal are all representative of the neoclassical approach. Marketti seeks to calculate the potential incomes which Africans lost by being enslaved. He uses the market price of slaves as his basis for calculating the incomes that slaves could have earned in the United States as free laborers. Implicitly, Marketti makes two peculiar assumptions: (1) He assumes Africans would have been present voluntarily in similar numbers in colonial labor markets in the absence of the forced migration engendered by the slave trade, and (2) even if Africans had been in the Americas as "free" laborers, he assumes that the hypothetical environment for income generation for blacks would have yielded wage rates equivalent to the prices the masters had to pay for blacks under slavery. Marketti's procedure also presumes that the pricing of slaves followed market fundamentals.

With respect to the second assumption, even today it can be asked whether relative prices find their determinants in market fundamentals. At minimum one can ask whether share prices on the New York Stock Exchange genuinely reflect careful and deliberate assessments of business's prospective yields by stock market participants. It is more likely that such an interpretation of the information content of share prices is rendered invalid by the circumstances described by John Maynard Keynes in the twelfth chapter of his *General Theory of Employment, Interest and Money*.[18]

Is there any reason to believe that the market for slaves was somehow immune from the impact of speculation in Keynes' sense? Can we treat the market for slaves, a market in capital assets, as invariant when transformed into a market for wage laborers? Given the fact that Marketti draws his data for slave prices from a year on the eve of the Civil War, there is no reason to believe that slave prices accounted solely, or even primarily, for the capitalized value of the annuity stream to be earned by the owner of a slave from working his human capital asset.

In their chapter Vedder, Gallaway, and Klingaman seek to estimate what whites, particularly Southern whites, gained in income from slavery. They conclude that the wealth of Southerners—at least those who were slaveowners—derived from slavery, compounded to the present, is virtually equal to the amount of wealth received from *all* sources today.

The three authors also contend that about one-quarter of the total income of whites in the Southern states was attributable to slave exploitation. How do Vedder, Gallaway, and Klingaman conceive of slave exploitation? They also adopt the Robinson-Pigou (neoclassical monopsony) concept, calculating the difference between the slaves' estimated marginal product and the estimated slave "wage." Based on this criterion, they find that the (neoclassical) rate of exploitation rose between 1820 and 1860. On the basis of their estimates they conclude that, whereas in 1820 slaves received 50 percent of their marginal product, by 1860 slaves received only 32 percent.

To arrive at their estimates, Vedder, Gallaway, and Klingaman also make arguable assumptions. In addition to their reliance on slave prices which leads them down Marketti's road, they also assume that the rate of return on slave production was *constant* at 7.51 percent throughout the last sixty years of U.S. slavery. They then calculate the marginal revenue product of the slave by multiplying this (assumed) constant rate of return times the slave price plus the slave "wage" (i.e., the cost of obtaining and maintaining the slave).

More interesting is their attempt to gauge the evolution of black-white income differences across 140 years. The imputation of an income to blacks under slavery in 1840, based on the estimated costs of slave maintenance, is questionable. So is their postbellum estimate of a black-white income ratio for 1880. Black per capita income is calculated as "the 1860 marginal revenue product reduced by 20.8% for the per capita commodity output decline in the south between 1860 and 1880 plus a further 20% for possible exploitation and discrimination," while white per capita income is calculated as "the 1860 white figure lowered by 20.8% for the estimated decline in per capita commodity output in the South" (p. 225). Nevertheless, they do construct a rough-and-ready secular description of the path of racial income inequality in the United States, per capita income ratios for the years 1840, 1860, and 1880, and family income ratios for 1907–1909, 1935–1936, 1947, 1964, and 1985. Comparing 1880 and 1985, the authors conclude that blacks' "relative economic status is not dramatically different than it was a century ago" (p. 000).

Both the Marketti and Vedder, Gallaway, and Klingaman calculations—the Marketti based on a concept of income lost to blacks and the Vedder based on a concept of income gains to whites from slavery—lead to enormous sums for reparations. Vedder and his coauthors arrive at a $3.2 million estimate in 1859 dollars for the total wealth accumulated from slavery in the South by the onset of the Civil War. This estimate is virtually identical with Ransom and Sutch's measure of Southern wealth from slavery. If the sum were compounded to the present and adjusted for inflation to convert it into a 1990 dollar measure, it would be a huge amount of money.

Larry Neal does exactly that in his chapter. He also makes assumptions akin to those of Marketti and Vedder, Gallaway, and Klingaman. For example, Neal assumes that all wages and prices would have been the same in the South prior to 1860, regardless of whether blacks were slaves or free. Nevertheless, he estimates that the present value of unpaid net wages to blacks before emancipation, after adjusting for inflation, would come to $1.4 trillion. This is a far larger figure than Neal's estimate of the net benefit to American society of free immigrant labor for the entire period 1790–1912. Note that if $1.4 trillion was distributed on a per capita basis to the nation's 25 million blacks in a lump sum, in payment for the enslavement of their ancestors, each of today's blacks would receive $56,000 (presumably tax free).

Other contributors to this volume are concerned less with black compensation for slavery than with compensation for discrimination during all the decades after emancipation. Estimates of gains to whites and/or losses to blacks from discrimination are no less enormous.

In Chapter 10 David Swinton contends that 40 to 60 percent of the disparity between current black and white median incomes is due to discrimination. Swinton espouses racial parity and proposes reparations as a mechanism to attain equality, reparations for both "the legacy of discrimination and enslavement for the living black population" (p. 000), since both processes severely inhibited black wealth accumulation. Swinton's conservative estimate of the social debt to blacks was $500 billion in 1983, a sum he argues should be redistributed to blacks to make rapid progress toward racial economic inequality.

Swinton's estimate is of a similar order of magnitude as that of the Berkeley Working Paper. It's authors calculate that the gains to whites from labor market discrimination alone during the forty-year period 1929–1969 comes to a present value of $1.6 trillion, after compounding at 3 percent and adjusting for inflation.

The enormity of these numbers suggests one major reason why the black case for reparation—like the Native American case for full restoration of tribal lands—has not received the same reception, as, say, the Japanese-American case. A once-and-for-all redistribution of $1.4 to $1.6 trillion from whites to blacks would mean a comprehensive recomposition of American economic life. This would have very different implications from the distribution of $48 billion to international Jewry by the West German government spread over thirty-six years. The mere financing of such a massive redistribution of income to black Americans would have vast social repercussions.

Some have argued that black Americans already have received compensation in the form of social welfare programs and affirmative action measures.[19] Stanley Masters makes a case for affirmative action as reparations in Chapter 13. But as Sheldon Danziger and Peter Gottschalk show in Chapter 12, means-tested transfer programs of the American variety are not targeted exclusively at blacks (or the black poor for that matter), nor have they redistributed income disproportionately to blacks. Swinton points out that, nevertheless, cash and in-kind transfers "are more like compensation for current damages experienced each year for failure to correct the historic damages." In fact, Swinton's $500 billion of American social debt to blacks was calculated net of an estimate of $150 billion in the present value of expenditures on social programs. Indeed, affirmative action certainly does not constitute full compensation for past damages. Fourteen years ago, Robert Browne bluntly observed that "the poverty programs which have thus far been offered cannot be considered to be in the nature of reparations payments."[20]

If reparations are paid to blacks for slavery and/or discrimination, should it go to *all* blacks or only to those who display evidence of distress borne of this bitter legacy? Why compensate apparently successful, middle-class blacks? For a philosophically sound scheme of reparations would it not be necessary, as Warren C. Whatley and Gavin Wright suggest in Chapter 5, to undertake the difficult task of sorting between immediate and ultimate winners and immediate and ultimate losers from slavery and discrimination. A complex analysis of class relations, coalitions, and political power may reveal that some whites ("po white trash") suffered under the slave regime and some blacks (the black bourgeoisie) prospered behind the walls of segregation. Perhaps a reparations scheme must take intraracial heterogeneity into account. After all, when the Senate voted in favor of reparations for Japanese-American internees, Senator Chic Hecht of Nevada complained that the result would be monetary compensation for some who are now "multimillionaires."[21]

Other reparations schemes have not inquired about the current status of the living descendants of the victims or, when they are still living, the victims themselves. A wealthy child or grandchild of a victim of a Nazi concentration camp is considered no less eligible for reparations because of his or her own affluence. The war crime is typically viewed as so heinous, in and of itself, that it would be callous to raise questions about the current financial status of descendants.

The causal connection between the legacies of slavery and discrimination and the ongoing unequal economic status for black Americans seems self-evident. Consequently, there is a natural tendency to conflate the issue of compensation for historic social crimes against blacks with the issue of the economic status of blacks today. But these are, quite reasonably, issues that can be treated separately.

Indeed, in Chapter 2, Stanley Engerman raises the troubling question of whether we can connect the legacy of slavery to the contemporary economic status of black Americans. Lynn C. Burbridge makes the disturbing argument in Chapter 14 that reparations could mask systemic flaws that would perpetuate racial inequality even after redistribution. There still would be a need for initiatives to address persistent disparities. But if a massive racial redistribution of wealth somehow had been implemented, would there be any political wherewithal to pursue initiatives to address remaining racial inequality? Would it not appear, after reparations, that blacks must take full responsibility for any persistent racial differences?

But, again, if $1.4 to $1.6 trillion in wealth were somehow transferred from whites to blacks, American society would not look the same. Customary patterns and modes of behavior necessarily would be altered. Even if blacks remained, on average, relatively poorer, they would not remain relatively poorer in the same type of society. After all, apart from the increased demand for genealogists which black reparations would engender, it really is the stuff of fantasy to imagine white America turning more than $1 trillion of wealth over to black America.

After all, slavery and discrimination have not been mere "distortions" for the U.S. economy, somehow extrinsic to the normal workings of the American economy. They have played an integral organic role in shaping American economic and social life and must be understood, as the Marxist sociologist Oliver Cox would have argued, on those terms.[22]

In 1979 the Joint Economic Committee of the U.S. Congress held hearings on the cost to the U.S. economy of racial discrimination. The Congressional Research Service reported that the lower levels of employment and income for blacks cost the U.S. economy $93.5 billion in 1978. Melvin Humphrey, director of research for the Equal Opportunity Commission, estimated that blacks lost $61 billion in income between 1969 and 1974 because of racial differences in job assignments and wage differentials. By making a similar calculation Victor Perlo estimated that blacks and, as a result, the U.S. economy, were deprived of $123 billion in purchasing power in 1979.[23]

These are pretty calculations, but they are all made on the assumption that if racial discrimination were eliminated everything else would be much the same. Discrimination appears as a pure deadweight loss to *all* Americans. No attention is given to the interdependence between the incomes of blacks and whites, and the possibility that the incomes of whites are higher because the incomes of blacks are lower.

Discrimination and its precursor, slavery, have played an essential role in American history in partitioning paths of opportunity by race and class, although the permanence of such effects remains controversial. To compensate blacks for this American legacy is not a matter of paying blacks a large sum of money and leaving affairs otherwise unchanged. To finance and redistribute wealth on the scale imagined by Swinton or Neal or the Berkeley Working Paper would change affairs—perhaps in ways far beyond our capacity to predict. Those who now possess America's wealth, of course, will resist all calls for reparations, contending they are outrageous, despite ample precedents. They have the most to lose today and perhaps the most to fear from an unknown postreparations future. To overcome their resistance and to have reparations paid to black America—to get the forty acres and a mule—would require a revolutionary transformation of American society unto itself. Even then, would $1 trillion genuinely pay for the dark side of the heritage of blacks in America?

NOTES

1. Robert S. Browne, "Wealth Distribution and Its Impact on Minorities," *The Review of Black Political Economy* 4, no. 4 (Summer 1974):34.

2. Ibid.

3. Ibid., p. 33.

4. Helen Dewar, "Senate Votes to Give Apology, Compensation to Interned Japanese Americans," *Washington Post*, April 21, 1988, p. A9. The U.S. Senate's version of the bill also included a provision to make payments of $12,000 to 450 living Aleut Indian evacuees with supplementary funds to compensate them for their wartime losses.

5. Associated Press, "West German Firm to Pay WWII Forced Laborers Nearly $12 Million," *Dallas Morning News*, June 12, 1988, p. 27A.

6. Ibid.

7. Lance Liebman, "Anti-Discrimination Law: Groups and the Modern State," in Nathan Glazer and Ken Young, eds., *Ethnic and Public Policy: Achieving Equality in the United States and Britain* (London: Heinemann Educational Books Ltd., 1983), p. 14.

8. Marjorie Williams, "The 40-Year War of Aiko Yoshimaga," *Washington Post* August 4, 1988, pp. C1, C14.

9. Ibid.

10. Dewar, "Senate Votes to Give Apology," p. A9.

11. Ibid.

12. Eric Williams, "The Golden Age of the Slave System in Britain," *Journal of Negro History* 25, no. 1 (January 1940):104.

13. Karl Marx, "The Civil War in the United States," *Surveys From Exile: Political Writings*, Vol. 2 (New York: Vintage Books, 1974), p. 352n.12.

14. Norman Girvan, "The Question of Compensation: A Third World Perspective," *Race* 16 (July 1974):53–82.

15. On the Williams hypothesis, see Williams, "The Golden Age" and Eric Williams, *Capitalism and Slavery* (Chapel Hill: University of North Carolina Press, 1944).

16. See, David Brion Davis, *Slavery and Human Progress* (New York: Oxford University Press, 1984).

17. Karl Marx, *Capital*, Vol. 1 (New York: Vintage Books, 1977), p. 280.

18. J. M. Keynes, *The General Theory of Employment, Interest and Money* (London: Macmillan, 1936), pp. 147–64.

19. Boris Bittker in *The Case for Black Reparations* (New York: Random House, 1973), made a case for antipoverty measures as reparations.

20. Browne, "Wealth Distribution," p. 34.

21. Dewar, "Senate Votes to Give Apology," p. A9.

22. Oliver Cox, *Caste, Class, and Race* (New York: Monthly Reader, 1970).

23. "The Cost of Racial Discrimination," hearing before the Joint Economic Committee, Congress of the United States (Washington, D.C.: GPO, October 19, 1979).

Part II

Economic History and the Current Benefits and Costs of Slavery

Part II explores whether we can measure the present real value of bene-fits produced by long past acts. The heart of the book is the attempt to make this measurement and to discuss policy implications. Obviously, however, the analytical chapters are forced to rely on some assumptions that are open to questioning and criticism. It is well then to begin by spotlighting three chapters that raise caveats and set a healthy tone of skepticism.

Stanley Engerman, Roger Ransom and Richard Sutch, and Sheryl Bailey-Williams focus on the kinds of concerns that quickly come to mind in any departure from conventional modes of thinking such as this. They prepare the ground for a critical reading of the chapters that follow.

2.

Past History and Current Policy: The Legacy of Slavery

STANLEY L. ENGERMAN

Historians, driven by the desire to be relevant, frequently point to the implications of historical events for current policies as well as advocate a variety of policies based on their interpretation of the past. This tendency to link current policies to distant historical events is perhaps nowhere as strong as it is in the case of governmental policies toward black Americans based on the perceived legacy of slavery. Making such direct linkages, however, does not necessarily lead either to good scholarship or to appropriate policy advocacy. Historical analysis can provide significant insights into the effects of institutional structures on individual and group behavior, insights that cannot be gained by examining the present without considering the past or by analyzing behavior under only one institutional regime. This strength of historical analysis can be a weakness when applied directly to contemporary politics.

Several related aspects of historical research suggest this conclusion. As should be apparent to anyone who has followed the debates about the history of slavery and emancipation, some disagreement exists even about basic facts. Moreover, interpretations of historical events are often colored by current policy interests. While no research is conducted in a vacuum, impervious to disciplinary and political perspectives, too direct a link between past and present interests can seriously distort the interpretations of the past. Moreover, this can leave scholars in awkward, if not outright embarrassing positions when the direction of current policy thinking shifts or when the present views of the most appropriate or correct ways to see the past are altered.

Not so long ago, it seemed easy to link the current plight of blacks in America solely to the consequences of the slave experience. With a stress on the absolute legal powerlessness of the enslaved and an emphasis on what could happen (and did happen, though with less frequency than was legally possible), historians provided the view that slavery meant a stripping of social and psychological resources, and was a fully destructive experience. This view was consistent with the interpretation of slavery as a form of "original sin," leaving an indelible scar on both blacks and whites, and became the historical buttressing for one generation's approach to policy advocacy. It became easy, even obvious, to connect contemporary problems with the pre-1865 experience, although this approach frequently meant ignoring the experiences of the century after emancipation. Yet such a view of an "original sin," fixing the long-term future within relatively narrow bounds, can be highly misleading. With its quite pessimistic assumption concerning what can (or cannot) be accomplished in the short run and with its shift of focus from recent events more directly related to present conditions, the emphasis on the consequences of the slave experience alone could be the worst possible guide to current policy. Moreover, within the past decade, mainly in reaction to the extremely negative portrayal which this view provided of the black experience, black and white historians have reinterpreted the slave experience and presented a view of the richness of black slave culture. This reinterpretation provides an important corrective to past depictions, although it perhaps goes too far and pays insufficient regard to certain negative aspects. This reinterpretation can also be incomplete as a guide to policy, as it sometimes avoids discussing the implications of these cultural patterns, however appropriate for the past, for developments under present conditions. The full impact of this major reinterpretation of the slave experience on policy discussions remains to be seen, but at present it suggests surprisingly little influence in changing the nature of the policies advocated.

We can point to two examples in which the earlier direct link of current issues with the legacy of slavery and a failure to consider the richness of historical experience had provided a misleading analysis. First, the economic position of blacks relative to whites has varied over time, with periods of absolute and relative gain being interspersed with periods, such as the 1890s and the 1930s, of sharp reversal.[1] This suggests that the impact of discrimination, and the responses of blacks to economic opportunity, were not constant over time, and that shifts in the economic and political sphere influenced the working out of the legacy of slavery.

A second example, more widely discussed, concerns the black family. The Moynihan Report of the mid-1960s presented a picture of the black family, its problems and its links to slavery, then widely held by scholars, black and white.[2] The great attention Moynihan paid to the slave experience may be seen as an attempt (failed) to avoid political disputes about current causation; at the time it was as nearly a noncontroversial statement as seemed possible on the topic. The attack on Moynihan's views of historical forces and present-day circumstances took a number of quite different forms, even among those who did not dispute the data presented.

Some argued that what he called the current problems of the black families—female-headed households and illegitimacy—were not really problems, and to view them as such reflected a white middle-class misreading of black life. These patterns, it was argued, either reflected a retention of preslave African patterns or were the outcome of healthy and beneficial adaptations to the postslave experience. Others argued that these measures reflected, not merely slavery, but mainly the process of urbanization and northward migration of the twentieth century, with their destructive impact on the black family structure. Other critiques of Moynihan's data and analysis were presented. For example, it was pointed out that the measures used to describe family problems, such as the percentage of female-headed households, then characterized only about one-fifth of black families and was not the prevalent pattern among blacks. Note, however, that the last view had implications in regard to black culture quite different from those previously mentioned, even while agreeing that Moynihan had erred.

There is no need here to evaluate the onslaught on Moynihan's views and the accuracy of the depictions of past and present. Rather, to bring the record up to date, the next decade and a half led to a major series of reinterpretations of slavery to show that what some regarded as the difficulties, if not the impossibility, of the slave family were not omnipresent and that the slave family was more frequently headed by a father, was long-lived, and influenced by the slaves' beliefs than previously thought.[3] Yet, in these fifteen years there was a very sharp increase in the measured percentage of female-headed households and the percentage of total births that were illegitimate in the black community, increases even sharper than in the years prior to the Moynihan Report.[4] Thus, compared to the early 1960s, we now have a quite different historical view of the legacy of slavery in regard to the black family, while the measures used to argue for a "black family problem" were sharply accelerating, about a century after slavery had ended. Moreover, it should be noted that this acceleration took place at a time of relative improvement in the income position of blacks, another apparent puzzle worth more study.

The case of the black family, in particular, demonstrates the pitfalls of linking historical research and current policy. This brief synopsis was intended to point out that tracing the legacies of slavery through the intervening century is neither easy nor obvious. In addition, more important for our concerns, to attribute everything to the legacy of slavery can shift attention from the impact of the present economic, social, and political forces affecting blacks.

The advocacy of policy should be based on current issues and needs, without trying to draw direct messages from the past. The use of past examples might serve as a useful rhetorical device, but even then they provide few clear implications for specific policies, as debates among, and between, blacks and whites today indicate. The recent discussions of "the declining significance of race," of the different performance of U.S.–born blacks and West Indian migrants in the U.S. North, and of the impact of "affirmative discrimination," all point to the complexity of finding *one* legacy of slavery and of using that legacy to define appropriate public policy.[5]

My own research over the past decade has been concerned with economic and demographic aspects of slavery in the United States and British West Indies and with the analysis of the differing responses to emancipation in the nineteenth century. This research has provided a basis for comparing the slave and postslave experience in several areas, which helps place the experience of each area in a broader context. While, for reasons already described, the direct policy implications might seem few, given the century and more that has passed, reflections on specific issues—the growth and decline of the slave economies, the initial adjustments to emancipation, and the patterns of change in the period since emancipation—are possible. These point to the critical role of political and cultural, as well as economic, forces.

Slavery was an economic system that was profitable for European overseas settlers for over four centuries and, economically, was expanding rapidly in the nineteenth century. While one may argue about how long slavery could have continued on strictly economic grounds, and whether slave economies were capable of adjusting to the growing importance of industry, it is clear that, in the middle of the nineteenth century, profits from slaveownership were high, slave-produced outputs were expanding, slave prices were rising, and the demand for slaves remained high.[6] As Eric Williams, among others, argued, slavery played a key (even if not an indispensable) role in the economic growth of England, the United States, and Western Europe. The slave trade was a major economic link among four continents, and the trade in slave-grown products, particularly sugar, tobacco, and cotton, was an important part of European and American commerce and consumption.[7]

The U.S. slave experience was unique in one important regard. While North America received only about 5 percent of all the slaves sent from Africa to the New World over the nearly four centuries of forced movement, so high was the rate of natural increase (and the United States was the one large slave society where any natural increase occurred) that in the nineteenth and twentieth centuries the United States had about one-third of all blacks in the New World.[8] This difference in demographic performance was due not only to lower mortality, but also to the very high fertility of North American slaves, rates as high as those of white Southerners of the time. As a result, there were charges of slave breeding and extreme interference with the family life of slaves, a link posited between slavery and the postemancipation black family. This depiction of slave breeding is currently under contention, but the extremely high fertility of U.S. slaves can also be explained as being the result of differences in the material treatment of slaves, in slave culture, and in slave family patterns.[9]

Recent work has demonstrated that slavery was a very profitable business investment for slaveowners throughout the Americas. Slaveowners accumulated wealth, and to justify the high and rising prices paid for slaves they pointed to the increased productivity and sales of slave-produced commodities on the world market. The calculations of profitability, and of its correlate, exploitation of slave labor, have featured directly in providing arguments for one policy proposal: the discussion in the late 1960s and early 1970s of the case for black reparations, based on the value of income which the slaveowning class took from the slaves.[10] This argument for black reparations, it might be noted, has not been made recently, even though the reparations issue came up again in the claim of Japanese Americans for compensation for the time they spent in World War II internment camps. The basis for reparations is quite different, however, from that for black reparations.

The economic basis of the reparations claim raises some interesting analytical issues, in addition to the obvious moral and political arguments. By looking at some of them briefly, we can better understand the slave economy. First, the claim for reparations based on the exploitation captured in the market price of slaves understates the real costs of slavery to the enslaved, even within conventional economic measurement. The nonpecuniary aspects of increased labor supply and the undesirable conditions of enforced gang labor were considerable.[11] Second, the slaveowners in America were not the only beneficiaries of slave labor. Benefits also accrued to consumers of cotton, sugar, and other plantation products throughout the world, as well as to the original providers of slaves, the slave-trading classes within Africa. Thus, while highly profitable to slaveowners, the economic "benefits" of slavery were widely diffused throughout the continents involved in the system of slave trading and trading in slave-grown products.

Slavery ended throughout the New World in the nineteenth century, although in no case is there any indication that the planters would have terminated it voluntarily to get out of an unprofitable situation.[12] The economic unimportance of slavery might account for its legislated demise in the Northern United States by the early nineteenth century, as well as in Central and South America, but unimportance is not unprofitability. Where slavery was important, more dramatic measures were needed: slave revolt in St. Domingue; metropolitan legislation for colonies in the case of the British, French, Danish, Swedish, and Dutch West Indies, as well as Puerto Rico and Cuba; civil war in the United States; and internal political turmoil in Brazil. In no case, however, was there an economic decay of the institution independent of political and military factors. Nor did the slaveowners take the major initiating action, either privately or in the political sphere.

In the late eighteenth and nineteenth centuries, it was frequently debated whether slavery would soon erode economically and whether slave or free labor would be more productive.[13] A frequent implication was that immorality and economic inefficiency (efficiency here in the sense of total output from a given body of land, not in the more important sense of the sum of the welfare of all individuals) went together, but the events pointed to a rather different conclusion. Immorality did not mean an inability to produce high levels of output and to enrich the ruling classes, and those awaiting the economic demise of slavery dramatically understated the time period before that would have been a possible occurrence. Not for the first nor the last time, slavery indicated that immoral institutions could be highly productive for the ruling classes and that economic collapse was not a necessary outcome.

Without political and military intervention (as in the case of the U.S. South) slavery would not soon have died on its own. The causes of the attack on slavery and the reasons for its success have been widely debated in recent years, but no really satisfactory linking of economic interest groups to legislated emancipation is to be seen.[14] This is an anomaly to our cynical age, especially to those who would apply everywhere an economist's belief in the omnipresence of financial self-interest. Slavery had been widely accepted for many centuries in all societies, but once the issue was seriously raised at the end of the eighteenth century it took a whole century before legal slavery disappeared throughout the Western world. One century is hardly a short time, particularly to those who lived in that period, but the transition to widespread condemnation, after millennia of unquestioned acceptance, does represent a remarkable change. There were some false starts and halts in the successful march to abolition, but ultimate success was achieved by rather broad-based coalitions of groups whose reform energies were also applied in numerous other causes.

The legislated emancipations generally involved the payment of compensation, but the belief for past property rights was so widespread that this reparation (in the form of cash, bonds, and labor time) went to the former slaveowners. In no case were ex-slaves given compensation of land or money. At least initially, attempts were made to use the legal process and newly created government agencies to improve the position of the freedmen—and the landowners of the time would be quite surprised at the widespread opinion among today's historians that the U.S. Freedmen's Bureau and the West Indian stipendiary magistrates were solely tools of their interest. Yet, clearly, in both regions, the political impact of the freedmen and their white supporters weakened over time. The clear goals of ending the slave trade and slavery were superseded by more complex issues that did not provide clear-cut legal targets, and the racism in American societies persisted.

No consensus has developed as to the long-term impact of the failure to provide some compensation to the ex-slaves, such as the "forty acres and a mule" which U.S. blacks anticipated after the end of the Civil War. That such a redistribution would have some desired effects on black social and economic life seems clear, but that it could have really helped solve the longer term problems is somewhat more doubtful. The Civil War marked the larger scale entry of white yeoman farmers into the cotton economy, on land rented, for cash or shares, and more frequently, owned. Yet the economic hardships suffered by these Southern whites in the last quarter of the nineteenth century, particularly in the 1890s, demonstrate that small-scale landownership was not necessarily a basis of long-term economic independence and achievement.[15]

The plantation system was profitable because of its effectiveness in placing labor on large-scale units to produce export crops.[16] In the Caribbean sugar was the major crop, while in the United States the principal slave-grown crop shifted from tobacco in the eighteenth century to cotton in the nineteenth century. Sugar plantations were usually large establishments by the standards of the time, but even tobacco and cotton were produced on units larger than the family-sized farm.

When slavery ended, in the United States and elsewhere, generally the ex-slaves moved to smaller family-sized farms, whether sharecropped, rented, or, in some cases, owned.[17] The move to smaller farms could mean either production of the same export crop, as was the case for ex-slaves growing cotton in the U.S. South, or, more general elsewhere, the production of a different set of crops, such as food-stuffs, for sale in local markets. In all but a few cases sharp declines in measured crop output accompanied emancipation, the declines being particularly sharp in the production of export crops. The exceptions were areas with high population densities (such as Barbados and Antigua) and, for quite different reasons relating to changes in sugar technology in the late nineteenth century, Cuba. Cotton, unlike sugar, could be grown on smaller farms, albeit with some decline in productivity, and the choices open to ex-slaves in the West Indies were more limited than those faced by ex-slaves in the South. Few ex-slaves anywhere moved into industrial pursuits, and agriculture remained the predominant sector of production long after slavery ended. The U.S. South did suffer from the initial declines in crop output, but, unlike most areas, there was not a relative shift out of export production in subsequent decades. While the plantation areas of the Deep South did not participate to the same extent as did the other parts of the slave South, the overall rate of economic growth was quite rapid relative to that of the other ex-slave areas.

Where the plantation re-emerged as the major unit of production in the West Indies (Trinidad and British Guiana), it was not based on the labor of ex-slaves but rather on what some describe as "a new system of slavery"—indentured labor brought in from China and India. That the continuation of plantation production for export in the West Indies did not provide the base for a long-term economic development is clear, but, as demonstrated by the case of Haiti, neither did a shift to peasant production even with political independence. Despite the many and well-known problems, it may be that the rate of growth of ex-slave income was higher in the United States than it was elsewhere in the Americas. Despite the many problems, black land-ownership rates did rise from roughly zero in 1860 to about 25 percent in 1900.[18]

With regard to the economic basis of the slave plantation, it is clear that coercion was necessary to get the slaves to labor on these large units. The emancipation response indicates that ex-slaves were quite willing to pay a price (in terms of material consumption foregone) to be able to avoid the working conditions and social arrangements of the plantation.[19]

That coercion was the basis of the slave plantation does not, however, have necessary implications for questions of slave care and treatment, for the evolution of a system of labor incentives, and for the attitudes of the slave toward work and income.[20] Nor does it mean that the coercion was so extreme as to destroy the slave culture or to extinguish slave resistance. If there is one point on which most recent students of slavery agree, it is that the enslaved were able to maintain and develop a set of beliefs in regard to religion, family, and other aspects of life.[21] That slavery was less destructive than earlier believed is now widely held. That, of course, does not mean agreement on the origins of these beliefs, nor on the manner in which they influenced the generations born after slavery.

Even when broad agreement is reached on questions of material treatment (particularly consumption), as in general they have for the United States, questions still remain as to the longer term implications of different methods of providing foodstuffs and other articles of consumption. Did, for example, the weakening of the link between labor input and consumption lead to the development of habits of shirking, and work avoidance, that were not changed in the postemancipation world? Did the allocation of foodstuffs by masters, somewhat independent of individual slave input, as was more frequent in the United States, lead to different attitudes toward labor than were developed in those areas such as the West Indies, where the masters frequently provided only garden plots and the slaves were themselves required to provide the necessary labor but then were able to market the products themselves? These are among the reasons recently given to explain the differences in the economic performance of West Indian migrants to the United States relative to that of U.S.–born blacks, as well as the lower incomes of blacks than of Eastern European immigrants in the United States. While the latter comparison clearly understates the long-term impact of racism and discrimination, the basic question of work attitudes remains critical, both for evaluating the postbellum responses and for understanding the background to current circumstances.

They are interesting questions for recent discussions of black culture, as well as for the interpretation of black drives for education, income, and mobility in the immediate postemancipation period and afterward.[22] Despite much recent work, neither the correct answers, nor the implications, are yet obvious. The West Indian–U.S. comparison must also allow for the subsequent differences in political representation, the demographic differences (one area, the West Indies, 90 percent black, the other, the South, about 40 percent black) with their implications for differences in ex-slave economic functions and occupations, the constraints of crop technology and world market conditions, and the different lengths of time from the African past. Difficulties in accounting for these factors have not stopped people from trying to draw policy implications from the past. Nor, conversely, has disagreement in analyzing the choices made by ex-slaves between market involvement and self-sufficiency after emancipation, an issue with quite different implications for discussing the burden of racism and its effects on levels of income, necessarily meant disagreement on questions of current policy. Nevertheless, as historical and contemporary discussions of culture and attitudes toward work seem to be taking on greater importance, the examination of these past patterns provides a necessary background. These discussions are, of course, not unique to the situation of blacks today, being the most recent replay of the discussions of the nineteenth and early twentieth centuries on the possibilities for the advancement of minority groups, and on the placement of minority groups within American society.[23]

Recent work on the post–Civil War era points to shifting patterns of difficulties for the black freedmen. It is sometimes suggested that emancipation made no difference for U.S. blacks, or even that their situation became even worse. There is an obvious sense in which the postemancipation pattern was mixed, and that some changes were (and have been) long deferred. Nevertheless, an examination of changes in black incomes, working conditions, and geographic mobility would indicate that such an extremely negative conclusion about Reconstruction and its aftermath is rather overdone. Initially, there was a short period of relative improvement, which was reversed with the political changes and racial hardening of the 1890s. In that decade dramatic restrictions were introduced affecting black voting, educational expenditures, and occupational opportunities.[24] These restrictions on black political influence, and on long-term human capital formation, came at a time when the cotton market collapsed, although some now argue that it was, in part, a reaction to the increasing assertiveness and resistance of Southern blacks.[25]

Other state and national political actions influenced the black economic position—some deliberately, others inadvertently. Among the most important were the restrictions introduced on foreign immigration in the 1920s, which, with the labor demands of World Wars I and II, and the 1930s legislation influencing Southern agriculture, generated the accelerated movement of blacks from the South to the urban North.[26] More directly in reaction to black political pressure were the various civil rights actions of the 1960s, which appear to have had some impact on the relative position of at least the more upwardly mobile members of the black community.

Without drawing the story up to the very present, several aspects of this summary of a century of postemancipation experience might be noted. This was not a period of monotonic change—either downward or upward—but rather one with quite varying experiences, and alterations of more and less rapid change around what would seem a generally rising trend pattern. The variations were related to changes in general economic conditions, affecting both blacks and whites, but were also influenced by the actions of political and judicial authorities. Not all blacks benefited to the same extent, but this, again, was not different from the patterns of other ethnic groups. What is still debated is the relative importance of political action, and, more specifically, the question of the most appropriate legislation for long-term improvements. It is perhaps this latter question which is most heatedly debated today, without clear agreement either on the implications that can be drawn from the past or on the most probable relationship between past and future measures. In addition, with the shift from laws to prevent discrimination to laws to provide more direct affirmative action, it has become increasingly difficult to generalize about the impact and desirability of politics and legislation without more specific knowledge as to their contents. There is some similarity here with the First Reconstruction, with its broad consensus on ending slavery disappearing when the legal complications of dealing with the behavior of white and freedmen became clear. Here again, however, both optimists and pessimists can read its message in their own different ways.

The quandary of simultaneously achieving the goals of appropriate historical balance and drawing attention to current policy concerns remains. To point out that the enslavement experience did not destroy the slaves or the slave community, and that there were economic and social gains in the century after emancipation, is not to be blind to difficulties and negative aspects. (For a counterexample of what could possibly have happened, one need only to look at the case of twentieth-century

South Africa.)[27] Nor need it lead to suggestions that there is no policy needed for today. Understanding the past and analyzing policy needs today can pose quite different questions, with quite different frames of reference and implicit comparisons.

As will be clear in the discussions that follow, there remain disagreements in the interpretation—and, at times, the facts—of the past, as well as in the drawing of current policy implications. In addition, even when we can reach an agreement on facts and interpretation, there will remain differences and debates on what the appropriate specific policy or sets of policies should be. Nevertheless, knowledge of the past should permit better understanding of the long-term forces at work. It is through this perspective, and not direct policy implications, that the contributions of historical research are to be made.

POSTSCRIPT

This chapter was originally prepared for a panel entitled "Policy Implications of Research on the Economics of Slavery and Discrimination," sponsored by the National Economic Association in December 1981. While there would no doubt be a number of changes made if I were to write the paper anew, I believe that there would be no dramatic changes in regards to major issues of substance and interpretation. Therefore, I have left the essay as written. For a very useful updating of data on many aspects of black life in the 1970s, based on the 1980 Census, see Reynolds Farley and Walter R. Allen, *The Color Line and the Quality of Life in America* (New York: Russell Sage Foundation, 1987), which contains a particularly interesting chapter on the comparison between U.S.-born and West Indian–born blacks.

Although I did comment that claims for black reparations based on a concept of exploitation measured by the value of income taken from slaves had not been made recently (as of the time of that writing), clearly the reparations issue remains one of continued interest. In part, no doubt, this reflects the actual payments committed to those Japanese Americans placed in internment camps during World War II. Thus, Congress recognized, at least in principle, a desire to redress wrongs previously committed and to provide some compensation for those victims still living. The restrictions to the actual victims of the crime and to those still living did mean that a number of the problems argued about in the discussion of direct payments to individuals as the means of undertaking black reparations did not arise. Avoided too were the complex questions of appropriately determining individual descendants and of defining "racial" boundaries. For this reason, perhaps, the recent discussions of black reparations have been aimed at a more generalized set of policies to aid black Americans, and a concern with general expenditure policies and affirmative action programs. There is, of course, a claim for such policies to offset past inequities, but, on the other hand, an argument for equity and social equalization today can also be based on current social and economic conditions, however they arose. Whether considered to be reparations for the past or as provisions for improvement of minority conditions today, both arguments point to the desirability of similar sets of social policies at present. Reparations based on the past, however, do make a very strong rhetorical point. It is for this reason that a knowledge of and concern with the analysis of slavery and past racial discrimination makes an important difference for our present-day policy discussions.

NOTES

I should like to thank Gary Gorton and Eric Hanushek for comments on an earlier draft of this chapter. Since this chapter draws extensively on previous publications, these will be cited as a guide to primary references.

1. For discussions of long-term relative black-white economic conditions, see, most recently, Stanley Lieberson, *A Piece of the Pie* (Berkeley: University of California Press, 1980) and Michael Reich, *Racial Inequality* (Princeton, N.J.: Princeton University Press, 1981). See also Robert Higgs, *Competition and Coercion: Blacks in the American Economy* (Cambridge, Eng.: Cambridge University Press, 1977). For discussions of the period since 1960, see, in particular, Richard Freeman, "Black Economic Progress Since 1964," *Public Interest* 52 (Summer 1978):52–68; James P. Smith and Finis Welch, "Black-White Male Wage Ratios: 1960–1970," *American Economic Review* 67 (June 1977):323–38; and Eric A. Hanushek, "Sources of Black-White Earnings Differences," *Social Science Research* (June 1982).

2. For the Moynihan Report and some of the initial reaction to its descriptions of the "black family" and to the policies suggested, see Lee Rainwater and William L. Yancey, *The Moynihan Report and the Politics of Controversy* (Cambridge, Mass.: MIT Press, 1967). For a subsequent analysis of the black family, which makes important points about kin networks in the black community but differs considerably in most of its interpretations from the earlier criticisms of Moynihan, see Carol B. Stack, *All Our Kin* (New York: Harper & Row, 1974).

3. See Herbert G. Gutman, *The Black Family in Slavery and Freedom, 1750–1925* (New York: Pantheon Books, 1976); Eugene D. Genovese, *Roll, Jordan, Roll* (New York: Pantheon Books, 1974); Robert W. Fogel and Stanley L. Engerman, *Time on the Cross*, Vol. 1 (Boston: Little, Brown, 1974), pp. 126–44; and John W. Blassingame *The Slave Community*, revised and enlarged ed. (New York: Oxford University Press, 1979). For a series of articles pointing to the impact of urbanization on the black family, see Theodore Hershberg, ed., *Philadelphia* (New York: Oxford University Press, 1981).

4. U.S. Bureau of the Census, *The Social and Economic Status of the Black Population in the United States, 1790–1978* (Current Population Reports: Special Studies, Series P-23; No. 80) (Washington, D.C.: GPO, 1979).

5. See William Julius Wilson, *The Declining Significance of Race*, 2d ed. (Chicago: University of Chicago Press, 1980); Orlando Patterson, "The Black Community: Is There a Future?" in Seymour Martin Lipset, ed., *The Third Century* (Stanford, Calif.: Hoover Institution Press, 1979), pp. 244–84; Thomas Sowell, "Three Black Histories," in Thomas Sowell, ed., *American Ethnic Groups* (Washington, D.C.: Urban Institute, 1978), pp. 7–64; and Barry Chiswick, "The Economic Progress of Immigrants: Some Apparently Universal Patterns," in William Fellner, ed., *Contemporary Economic Problems* (Washington, D.C.: American Enterprise Institute, 1979), pp. 357–99.

6. See Fogel and Engerman, *Time on the Cross*, and Stanley L. Engerman, "The Southern Slave Economy," in Harry P. Owens, ed., *Perspectives and Irony in American Slavery* (Jackson: University Press of Mississippi, 1976), pp. 71–101. While the profitability of the

antebellum Southern economy now seems widely accepted, there does remain debate about how long it was possible to have sustained this expansion. See, for example, Gavin Wright, *The Political Economy of the Cotton South: Households, Markets and Wealth in the Nineteenth Century* (New York: W. W. Norton, 1978).

7. Eric Williams, *Capitalism and Slavery* (Chapel Hill: University of North Carolina Press, 1944). See also Douglass C. North, *The Economic Growth of The United States, 1790–1860* (Englewood Cliffs, N.J.: Prentice-Hall, 1961), and Richard B. Sheridan, *Sugar and Slavery* (Baltimore: Johns Hopkins University Press, 1973).

8. See Philip D. Curtin, *The Atlantic Slave Trade* (Madison: University of Wisconsin Press, 1969); Fogel and Engerman, *Time on the Cross*, Vol. 1, ch. 1; and Robert W. Fogel and Stanley L. Engerman, "Recent Findings in the Study of Slave Demography and Family Structure," *Sociology and Social Research* 63 (April 1979):566–89.

9. On slave breeding, see Richard Sutch, "The Breeding of Slaves for Sale and the Westward Expansion of Slavery, 1850–1860," in Stanley L. Engerman and Eugene D. Genovese, eds., *Race and Slavery in the Western Hemisphere* (Princeton, N.J.: Princeton University Press, 1975), pp. 173–210, as well as my "Comments on the Study of Race and Slavery," in the same volume, pp. 495–530. See also Fogel and Engerman, *Time on the Cross*, Vol. 1, pp. 78–86, and Herbert Gutman and Richard Sutch, "Victorians All? The Sexual Mores and Conduct of Slaves and Their Masters," in Paul David et al., *Reckoning with Slavery* (New York: Oxford University Press, 1976), pp. 134–62. For comparative discussions of slave fertility patterns, see Herbert S. Klein and Stanley L. Engerman, "Fertility Differentials Between Slaves in the United States and the British West Indies: A Note on Lactation Practices and Their Possible Implications," *William and Mary Quarterly* 35 (April 1978):357–74, and Richard H. Steckel, "The Fertility of American Slaves," in Paul Uselding, ed., *Research in Economic History*, Vol. 7 (Greenwich, Conn.: JAI Press, 1982). In discussing the impact of slavery on fertility, it is necessary to distinguish deliberate interference with slave mating from other aspects of slavery which might lead to higher fertility (for example, the loosening of those budget constraints that would raise the age of marriage of the free population). These need not interfere directly with slave family decisions and, since most planters seemed to have believed that stable marriages led to higher fertility, the planter desire for larger numbers of slaves need not itself have led to antifamily policies. See, for example, the discussions in Part I of Herbert Gutman, *The Black Family in Slavery and Freedom, 1750–1925* (New York: Random House, 1977).

10. See, for example, the articles by Richard America, Brian G. M. Main, Jim Marketti, and Robert S. Browne in the special issue on reparations, *Review of Black Political Economy* 2 (Winter 1972). See also Julian Simon and Larry Neal, "A Calculation of the Black Reparations Bill," *Review of Black Political Economy* 4 (Winter 1974):75–86. For an extended analysis of the reparations issue, see Boris I. Bitker, *The Case for Black Reparations* (New York: Vintage Books, 1973).

11. See Fogel and Engerman, *Time on the Cross*, Vol. 1, ch. 6.

12. For a discussion of some of these measures, see Robert William Fogel and Stanley L. Engerman, "Philanthropy at Bargain Prices: Notes on the Economics of Gradual Emancipation," *Journal of Legal Studies* 3 (June 1974):377–401.

13. For an analysis of these debates, see Stanley L. Engerman and David Eltis, "Economic Aspects of the Abolition Debate," in Christine Bolt and Seymour Drescher, eds., *Anti-Slavery, Religion, and Reform* (Hamden, Conn.: Shoe String Press, 1980), pp. 272–93.

14. See, e.g., David Brion Davis, *The Problem of Slavery in the Age of Revolution, 1770–1823* (Ithaca: Cornell University Press, 1975), and Seymour Drescher, *Econocide: British*

Slavery in the Era of Abolition (Pittsburgh: University of Pittsburgh Press, 1977), and the ongoing work of these two scholars.

15. See, e.g., C. Vann Woodward, *Origins of the New South, 1877–1913* (Baton Rouge: Louisiana State University Press, 1951); Robert C. McMath, Jr., *Populist Vanguard* (Chapel Hill: University of North Carolina Press, 1975); and Lawrence C. Goodwyn, *Democratic Promise* (New York: Oxford University Press, 1976).

16. See Fogel and Engerman, *Time on the Cross*; Wright, *Political Economy of the Cotton South*; Paul David et al., *Reckoning with Slavery*, and the subsequent series of articles and comments in *The American Economic Review*, June 1977, March 1979, and September 1980.

17. The following paragraphs draw heavily upon Stanley L. Engerman, "Economic Aspects of the Adjustments to Emancipation in the United States and the British West Indies," *Journal of Interdisciplinary History* (forthcoming). See, on the United States, Robert L. Ransom and Richard Sutch, *One Kind of Freedom* (Cambridge, Eng.: Cambridge University Press, 1977); Higgs, *Competition and Coercion*; Stephen J. DeCanio, *Agriculture in the Post-Bellum South* (Cambridge, Mass.: MIT Press, 1974), and the articles in the two special issues of *Explorations in Economic History*, January and April 1979.

18. See Higgs, *Competition and Coercion*, pp. 95–134, and Claude F. Oubre, *Forty Acres and a Mule* (Baton Rouge: Louisiana State University Press, 1978), pp. 158–81.

19. As the possible decrease in labor force participation would indicate, there was some desire to substitute consumption in the form of leisure for consumption in the form of goods. It should be noted that the magnitude and reasons for any decline in labor input, and the implications for family life, persistence of debt, and black health and mortality remain under debate. See Ransom and Sutch, *One Kind of Freedom*; Gavin Wright, "Freedom and the Southern Economy," *Explorations in Economic History* 16 (January 1979):90–108; and Claudia Goldin, " 'N' Kinds of Freedom: An Introduction to the Issues," *Explorations in Economic History* 16 (January 1979):8–30.

20. See Stanley L. Engerman, "The Realities of Slavery: A Review of Recent Evidence," *International Journal of Comparative Sociology* 20 (March-June 1979):46–66.

21. See, in addition to the books cited in note 3, Lawrence W. Levine, *Black Culture and Black Consciousness* (New York: Oxford University Press, 1977). See also Sidney W. Mintz and Richard Price, *An Anthropological Approach to the Afro-American Past: A Caribbean Perspective* (Philadelphia: Institute for the Study of Human Issues, 1976).

22. On the immediate postemancipation response in the United States, see Leon F. Litwack, *Been in the Storm So Long* (New York: Alfred A. Knopf, 1979).

23. See the discussions in Arthur Mann, *The One and the Many* (Chicago: University of Chicago Press, 1979).

24. See C. Vann Woodward, *The Strange Career of Jim Crow*, 2d rev. ed. (New York: Oxford University Press, 1960), and J. Morgan Kousser, *The Shaping of Southern Politics* (New Haven, Conn.: Yale University Press, 1974).

25. Howard Rabinowitz, *Race Relations in the Urban South, 1865–1890* (New York: Oxford University Press, 1978).

26. Jay R. Mandle, *The Roots of Black Poverty: The Southern Plantation Economy After the Civil War* (Durham, N.C.: Duke University Press, 1978).

27. George M. Fredrickson, *White Supremacy* (New York: Oxford University Press, 1981).

3.

Who Pays for Slavery?

ROGER L. RANSOM AND
RICHARD SUTCH

One of the distinctive features of black slavery as it emerged in the North American British colonies was that slaves were regarded as the private property of their owners. This "property right" over humans was reaffirmed in the American Constitution of 1790 and consistently upheld by the courts for the next seventy years. The first census of the United States, taken in 1790, enumerated one out of every six inhabitants—a total of 700,000 black Americans—as a slave. By the time of the census of 1860, almost 4 million Americans were slaves.[1]

The system of chattel labor which operated in the United States from 1790 to 1860 was, to an extraordinary degree, guided by the calculus of the marketplace. An abundance of research over the past three decades has made it clear that slaveholders viewed their slaves as capital assets. The purchase of that asset required an investment of financial capital not unlike the financial outlay necessary for land and equipment. Moreover, researchers have shown that an investment in slave property brought a financial return that equaled or exceeded the return available from other potential investments.[2]

The conclusion that American slavery was profitable to slaveowners carries with it several significant implications of particular interest for the theme addressed in this volume. Most obvious perhaps is the implication that slavery in the Southern states would not die of its own accord. As long as slaves were a self-reproducing asset able to produce a surplus above and beyond the costs of their maintenance, and as long as slave markets operated efficiently, slavery would be an economically viable institution. This means that the elimination of slavery required either abrogation of a constitutionally protected property right or a government-financed purchase and manumission of the entire slave population. The financial magnitude of the manumission option was staggering. Table 3.1 gives the value of the slave stock as a fraction of the value of all private assets within the United States in 1840, 1850, and 1860. Slaves accounted for roughly 15 percent of total assets. Since slaveholders had no reason to willingly part with their slave capital, any emancipation scheme that required the purchase of these assets involved a huge sum.

ECONOMIC EXPLOITATION OF AMERICAN SLAVES

The market price of a slave represented the buyer's calculation of the present value of the stream of income which the buyer could extract from the slave. Since this income is the difference between the slave's productivity and the maintenance cost of food, shelter, and the like provided by the owner, the price of a slave summarizes the capitalized value of the economic exploitation inherent in the slave system.[3] This capitalized value in 1860 was $3 billion which can be thought of as the stock of the potential exploitation embodied in the 4 million slaves alive on that date.

As used here, the term *economic exploitation* means that part of labor's product which is not returned to the slave as food, shelter, and other consumption items. We have estimated that in 1859 the exploited amount averaged $33.51 per slave. This produces a calculated rate of return of 6.6 percent on the current value of the average slave.[4] If we assume that this rate of return was typical for the antebellum period, we can estimate the dollar value of exploitation from the crop output produced by slaves in each year using evidence on the slave population and the average price of

Table 3.1
Estimates of the Value of the Slave Stock and the Aggregate Value of Private Assets, Current Prices, 1840, 1850, and 1860

(Millions of Dollars)

Year	Value of Slave Stock	Privately Held Assets	Slaves as Percentage of Assets
1840	997	6,145	16.2
1850	1,286	9,976	13.0
1860	3,059	20,999	14.6

Sources: *Value of slaves:* Ransom and Sutch (1988: Table A-1). This source gives a value based on a three-year moving average of the annual prices reported in Table A-1 of this chapter.

Privately held assets: The figure given is the sum of the estimate of the value of national wealth (variant A) made by Gallman (1986: Table 4.A.1, p. 204) plus the value of the slave stock (column 1) plus our estimate of the value of the stock of consumer durables (Ransom and Sutch, 1984: Table D-2) plus the federal debt outstanding (U.S. Census, 1975, Series Y493) plus our estimate of the state and local government debt outstanding (Ransom and Sutch, 1984: Table D-3).

slaves.[5] In addition to this stream of exploited crop output, slaveowners also received the value of any children born to slaves each year.[6] Our estimates of the annual stream of crop exploitation—together with estimates of the gains from the value of children born to slaves each year—are presented in Table A.1 of the Appendix for the years 1806 through 1860.

Figure 3.1 presents the annual value of exploited income as a percentage of gross national product (GNP) each year.[7] The amount exploited from slaves, expressed as a fraction of GNP, averaged 3.5 percent a year, with a rising trend evident over the fifty-five-year period covered by our calculations. At first glance, 3.5 percent of GNP might seem to be a rather modest figure. One must remember, however, that this stream of exploitation went directly to a small fraction of the white population: those who owned the slaves. Moreover, the exploitation continued over a longer period of time; the value of exploitation summed over the entire period was about $3.4 billion by 1860.

A simple summing of the value of exploited product each year does not, of course, take account of the opportunity cost of earnings foregone over time. If we calculate the *present value* of past exploitation in 1860, the total would be $17.4 billion.[8] This figure is consistent with the order of magnitude of similar estimates of exploitation calculated by James Marketti elsewhere in this volume; however, the interpretation of such estimates is unclear at best.[9] Using an estimate of the present value of exploitation over a long period of time implies that the present generation should be held responsible for the sins of all past generations. Moreover, such a procedure attaches enormous weight to the exploitation that occurred at the outset of

Figure 3.1
Exploitation of Slaves as a Percentage of U.S. GNP, 1805–1860

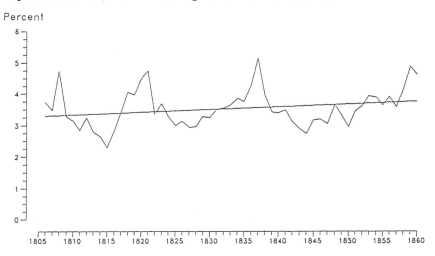

Sources: See sources for Table A.1.

the period in question. Such computations are extremely sensitive to the choice of an interest rate. These problems are greatly compounded when the present value of exploitation is computed as of the present.[10]

Some important insights into the nature of slave exploitation can be gained by looking at the components that make up our estimate of economic exploitation. As an illustration, in Table 3.2 we present a schematic breakdown of the division of out-

Table 3.2
Exploitation of Slave Output in 1859

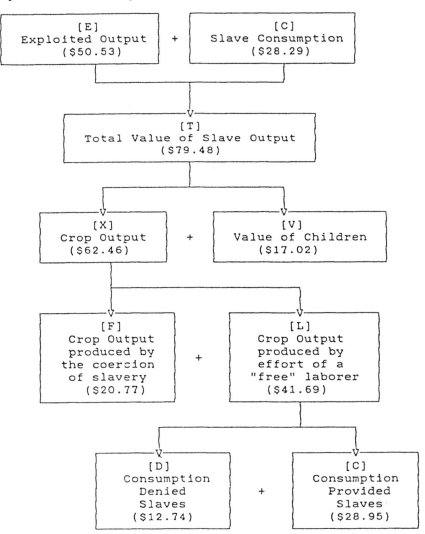

put between slave and master. We begin by noting that, according to our definition of exploitation, the total output of a slave can be thought of in two ways. On the one hand, the slave's output must be equal to the consumption provided by the master as well as any exploited output taken by the master. Viewed another way, the total output of a slave must also equal the value of crop output as well as the value of slave children born each year. This identity is shown at the top of Table 3.2. The first thing we observe about exploitation is that the master expropriated all the economic value attached to an infant slave.

What about the crop output of the slave? Clearly, it was in the interest of the slaveowner to get the maximum level of crop output from the labor of slaves. To do so, masters relied on the coercion of slavery to extract more labor from the slave population than would have been forthcoming from a comparable free population. The crop output of the slave, therefore, can be thought of as consisting of that part which would be produced by someone working as a "free" laborer, and that part which resulted from the extra labor extracted through the coercion of slavery. The output resulting from coerced slave labor was a part of the exploitation of slavery. This leaves us with the share of output which would have been produced by the labor of a "free" worker. The slave received only a consumption allowance from his or her master. To the extent that output exceeded the value of this fixed consumption, the slave was being denied consumption by the master. This "denied consumption" was the final component of exploitation of slaves by their masters.[11]

We can calculate these components of slave exploitation. In Table 3.2 we indicate the values for each component in the single year 1859; the estimates for other years back to 1806 are presented in Tables A.1 and A.2 of the Appendix. We know that the crop output per slave in 1859 was $62.46 and that the value of children born per slave in that year was $17.02.[12] Thus, the value of slave output in that year was $79.48. To estimate the portion of crop output which was produced by free and coerced labor, we can compare the amount of labor offered by the free black population of the 1870s to that offered by the slave population in the 1850s. Free blacks offered about 30 percent *less* labor per capita than the level common under slavery.[13] This implies that $20.77 of output would be attributable to coerced labor, and $41.69 of output could be attributed to the "free" laborer's effort. However, the slave received only $28.29 in consumption items. The balance—$12.74—was consumption which was denied the slave. In 1859, then, the fraction of total slave output—including the value of children—which was taken as exploitation by the master equaled 63.6 percent. The fraction of the crop output expropriated by the master was 53.7 percent.

These estimates of slave exploitation in 1859 may be extrapolated back to the first decade of the nineteenth century. Table 3.3 presents estimates of consumption, exploitation, total output, and the value of slave children produced per slave for the six census dates between 1809 and 1859. Annual estimates of the crop output per slave, the output attributable to coerced slave labor and that of a free laborer, together with the consumption returned to the slave, are presented in Figure 3.2 for the period 1806 through 1860.[14]

Table 3.3
Price, Exploitation, Consumption, and Output of a Slave, Census Years 1809 to 1859

Year	Average Price of Slave [$/slave]	Total Exploit- ation [$/slave]	Consump- tion Provided [$/slave]	Total Slave Output [$/slave]	Children Born [$/slave]	Crops Produced [$/slave]
1808–10	303	19.23	34.06	53.29	8.53	44.76
1818–20	426	26.98	36.99	63.97	11.17	52.80
1828–30	269	17.03	25.97	42.99	6.78	36.21
1838–40	433	27.37	29.66	57.03	9.87	47.16
1848–50	392	24.80	23.31	48.11	9.51	38.60
1858–60	741	46.74	29.43	76.17	15.74	60.43

Sources: See sources for Table A.1.

What can we say about the exploitation of slaves over the period 1806 to 1860? Clearly, the absolute level of exploitation per slave was increasing over time, and the sources of that increase are evident. The most significant change was a marked increase in the level of consumption denied slaves. During the first three decades of the period, slave rations nearly equaled the product that would have resulted from their "free" labor. Indeed, for several years between 1810 and 1820, denied consumption was actually negative. This changed in the 1830s, when denied consumption rose sharply. After a decline during the depression of 1837–1843, denied consumption was again rapidly increasing through the late 1840s and 1850s. The output attributable to coerced labor also rose in those periods, adding to the total product that could be expropriated by the master. The effect of this increase in expropriated product can be seen in Figure 3.3, which presents estimates of the rate of exploitation calculated both as a fraction of total slave output and of crop output alone. Both calculations confirm the fact that exploitation increased throughout the period of our analysis. In the first decade of the nineteenth century, the exploited product represented about 20 percent of crop output and 30 percent of the total value of output (including the value of children born). By the time of the Civil War these percentages had more than doubled; 54 percent of the slave's crop output went to the owner and 64 percent of the total product went to the master.

Over time, these high rates of exploitation produced, as we have seen, an enormous accumulation of exploited product that supported the operation of the slave system. To focus only on the size of the exploited product, however, is to miss another, equally important, aspect of slave exploitation which has important implications if one thinks in terms of *ending* the exploitation of slavery.

In a free economy the "value" of children born to blacks would not be assets owned by slave masters, and the labor effort of free laborers would be substantially

Figure 3.2
Crop Output and Consumption per Slave, Current Dollars, 1806–1860

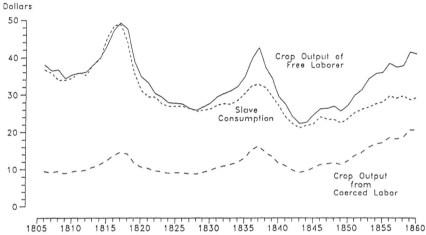

Sources: See sources for Table A.1.

less than that under slavery. These two components, which totaled just under $30 per slave in 1859 (or 37 percent of the total value of slave product), would (from the perspective of the slaveholder) simply disappear if slavery were eliminated. The costs associated with the disappearance of this gain to the slaveholder not only blocked any realistic hope of peaceful emancipation in the United States, but it also had profound implications for the impact of emancipation on the American economy in 1865.

THE ECONOMICS OF EMANCIPATION

We have seen that slaves were valuable assets in 1860. Emancipation required that ownership of those assets be surrendered by slaveowners in any of three ways: (1) slaveowners could free their slaves as an act of charity; (2) the government could expropriate the slaves and free them with no restitution to the former owners; or (3) the government could pay the slaveowners the value of their assets and then free the slaves. American slaveowners were not sufficiently altruistic to give up their wealth, and they surely had sufficient political power to protect their property from government confiscation. As a practical matter, only the purchase of slaves by the government represented a plan for emancipation which would avoid serious conflict.

The economic logic behind a proposal to emancipate slaves through purchase rests on a choice-theoretical approach to economic decisions. This approach holds that institutional change is best understood as a process propelled by people who seek to capture the gains from establishing new institutional arrangements and who

Figure 3.3
Gross and Net Exploitation Rates of Slaves, 1805–1860

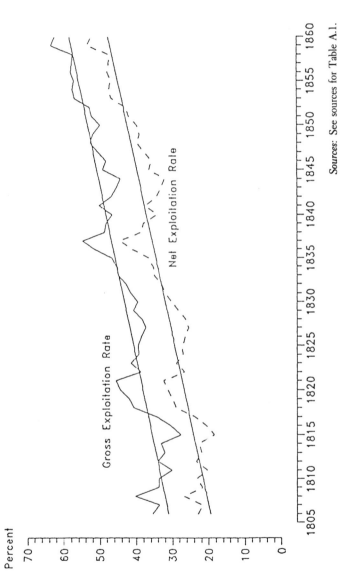

Percent

Gross Exploitation Rate

Net Exploitation Rate

1805 1810 1815 1820 1825 1830 1835 1840 1845 1850 1855 1860

Sources: See sources for Table A.1.

form coalitions with others in order to get what they want.[15] If certain individuals or groups would lose as a consequence of the change, then the advocates could gain their acquiescence by offering to compensate the "losers" by sharing the potential gains from the institutional change. Institutional change, in this view, must be a positive economic force, working to improve efficiency, to increase economic output, and to accelerate economic growth. If the losers are actually compensated, everyone gains in the process. The implication is obvious: An orderly abolition requires that the losses imposed on slaveowners by the exercise of eminent domain be restored through some system of compensation. However, there is no need to provide cash payments to the freed slaves. Slaves will gain enormously from emancipation simply by becoming free. Consequently, no further "bribe" is required to gain the support of slaves.

A major problem with the buy-out scheme was finding someone to pay for it. The choice-theoretical model requires that the gainers actually "bribe" the losers into accepting the new arrangement. Implicitly, this assumes that the change being sought will increase economic efficiency—and therefore total output. The "bribe" can then be financed from the increased output. No one is a net loser; some are net gainers. Unfortunately, emancipation did not fit the requirements for ·change by consensus. The *welfare* of the slave population was unquestionably improved with emancipation. But, as we have already seen, *per capita output* among the free black population would fall since, as free people, ex-slaves would no longer be forced to offer the extra labor obtained through the coercion of slavery. The resulting decline in output meant that compensated emancipation in the United States could not have been effected by a simple transfer of income from those who gained to those who lost. The exploitation of slavery had been capitalized into the price of a slave. If the slaveowner were to be paid the full price of his slaves, some "cost" to society would remain in the form of the exploited output which would not be produced after emancipation.

COMPUTING THE COSTS OF COMPENSATED EMANCIPATION

The major cost of compensated emancipation would be the need to pay slaveholders the full value of their slaves. Our estimate of the total value of slave capital in the slave states in 1860 is $3.059 billion. In that year the total commodity output of the entire country was no larger than $1.4 billion (Gallman, 1960). Obviously, the only feasible way to pay slaveholders such a large sum would have been for the government to issue interest-bearing bonds that would be given to the slaveowner in exchange for freeing his slaves. Bondholders would receive the prevailing interest rate for government securities, which we estimate as 6 percent.

The costs of this plan are evident enough; at 6 percent the annual interest on the bonds would amount to $183.5 million.[16] The revenues required to finance an issue of "emancipation bonds" would have presumably been raised through domestic taxation or additional borrowing. In examining how these costs might have been distributed among the population, it is useful to distinguish three distinct groups. In 1860 there were 384,884 *slaveholders* in the United States,[17] who owned 3.95 million *slaves* (see Appendix Table A.1). The *nonslaveholding free population* of the United States was 27.2 million, 20.2 million of whom lived outside the Southern states.[18]

The difficulties with financing a "consensus emancipation" scheme in which the group benefiting from the change (slaves) uses the benefits from emancipation to repay the losers (the slaveowner) are immediately apparent. In this case, the emancipation-bond tax would fall entirely on the freed blacks. The annual per capita tax would amount to $46.47, or about the level of our estimate of the *total per capita income* of black sharecroppers in 1879.[19] This result is consistent with the implications of an asset-pricing model of slavery. Placing the entire burden of the bond tax on freedmen would be equivalent to replicating slavery, since the exploitative level of labor intensity with slavery was capitalized into the slave price. To pay for their emancipation, blacks would have to give up one of the most precious fruits of freedom—the increased leisure possible when the coercion of slavery was removed.

Under a "full compensation" scheme, the ex-slaveowners and the freedmen would be exempted from the bond tax. Levying the tax on the nonslaveholding free population of the United States in 1860 would create a per capita burden of $6.75, or 4.8 percent of the estimated per capita income of $140 in 1859. How should we view a burden of this magnitude? Claudia Goldin, in considering cost estimates not very different from ours, concluded that: "It appears . . . that the Union erred. It did not look to other slaveocracies for advice in solving its slave problem, for the realized costs of the Civil War were far greater than those of various emancipation schemes."[20] If one is weighing the costs of paying the slaveowners the value of their slaves in order to avoid the Civil War, then Goldin's conclusion seems warranted. Even the most conservative estimates place the direct costs of that conflict (*excluding* the costs connected with loss of life) at well over $4 billion.[21] Clearly, had either side accurately foreseen the full costs of the war and used the choice-theoretical model of institutional change to reach a decision, they would not have fought the war. But the same logic that shows war to be a mistake also suggests that Americans would not choose to spend $3.059 billion for compensated emancipation in 1860.

Expressing the bond tax as a fraction of total income is a misleading way to express the relative size of the burden of that tax in 1860. A more meaningful way to express the burden would be to view that sum in the context of the level of government spending at that time. Lance E. Davis and John Legler (1966) have constructed estimates of government expenditures and revenues from 1815 to 1900. Their estimates show that per capita expenditures and revenues of the federal government in 1860 were about $2.20, and expenditures by *all* levels of government totaled only slightly more than $9 per capita.[22] Viewed in this perspective, the "full compensation" plan would require a vast increase in the level of government. Federal outlays would have to triple, and the total of all government outlays would be increased by 75 percent.

EMANCIPATION, REPARATIONS, AND "ECONOMIC" MORALITY

Putting aside the costs of financing emancipation, there remains a more serious objection to a compensated emancipation scheme: The wrong people are getting paid for freeing the slaves. Why should the very group that perpetuated slavery and most directly reaped the fruits from its exploitation now be paid a price that includes the value of future exploitation which is included in the price of a slave? By itself, a price tag of $3.416 billion to free slaves is a forbidding sum; paying it to the owners of slaves would be still more objectionable to those who viewed abolition as a moral issue.

The problem, of course, is that others continued to insist that abolition was an economic question. To them, the expropriation of property inherent in an uncompensated emancipation was unethical. The authority cited in defense of slave property, of course, was no less than the United States Constitution. The hopes for emancipation in 1860 were obviously dim. The Constitution gave support to those who insisted on restitution for property that was expropriated. The capitalization of slave returns into their market price made the cost of "buying off" slaveowners prohibitively high, even when spread over the entire population. To those who pushed for emancipation, the morality of paying slaveowners a large sum to free the slaves was, to say the least, questionable. The "economics of emancipation" dictated that those who objected to slavery would either have to live with it because it was too expensive to do away with, or they must find some way of forcing slaveowners to relinquish their slave capital for less than the market price.

One question that lay behind the estimates of exploitation presented earlier in this chapter and elsewhere in this volume is whether anyone is "owed" something as a consequence of slavery. Can we find a "balancing of the books" in all this? By now it must be apparent that we must approach the exercise with caution. If such a reckoning is made, it should be calculated as of 1860–1865, not 1985. Adding 125 years of compounded interest to the totals only obfuscates the argument. Moreover, we must take account of all three groups who gained and lost in the struggle over slavery in America.

Slaves got their freedom. While liberty was hardly a trivial gain, the freedmen received no reparations. Black Americans had been exploited for two and a half centuries by their white masters, and that exploitation was increasing at the end of the antebellum period. Counting only the last half century of that exploitation, and taking no account of interest forgone, the value of exploited income taken from slaves amounted to $3.4 billion in 1860. The present value of that exploitation would be over $17 billion.

Slaveowners lost their investment with the uncompensated emancipation of slaves in 1865. The value of investment by Southern slaveowners in the slave labor force in 1860 totaled $3 billion. Southerners claimed that expropriation of that property justified reimbursement of the value of those lost assets. While we might dispute the morality of such payments, we should recognize that the economic impact of losing such a large fraction of their assets had a profound impact on their behavior after the war.

Northern whites, a group that has been largely omitted from our discussion thus far, "paid" for emancipation with their lives and resources to finance the military effort of the Civil War. Peaceful emancipation through the purchase of slaves was clearly not feasible in 1860. The costs of the Civil War should therefore be figured as part of the "price" paid for the emancipation of black slaves. That, too, was not a trivial sum. The war consumed 360,000 lives and some $2 billion of direct costs on the Union side alone; the total "costs" for all Americans was more than 600,000 lives and at least $7 billion of spent resources by 1865.

What can we conclude from this discussion? The numbers we have presented in this chapter are at best rough approximations of concepts that are themselves subject to a considerable range of interpretations. With that in mind, we offer three final thoughts. First, black slaves who were the victims of slavery suffered from severe economic exploitation in the form of labor extracted through the coercion of slavery, together with consumption denied them by their masters. Second, this economic measure of exploitation cannot fully capture either the injuries to blacks as a consequence of slavery or the costs incurred by whites in the removal of slavery. Finally, if there is a single lesson from our conjectures about slavery and emancipation, it is that moral and economic pressures do not always work toward the same ends. In the case of slavery in the antebellum United States, it is apparent that economic factors worked very powerfully to sustain an immoral institution, and the elimination of slavery entailed a war that imposed staggering costs on the generation of Americans who fought and died in that conflict. The "costs" of slavery were not, in the final analysis, imposed solely on blacks.

NOTES

This research has been supported by the National Science Foundation, the Institute of Business and Economic Research of the University of California at Berkeley, and the John Simon Guggenheim Memorial Foundation.

1. U.S. Census (1918): Table 6, p. 57; U.S. Census (1975): Series A-6, p. 8. These figures for the entire United States are misleading as a guide to the importance of blacks in the slaveholding states, where approximately one out of three inhabitants in 1860 was a slave.

2. Historians once believed that slavery in the antebellum period was not profitable. The most frequently cited writings in this school of thought are those of Ulrich Bonnell Phillips (1905 and 1918), Charles Ramsdell (1929), and Charles S. Sydnor (1933). In 1958 Alfred H. Conrad and John R. Meyer published a path-breaking article demonstrating that slavery was profitable. Conrad and Meyer were the first to clearly elucidate a model of slavery in which the slaveholder was viewed as a profit-maximizing investor. Major quantitative studies that bolstered and extended the findings of Conrad and Meyer include those by Yasukichi Yasuba (1961), Robert Evans (1961), Richard Sutch (1965), and James Foust and Dale Swann (1970). These essays and several more are collected in Hugh G. Aitken (1971). An excellent review of the first fifteen years of the debate can be found in Robert W. Fogel and

Stanley L. Engerman (1971). *Time on the Cross* (1974) contains Fogel and Engerman's own estimate of the rate of return to slave property. Our own estimate of the rate of profit is from Ransom and Sutch (1977, pp. 212–14). For a discussion of the larger implications of the capital asset model of slavery, see Ransom and Sutch (1988).

3. Scholars agree that slaves were able to produce a surplus well beyond the costs of maintenance. See the findings reported in Fogel and Engerman (1974, ch. 5); Ransom and Sutch (1977, ch. 1 and Appendix A); Richard Vedder and David Stockdale (1975); and Gavin Wright (1977, ch. 3). The present value calculations referred to in the text include the expected returns from slave children. We are aware, of course, that economic exploitation is a narrow view of the exploitation inherent in any system of slavery.

4. Ransom and Sutch (1977, pp. 212–13). The formula calculating the rate of return of a slave in any given year is:

$$r = \frac{(1 + a)}{1 - (E_o/P_s)} - 1$$

where:

r = rate of return on slave property
a = annual rate of growth of the slave population
E = amount of "exploited" income; equal to labor's product less the cost of maintenance
P = the market price of the slave

In 1859 a equaled 2.124 percent (see Table A.1). In *One Kind of Freedom* we used $865 as the price of a slave, which yielded a rate of return of 6.3 percent. The estimate of 6.6 percent presented in the text is calculated using the 1859 price of $801, based on the price estimates for slaves presented in Table A.1 of this chapter.

5. Rearranging terms in the formula of footnote 4, we can see that:

$$E_o = P_s * \left[1 - \frac{(1 + a)}{(1 + r)} \right]$$

Table A.1 provides annual estimates of the price of slaves and the slave population; r is equal to 6.6 percent.

6. The value of children is estimated as the rate of growth of the slave population in a given year times the average price of a slave in that year. In the notation of note 4 that is:

$$V = P_s * (1 + a)$$

7. The estimates of slave exploitation presented in Table A.1 assume that slaves received no income; they received only an annual allowance equal to the value of consumption supplied by their owners. The exploitation estimates also assume that the value of slave children born each year accrued as income to the owner. Consequently, the estimates of GNP used to construct the ratio presented in Figure 3.1 have been augmented by the addition of slave consumption plus the capital gains from growth in the slave labor stock. The denominator is the free population of the United States.

8. Assuming an interest rate of 6.6 percent—the return estimated for slaves—the present value in 1860 of exploitation in any given year n would be:

$$PV_n = E_n * (1.066)^e$$

where E is the exploited output in year n and e is equal to $(1860 - n)$. The present value of all exploitation for 1806 to 1860 is the sum of the present value for each year.

9. Marketti estimates that the present value of exploited income between 1790 and 1860 ranged between $18.7 billion (at a 2.5 percent interest rate) and $53 billion (at a 6 percent interest rate) in 1860 (1984: Table V).

10. Thus, for example, Marketti (see Chapter 7) triples his 1860 estimates to account for compounding between 1860 and 1983. Larry Neal (see Chapter 6) presents a different measure of exploitation, but the importance of compounding is equally evident in the estimated present value in 1914 of exploitation which occurred between 1690 and 1840 (Table 6.3). Our point is that even minor differences in the estimates for the base periods create huge differences in the present value one hundred or more years later.

11. Note that "denied consumption" could be negative. In such a case, the rations of the slave exceeded what would be produced by free labor on the farm, and the slave was, in a sense, being subsidized by his or her master.

12. The figures for crop output per slave in 1859 are based on the estimates of slave output reported in Ransom and Sutch (1977: Table A.4, p. 210). The calculation of the value of children per slave is discussed in note 6 above.

13. In One Kind of Freedom we found that the labor offered by free blacks in 1879 was between 25 to 37 percent less than that offered by the slave population in the 1850s. The calculation in Table 3.2 assumes a reduction of 30 percent for 1859.

14. Note that in Figure 3.2 the distance between the level of consumption and the output of free labor is equal to the "denied consumption" as defined in Table 3.2.

15. A considerable literature on this approach, which first gained attention with James Buchanan and Gordon Tullock's The Calculus of Consent (1962) and Mancur Olson's The Logic of Collective Action (1964). Lance Davis and Douglass North applied this logic to the question of institutional change in 1971.

16. We assume that the government would issue consoles with no maturity; if the bonds were to be retired, the annual costs would be slightly higher. We also neglect any costs of administering the plan. Claudia D. Goldin considers an emancipation plan in which thirty-year bonds are given to slaveholders. The costs of her scheme, which is based on a value of the slave stock equal to $2.7 billion, would be $195 million (Goldin, 1973: 73).

17. U.S. Census Office (1860: 247).

18. U.S. Bureau of the Census (1975: I, Series A199-A201, pp. 25-37).

19. Expressed in 1859 dollars, the per capita income of a black sharecropper in 1879 was $42.22 (Ransom and Sutch, 1979: 224-25).

20. Goldin (1973: 84). Goldin estimated a per capita burden on the same order of magnitude as our estimate: $7.25 if the population as a whole is taxed; $9.66 if all Southerners are excluded (1973: 74-76).

21. Goldin and Lewis estimate the "direct cost" of the war as $4.4 billion. Adding an allowance for loss of life increases this estimate to $6.7 billion (1975: 304, 308). They also construct a much larger estimate of what they term the "indirect costs" of the war; however, these costs include effects in addition to the wartime destruction. Gerald Gunderson estimates the costs as $4.2 billion (1974: 948-50).

22. Davis and Legler presented per capita estimates of revenues and expenditures for each region of the United States. Our aggregate figures were constructed using the population data in U.S. Bureau of the Census (1975: I, Series A-172 and A-195, pp. 22–37). Estimates of expenditure for all levels of government are for 1859. These estimates are considerably more conjectural than the figures for federal expenditures. See Davis and Legler (1966, Tables 1 and 2, pp. 529–31; and Table 8, pp. 548–49).

REFERENCES

Aitken, Hugh G. *Did Slavery Pay?* New York: John Wiley & Sons, 1971.

Bateman, Fred, and Weiss, Thomas. *A Deplorable Scarcity: The Failure of Industrialization in the Slave Economy.* Chapel Hill: University of North Carolina Press, 1981.

Berry, Thomas Senior. "Revised Annual Estimates of American Gross National Product and Preliminary Annual Estimates of Four Major Components of Demand: 1789–1889." *Bostwick Papers*, No. 3: Bostwick Press, 1978.

Buchanan, James, and Tullock, Gordon. *The Calculus of Consent.* Ann Arbor: University of Michigan Press, 1962.

Conrad, Alfred H., and Meyer, John R. "The Economics of Slavery in the Ante Bellum South." *Journal of Political Economy* 66 (April 1958):95–130.

Davis, Lance E., and Legler, John. "The Government in the American Economy, 1815–1902: A Quantitative Study." *Journal of Economic History* 26 (December 1966):514–52.

————, and North, Douglass C. *Institutional Change and American Economic Growth.* New York: Cambridge University Press, 1971.

Engerman, Stanley L. "Some Considerations Relating to Property Rights in Man." *Journal of Economic History* 33 (March 1973):43–65.

Evans, Robert J. "The Economics of American Negro Slavery." In Universities-National Bureau Committee for Economic Research, *Aspects of Labor Economics.* Princeton, N.J.: Princeton University Press, 1961.

Fogel, Robert W., and Engerman, Stanley L. "The Economics of Slavery." In Robert William Fogel and Stanley L. Engerman, eds., *The Reinterpretation of American Economic History.* New York: Harper & Row, 1971, pp. 311–41.

————. *Time on the Cross.* 2 vols. Little, Brown, 1974.

Foust, James, and Swann, Dale. "Productivity and Profitability of Antebellum Slave Labor: A Micro Approach." *Agricultural History* 44 (January 1970):39–62.

Gallman, Robert E. "Commodity Output, 1839–1899: In National Bureau of Economic Research." *Trends in the American Economy in the Nineteenth Century.* Studies in Income and Wealth. Princeton, N.J.: Princeton University Press, 1960.

————. "The United States Capital Stock During the Nineteenth Century." In Robert E. Gallman and Stanley L. Engerman, eds., *Long-Term Factors in American Economic Growth.* National Bureau of Economic Research, Studies in Income and Wealth Number 51. Chicago: University of Chicago Press, 1986.

Goldin, Claudia D. "The Economics of Emancipation." *Journal of Economic History* 33 (March 1973):66–85.

————, and Lewis, Frank. "The Economic Costs of the American Civil War: Estimates and Implications." *Journal of Economic History* 35 (June 1975):299–326.

Gunderson, Gerald. "The Origins of the American Civil War." *Journal of Economic History* 4 (December 1974):915–950.

Olson, Mancur. *The Logic of Collective Action.* Cambridge, Mass.: Harvard University Press, 1964.

Phillips, Ulrich Bonnell. "The Economic Cost of Slaveholding in the Cotton Belt." *Political Science Quarterly* 20 (June 1905):257–75.

―――. *American Negro Slavery: A Survey of the Supply, Employment, and Control of Negro Labor, as Determined by the Plantation Regime.* New York: D. Appleton, 1918.

Ramsdell, Charles. "The Natural Limits of Slavery Expansion." *Mississippi Valley Historical Review* 16 (September 1929).

Ransom, Roger L., and Sutch, Richard. *One Kind of Freedom: The Economic Consequences of Emancipation.* Cambridge, Eng.: Cambridge University Press, 1977.

―――. "Growth and Welfare in the American South of the Nineteenth Century." *Explorations in Economic History* 16 (April 1979):207–36.

―――. "A System of Life-Cycle National Accounts: Provisional Estimates, 1839–1938." *Working Papers on the History of Savings* 2 (December 1984). University of California, Berkeley: Institute for Business and Economic Research.

―――. "Capitalists Without Capital: The Burden of Slavery and the Impact of Emancipation." *Agricultural History* (Summer 1988).

Saraydar, Edward. "A Note on the Profitability of Antebellum Slavery." *Southern Economic Journal* 30 (April 1964):325–32.

Sutch, Richard. "The Profitability of Slavery—Revisited." *Southern Economic Journal* 31 (April 1965):365–77.

Sydnor, Charles S. *Slavery in Mississippi.* New York: Appleton Century, 1933.

Temin, Peter. "The Postbellum Recovery of the South and the Cost of the Civil War." *Journal of Economic History* 36 (December 1976):898—907.

U.S. Bureau of the Census. *Historical Statistics of the United States, Colonial Times to 1970.* 2 vols. Washington, D.C.: GPO, 1975.

Vedder, Richard K., and Stockdale, David. "The Profitability of Slavery Revisited: A Different Approach." *Agricultural History* 49 (April 1975).

Wright, Gavin. "New and Old Views on the Economics of Slavery." *Journal of Economic History* 33 (June 1973):452–66.

―――. *The Political Economy of the Cotton South: Households, Markets and Wealth in the Nineteenth Century.* New York: W. W. Norton, 1978.

Yasuba, Yasukichi. "The Profitability and Viability of Plantation Slavery in the United States." *Economic Studies Quarterly* 12 (September 1961):60–67.

Appendix Table A.1
Annual Estimates of the Average Price of a Slave, Value of Crop Exploitation, Value of Children Born, and the Consumption Provided a Slave, 1806–1860

Year	Number of Slaves [000]	Average Price of Slave [$/slave]	Value of Crop Exploit- ation [$/slave]	Value of Children Born [$/slave]	Value of Total Exploit- ation [$/slave]	Consump- tion Provided [$/slave]
1806	1,062	317	10.90	9.25	20.15	36.69
1807	1,093	286	9.82	8.34	18.16	35.80
1808	1,125	360	12.36	10.49	22.85	33.86
1809	1,158	272	9.36	7.95	17.31	33.91
1810	1,191	277	10.37	7.16	17.53	34.41
1811	1,222	246	9.23	6.37	15.61	36.15
1812	1,254	286	10.71	7.40	18.11	35.21
1813	1,286	284	10.64	7.35	17.99	37.90
1814	1,320	309	11.59	8.00	19.59	39.60
1815	1,354	272	10.20	7.04	17.24	45.18
1816	1,389	337	12.61	8.71	21.32	48.53
1817	1,425	403	15.09	10.42	25.50	48.85
1818	1,461	477	17.88	12.34	30.22	43.90
1819	1,499	407	15.26	10.54	25.80	35.80
1820	1,538	393	14.28	10.64	24.93	31.27
1821	1,580	389	14.14	10.54	24.68	29.52
1822	1,622	294	10.67	7.95	18.61	29.48
1823	1,666	309	11.24	8.38	19.62	27.66
1824	1,711	275	10.00	7.45	17.45	27.01
1825	1,758	277	10.06	7.50	17.55	26.98
1826	1,805	268	9.76	7.27	17.03	27.07
1827	1,854	248	9.02	6.72	15.74	26.40
1828	1,905	253	9.19	6.85	16.04	25.70
1829	1,956	281	10.22	7.62	17.84	25.94
1830	2,009	273	11.32	5.89	17.20	26.26
1831	2,052	308	12.77	6.64	19.41	27.30
1832	2,097	330	13.69	7.12	20.82	27.76
1833	2,142	359	14.90	7.75	22.65	27.65
1834	2,188	378	15.67	8.15	23.82	28.69
1835	2,235	424	17.59	9.15	26.74	30.50
1836	2,284	547	22.69	11.81	34.50	32.50
1837	2,333	634	26.32	13.69	40.02	32.82
1838	2,383	484	20.06	10.44	30.50	32.00
1839	2,435	440	18.24	9.49	27.73	29.68
1840	2,487	377	14.21	9.67	23.88	27.29
1841	2,551	385	14.52	9.88	24.40	24.17
1842	2,617	314	11.82	8.05	19.86	22.47
1843	2,684	280	10.53	7.17	17.70	21.25
1844	2,753	276	10.41	7.09	17.49	21.91
1845	2,823	342	12.87	8.76	21.63	22.35
1846	2,896	358	13.48	9.17	22.65	24.21
1847	2,970	382	14.40	9.81	24.21	23.65
1848	3,046	413	15.54	10.58	26.12	23.49
1849	3,124	387	14.57	9.92	24.48	22.63
1850	3,204	377	15.78	8.02	23.80	23.81
1851	3,272	440	18.39	9.34	27.73	25.35
1852	3,342	471	19.68	10.00	29.68	26.27
1853	3,413	565	23.63	12.00	35.64	26.84
1854	3,485	601	25.12	12.76	37.88	27.74

Appendix Table A.1 (continued)

Year	Number of Slaves [000]	Average Price of Slave [$/slave]	Value of Crop Exploit- ation [$/slave]	Value of Children Born [$/slave]	Value of Total Exploit- ation [$/slave]	Consump- tion Provided [$/slave]
1855	3,559	600	25.10	12.75	37.85	28.27
1856	3,635	655	27.43	13.93	41.36	29.86
1857	3,712	636	26.61	13.52	40.13	29.35
1858	3,791	645	26.97	13.70	40.66	29.90
1859	3,872	801	33.51	17.02	50.53	28.95
1860	3,954	773	32.51	16.51	49.03	29.45

Sources: *Number of Slaves* and *Average Price per Slave* is from Ransom and Sutch (1988: Table A-1).
Value of Crop Exploitation per Slave is calculated as:

$$E_O = P_S * \left[1 - \frac{(1 + a)}{(1 + r)} \right]$$

Where P_S is the average price of a slave; a is the growth in the slave population each year, and r is the rate of return on slave property which is assumed to be 6.6 percent.

Number of Children Born per Slave is calculated as the average price of a slave times the rate of growth of the slave labor stock.

Value of Total Exploitation per Slave is the sum of crop exploitation and the value of children born.

Value of Consumption per Slave is based on the estimate of $28.29 in 1859 from Ransom and Sutch (1977). The data for previous years have been adjusted to reflect changes in the prices of commodities included in the slave consumption estimates. See Ransom and Sutch (1984: Table E-2).

Appendix Table A.2
Value of Slave Output Produced by Free and Coerced Labor, Consumption Denied Slaves, 1806–1860

Year	Total Value of Slave Output [$/slave]	Value of Crops Produced [$/slave]	Crop Product due to Coercion [$/slave]	Crop Product due to Labor [$/slave]	Denied Consumption [$/slave]
1806	56.85	47.59	9.52	38.07	1.38
1807	53.96	45.63	9.24	36.39	0.58
1808	56.71	46.22	9.47	36.74	2.88
1809	51.22	43.28	8.98	34.30	0.38
1810	51.94	44.78	9.40	35.38	0.96
1811	51.75	45.38	9.64	35.74	-0.41
1812	53.32	45.92	9.87	36.05	0.84
1813	55.89	48.54	10.56	37.99	0.09
1814	59.19	51.19	11.26	39.93	0.33
1815	62.42	55.38	12.32	43.06	-2.12
1816	69.85	61.14	13.76	47.39	-1.15
1817	74.35	63.94	14.55	49.39	0.54
1818	74.12	61.78	14.21	47.57	3.67
1819	61.60	51.06	11.87	39.19	3.39
1820	56.19	45.55	10.70	34.85	3.58
1821	54.20	43.66	10.37	33.29	3.77
1822	48.09	40.14	9.63	30.51	1.03
1823	47.28	38.90	9.43	29.47	1.81
1824	44.46	37.01	9.07	27.95	0.93
1825	44.54	37.04	9.17	27.87	0.89
1826	44.09	36.82	9.21	27.62	0.55
1827	42.14	35.42	8.94	26.48	0.07
1828	41.74	34.89	8.90	26.00	0.29
1829	43.78	36.16	9.31	26.85	0.91
1830	43.46	37.57	9.77	27.81	1.55
1831	46.71	40.07	10.52	29.55	2.25
1832	48.58	41.45	10.99	30.47	2.71
1833	50.30	42.55	11.38	31.16	3.52
1834	52.51	44.36	11.98	32.38	3.69
1835	57.24	48.09	13.10	34.99	4.48
1836	67.00	55.19	15.18	40.01	7.52
1837	72.84	59.14	16.41	42.73	9.91
1838	62.50	52.06	14.58	37.49	5.49
1839	57.41	47.92	13.54	34.38	4.70
1840	51.17	41.50	11.83	29.67	2.38
1841	48.58	38.69	11.12	27.57	3.39
1842	42.33	34.29	9.94	24.34	1.87
1843	38.95	31.78	9.30	22.49	1.24
1844	39.41	32.32	9.53	22.79	0.87
1845	43.98	35.21	10.48	24.74	2.39
1846	46.86	37.68	11.30	26.38	2.17
1847	47.87	38.06	11.51	26.55	2.89
1848	49.61	39.03	11.90	27.12	3.64
1849	47.11	37.19	11.44	25.76	3.13
1850	47.61	39.59	12.27	27.32	3.51
1851	53.08	43.74	13.67	30.07	4.72
1852	55.95	45.95	14.48	31.48	5.21
1853	62.47	50.47	16.02	34.45	7.61
1854	65.62	52.86	16.91	35.94	8.20

Appendix Table A.2 (continued)

Year	Total Value of Slave Output [$/slave]	Value of Crops Produced [$/slave]	Crop Product due to Coercion [$/slave]	Crop Product due to Labor [$/slave]	Denied Consumption [$/slave]
1855	66.12	53.37	17.21	36.16	7.89
1856	71.23	57.29	18.62	38.67	8.81
1857	69.47	55.96	18.33	37.63	8.28
1858	70.56	56.87	18.77	38.10	8.20
1859	79.48	62.46	20.77	41.69	12.74
1860	78.48	61.97	20.76	41.21	11.75

Sources: *Total Value of Slave Output* is the value of exploited product plus slave consumption reported in Table A.1.

Value of Crop Output is the total value of slave output less the value of children reported in Table A.1.

Value of Output from Coerced Labor is the fraction of crop output resulting from labor that would not be provided by a free laborer. In 1879 the total work-hours per capita offered by the free black population was between 28 and 37 percent less than the labor offered by slaves (Ransom and Sutch, 1977: 45). We assumed a reduction in work-hours of 20 percent in 1806, rising to 30 percent in 1860.

Value of Output from Free Labor is total crop output less the output produced with coerced labor.

Appendix Table A.3
Exploitation of Slaves as a Percentage of Gross National Product, 1806–1860

Year	Gross National Product	Augmented Gross National Product	Total Value of Exploitation	Exploitation as Percent of Augmented GNP
1806	562	572	21.40	3.74
1807	561	570	19.85	3.48
1808	530	542	25.70	4.74
1809	599	608	20.04	3.29
1810	650	659	20.88	3.17
1811	661	669	19.08	2.85
1812	687	696	22.70	3.26
1813	820	829	23.14	2.79
1814	963	974	25.85	2.66
1815	1,012	1,022	23.34	2.29
1816	1,033	1,045	29.60	2.83
1817	1,055	1,070	36.33	3.40
1818	1,073	1,091	44.17	4.05
1819	958	974	38.68	3.97
1820	841	857	38.34	4.47
1821	806	823	38.98	4.74
1822	889	902	30.20	3.35
1823	873	887	32.69	3.69
1824	894	907	29.87	3.29
1825	1,014	1,027	30.86	3.00
1826	967	980	30.74	3.14
1827	980	992	29.18	2.94
1828	1,016	1,029	30.55	2.97
1829	1,046	1,061	34.89	3.29
1830	1,053	1,065	34.56	3.25
1831	1,126	1,140	39.83	3.50
1832	1,213	1,228	43.65	3.55
1833	1,312	1,329	48.52	3.65
1834	1,333	1,351	52.12	3.86
1835	1,574	1,594	59.77	3.75
1836	1,817	1,844	78.79	4.27
1837	1,781	1,813	93.36	5.15
1838	1,800	1,825	72.70	3.98
1839	1,944	1,967	67.51	3.43
1840	1,725	1,749	59.39	3.40
1841	1,759	1,784	62.25	3.49
1842	1,637	1,658	51.97	3.13
1843	1,618	1,637	47.51	2.90
1844	1,737	1,757	48.15	2.74
1845	1,896	1,921	61.07	3.18
1846	2,020	2,047	65.59	3.20
1847	2,320	2,349	71.91	3.06
1848	2,140	2,172	79.57	3.66
1849	2,265	2,296	76.49	3.33
1850	2,556	2,582	76.27	2.95
1851	2,590	2,621	90.73	3.46
1852	2,709	2,742	99.18	3.62
1853	3,052	3,093	121.62	3.93
1854	3,347	3,391	132.01	3.89

Appendix Table A.3 (continued)

Year	Gross National Product	Augmented Gross National Product	Total Value of Exploit- ation	Exploit- ation as Percent of Augmented GNP
1855	3,653	3,698	134.73	3.64
1856	3,802	3,853	150.35	3.90
1857	4,109	4,159	148.95	3.58
1858	3,692	3,744	154.15	4.12
1859	3,949	4,015	195.63	4.87
1860	4,147	4,212	193.84	4.60

Sources: Gross National Product: Berry (1978).

Augmented Gross National Product: The sum of GNP (column 1) plus the value of the increase in the slave stock for each year calculated from Table A.1.

Total Value of Exploitation: Calculated from Table A.1.

Appendix Table A.4
The Rate of Exploitation of Slaves, 1806–1860

Year	Value of Exploitation Per Slave		Rate of Exploitation Per Slave	
	Total [$/slave]	Crop [$/slave]	Gross [%]	Net [%]
1806	20.15	10.90	35.45	22.90
1807	18.16	9.82	33.65	21.53
1808	22.85	12.36	40.29	26.74
1809	17.31	9.36	33.79	21.63
1810	17.53	10.37	33.74	23.15
1811	15.61	9.23	30.16	20.35
1812	18.11	10.71	33.96	23.33
1813	17.99	10.64	32.19	21.93
1814	19.59	11.59	33.10	22.64
1815	17.24	10.20	27.62	18.42
1816	21.32	12.61	30.52	20.62
1817	25.50	15.09	34.30	23.60
1818	30.22	17.88	40.77	28.94
1819	25.80	15.26	41.89	29.89
1820	24.93	14.28	44.36	31.36
1821	24.68	14.14	45.53	32.39
1822	18.61	10.67	38.71	26.57
1823	19.62	11.24	41.49	28.90
1824	17.45	10.00	39.25	27.02
1825	17.55	10.06	39.42	27.16
1826	17.03	9.76	38.61	26.50
1827	15.74	9.02	37.34	25.46
1828	16.04	9.19	38.42	26.34
1829	17.84	10.22	40.74	28.26
1830	17.20	11.32	39.58	30.12
1831	19.41	12.77	41.55	31.86
1832	20.82	13.69	42.85	33.03
1833	22.65	14.90	45.03	35.02
1834	23.82	15.67	45.36	35.32
1835	26.74	17.59	46.71	36.57
1836	34.50	22.69	51.50	41.12
1837	40.02	26.32	54.94	44.51
1838	30.50	20.06	48.80	38.54
1839	27.73	18.24	48.30	38.06
1840	23.88	14.21	46.66	34.23
1841	24.40	14.52	50.23	37.52
1842	19.86	11.82	46.92	34.47
1843	17.70	10.53	45.45	33.14
1844	17.49	10.41	44.39	32.20
1845	21.63	12.87	49.19	36.54
1846	22.65	13.48	48.34	35.76
1847	24.21	14.40	50.58	37.85
1848	26.12	15.54	52.66	39.82
1849	24.48	14.57	51.97	39.16
1850	23.80	15.78	49.99	39.87
1851	27.73	18.39	52.24	42.04
1852	29.68	19.68	53.04	42.83
1853	35.64	23.63	57.04	46.82
1854	37.88	25.12	57.72	47.52

Appendix Table A.4 (continued)

Year	Value of Exploitation Per Slave		Rate of Exploitation Per Slave	
	Total [$/slave]	Crop [$/slave]	Gross [%]	Net [%]
1855	37.85	25.10	57.25	47.04
1856	41.36	27.43	58.07	47.87
1857	40.13	26.61	57.76	47.55
1858	40.66	26.97	57.63	47.42
1859	50.53	33.51	63.58	53.65
1860	49.03	32.51	62.47	52.47

Sources: Value of Exploitation per Slave: see sources for Table A.2.

Notes: Gross Rate of Exploitation is defined as the total value of exploitation per slave divided by the total value of slave output (col. 1 of Table A.2).

Net Rate of Exploitation is defined as the value of crop exploitation divided by the value of crop output per slave (col. 2 of Table A.2).

4.

An Appraisal of the Estimated Rates of Slave Exploitation

SHERYL BAILEY-WILLIAMS

Economists have investigated numerous aspects of the slave labor system of the antebellum period. One result of this extensive research has been the estimation of the percentage of earned labor income expropriated from slaves by the slaveowner on Southern plantations. This percentage of expropriated labor income is termed the rate of slave exploitation. A wide range of rates of exploitation has been calculated, with the estimates ranging from 10 to 72 percent. Although the estimated rates vary, all previous estimates are theoretically grounded in the neoclassical concept of the exploitation of labor in imperfect labor markets. In the neoclassical model, the amount of income expropriated from a worker by a monopsonistic employer is defined as the difference between labor's marginal revenue product and the wage paid by the monopsonist. However, the fundamental neoclassical supposition that individuals are free to pursue their own self-interest and thus have freedom of choice is not fulfilled by the institution of slavery. Hence, the model cannot be blindly invoked as the theoretical guide to the assessment of the economic consequences of slavery.

It is extremely important to conduct an accurate appraisal of the amount of labor income which the slaveholder expropriated from the slaves. It is necessary to have the appropriate scholarly analysis of this particular economic system. However, the resulting estimates of the economic costs of slavery borne by the slave and the concomitant economic benefits enjoyed by the antebellum slaveholding class also have significant ramifications for present-day public policy on affirmative action and racial discrimination. Since the results of this type of research have an impact on the shape of contemporary public policy, it is imperative that the appropriate methodology be employed.

This chapter examines the neoclassical model that lies behind the estimated rates of slave labor exploitation and identifies the inconsistencies that exist between the underlying theoretical assumptions and the actual circumstances under analysis. The full appraisal of the basic neoclassical assumptions will indicate that the unmodified neoclassical model is inadequate for the analysis of the economic benefits and costs of slavery and that an alternative theoretical paradigm must be developed in order to arrive at a more accurate assessment of the economic consequences of the American slave experience.

THE NEOCLASSICAL DEFINITION OF EXPLOITATION

The neoclassical model is based on the marginal productivity theory of labor demand.[1] One of the model's key assumptions is that the firm's demand for labor is derived from the marginal revenue product of labor for its particular production process. In the world of perfect competition, in both the product and labor markets, the marginal revenue product of labor is equal to the marginal physical product of labor times the selling price of each unit of output. In addition, the prevailing wage rate is set in the market at the intersection of the labor market demand and supply curves, and the individual producer faces a perfectly elastic supply curve for labor at the going wage rate. Hence, the profit-maximizing producer continues to employ workers until the marginal revenue product of the last worker hired is equal to the going wage rate.

Prior to the full development of the theory of the firm under imperfect competition in the late 1930s, A. C. Pigou (1920, p. 556) classified the exploitation of labor as the difference between the value of the marginal physical product of labor times the product price and the wage rate actually paid. Yet, under the conditions of an imperfect product market, the firm faces a downward-sloping product demand curve. The marginal revenue product of labor is not equal to the marginal physical product of labor times product price, but is less than this amount because the firm's marginal revenue is less than the product's price for all outputs greater than one. According to the theory, the relevant concept to the firm, however, is the amount by which total revenue changes as a result of an additional worker being hired. Even if the labor market is competitive and the producer sets the prevailing wage equal to the marginal revenue product of labor, the wage will never equal the marginal physical product of labor times product price since the output is sold in an imperfectly competitive environment.

Following the development of the theory of imperfect competition, the concept of exploitation was modified to be defined as the discrepancy between the marginal revenue product of labor and the wage actually paid. As indicated by Gordon F. Bloom (1941, pp. 414–15), the Pigouvian definition of exploitation is less useful because under that criterion labor exploitation "will be almost universal" and the exploitation can be eliminated only by removing the impediments to perfect competition.

Given the updated definition of exploitation, the source of any discrepancy between the marginal revenue product of labor and the wage paid is most generally identified as the monopsonistic position of the employer.[2] The neoclassical monopsonist faces the upward-sloping labor market supply curve. He or she therefore finds that the marginal cost of an additional unit of labor is greater than the average cost of labor (that is, the wage to be paid) because the higher wage paid to lure an additional worker to supply his or her labor to the firm must be paid to all previous workers hired as well, assuming no wage discrimination. Thus, the profit-maximizing monopsonist will equate the marginal revenue product of labor to the marginal cost of labor. As a result, the monopsonist will hire fewer workers than would be hired in a competitive labor market and will pay a wage that is below the competitive level. In addition, the monopsonistic wage will be less than labor's marginal revenue product. The extent to which the wage paid by the monopsonist is less than the marginal revenue product of labor is the measure of the degree of monopsonistic labor exploitation. Given this approach, the rate of labor exploitation can thus be calculated as the ratio of the amount of income expropriated from the worker to labor's marginal revenue product.[3]

ESTIMATED RATES OF SLAVE EXPLOITATION

Given the fundamental neoclassical definition of exploitation as the divergence between labor's marginal revenue product and the wage actually received by labor, various researchers have estimated the percentage of earned labor income expropriated from slaves by the slaveowners on the Southern antebellum farms. Although the techniques employed differ slightly, they are all based on the neoclassical categorization of labor exploitation as resulting from an employer's monopsonistic position. In general, the method employed entails calculation of the value of labor's share of total farm output, that is, the value of total output attributable to the labor input. This implies the marginal revenue product of the last worker employed. Labor's estimated marginal revenue product is compared with an estimate of actual slave "income" (value of slave consumption), and the degree of exploitation is then calculated.

This general procedure relates directly to the neoclassical paradigm. Within the context of the monopsony model, the marginal revenue product of the last worker is equal to the marginal cost of labor at the profit-maximizing quantity of labor; the wage actually paid then comes from the labor supply curve at the indicated quantity of labor. The amount of labor income expropriated from the workers by the monopsonist is measured by the difference between labor's marginal revenue product and the actual wage paid; the rate of exploitation is the amount of expropriated labor income taken as a percentage of the marginal revenue product of labor.

Estimated rates of slave exploitation have been advanced by Robert W. Fogel and Stanley Engerman (1974), Richard K. Vedder (1974), and Roger L. Ransom and Richard Sutch (1978). These researchers employ a variety of techniques. Vedder and Ransom and Sutch directly apply the neoclassical model, whereas Fogel and Engerman employ a variant of the basic neoclassical concept of exploitation.

Vedder (1975) uses estimates of farm production function coefficients in order to calculate labor's share of total farm output. He generally selects a value within the range of previous estimates of slave maintenance costs for the actual slave "wage." The estimated average rate of slave expropriation is 65 percent for the year 1860. Using different estimates of labor's share and of average slave compensation, Vedder derives alternative estimates of the rate of slave exploitation, ranging from a lower bound estimate of 43.2 percent to an upper bound estimate of 72.2 percent.

Having reservations about the production function approach, Ransom and Sutch (1978) employ an accounting method in order to estimate the value of labor's share of total output. They estimate the value of total farm output and then deduct the cost of capital, depreciation on land, imputed interest costs, and supervisory costs; the residual is the estimated value of total output attributable to the labor input. Their estimated values of slave consumption are based on Sutch's (1975) thorough analysis of Fogel and Engerman's estimates of slave maintenance costs. The resulting estimates of the average rate of exploitation of slaves in 1859 are 53.7 percent for all slave farms and 59.2 percent for large plantations (pp. 203–12).

Fogel and Engerman (1974) follow the neoclassical model and classify the amount of income expropriated from the slave at any point in time as the difference between the marginal revenue product of labor and the actual slave "wage." However, they submit that, since the purchase of a slave was a long-term investment, the relevant measure for the analysis of slavery is the "expected present value [at birth] of the income expropriated from a slave over the course of his lifetime" (Vol. 2, pp. 119–20). Fogel and Engerman also maintain that this measure is equal to the value of a slave's "birthright," or the average price of a newborn slave. The rate of exploitation is calculated as the ratio of the value of the birthright to the expected present value at birth of the average slave's marginal revenue product over his or her entire lifetime. The average rate of slave exploitation is thereby estimated to be 12 percent. Fogel and Engerman adjust this estimate down to 10 percent in order to account for the "offsetting services" that slaves received from the slaveowner.[4]

Fogel and Engerman also calculate an "undiscounted" version of the exploitation rate as the ratio of the sum of expected expropriated income over the slave's lifetime to the sum of expected total income (marginal revenue product) over the slave's lifetime. The reported figure is 49 percent.[5]

An estimate of the unmodified neoclassical rate of exploitation can also be derived from the myriad estimates calculated by Fogel and Engerman in *Time on the Cross* (1974). Ransom and Sutch (1978) calculate the value of slave marginal revenue product implied by Fogel and Engerman's production function estimate of a labor share of 58 percent on slave farms, using their estimates of the average value of total farm output on all slave farms and on large plantations. Combined with Fogel and Engerman's estimates of the value of slave consumption on both categories of Southern farms, these calculations yield estimated rates of the average slave exploitation of 54 percent for all slave farms and 50 percent for large plantations.[6]

PREVIOUS ESTIMATES INVOLVE THE INAPPROPRIATE APPLICATION OF THE NEOCLASSICAL PARADIGM

It can be concluded from the previous discussion that the neoclassical model is the central force behind all of the previously estimated rates of slave exploitation. In order for these estimates to be of any analytical value, it is of paramount importance that the principal theoretical model be applicable to the situation of slavery. A close examination of the underlying neoclassical paradigm will reveal that the fundamental assumptions of neoclassical theory are not fulfilled by the circumstances of slavery. Therefore, the applicability of the unmodified model is questionable.

The assumption that each individual possesses the freedom to pursue his or her own self-interest and therefore is free to make choices can be regarded as being an integral part of neoclassical theory. It is further assumed that each individual's preferences are considered and are expressed through his or her market behavior. Moreover, the neoclassical model postulates that individuals in the economy freely choose which goods they will consume and when and that each person voluntarily decides how they will allocate their labor (and other resources) to be used in production processes. In addition, it is presumed that all transactions that take place between individuals have been entered into freely and voluntarily.[7]

In the context of the monopsony model, it is assumed that the monopsonist faces an upward-sloping market labor supply curve, indicating that the quantity of labor supplied to the monopsonist varies directly with the wage rate. This market supply curve is defined as the sum of the individual labor supply curves. Given the underlying presupposition of freedom of choice, the neoclassical model of labor supply indicates that the representative individual will choose that combination of market work (which generates income that is used to buy goods) and nonmarket activities (leisure) which maximizes his or her utility, subject to time and price constraints. The effect of an increase in the wage paid for any particular job can be traced through the individual utility-maximization model, and an upward-sloping individual labor supply curve can thereby be derived for that occupation.[8]

In surveying the possible uses of their labor, the neoclassical model postulates that individuals consider both the monetary return as well as the working conditions ("nonpecuniary aspects") of alternative opportunities. Workers are assumed to view the nonmonetary characteristics of a job opportunity as being advantageous or disadvantageous. Changes in the working conditions of an occupation will cause its neoclassical labor supply curve to shift. In general, it is hypothesized that as individuals seek to maximize their well-being (subject to the relevant constraints), they choose the employment opportunity that produces the greatest net advantage to themselves. As indicated by Ingrid H. Rima (1981):

The net advantage of any employment opportunity reflects the net money income (i.e., gross income minus the cost of education, training, and moving) plus or minus the value the worker attaches to its *nonmonetary* advantages and disadvantages. People choose among different opportunities on the basis of their net advantages. If workers are free to move among occupations and locations, the choice mechanism tends to equalize the net advantage among different opportunities (p. 91).

This hypothesis of equal net advantage originated with Adam Smith.

With regard to the analysis of the economics of slavery, the neoclassical monopsony model is of questionable applicability. In applying the monopsony model to the analysis of the degree of labor exploitation suffered by the slaves, it is implicitly assumed that the slaves freely chose to supply their labor to the antebellum Southern farms and that the quantity of slave labor supplied varied directly with the wage paid to slaves. This implicit framework obviously does not apply to the institution of slavery which is primarily characterized by its involuntary, compulsory nature. The assumed labor supply curve of the monopsony model does not exist for slave labor because the slaves had absolutely no choice in the whole matter. None of the neoclassical suppositions underlying a freely determined labor supply curve is fulfilled by the circumstances of slavery. The slaves were not free to pursue their own self-interest; their individual preferences did not count and were not expressed in the marketplace; they did not freely choose which goods they consumed and when; they could not voluntarily decide how their labor would be allocated among the alternative production processes and between work and leisure; nor did they enter into their transactions with others (both market and nonmarket) freely and voluntarily.

Hence, the monopsony model cannot accurately describe the "wage-employment" decisions of the slaveholder. The slaveowner did not face a free labor market. Since the labor supply curve indicating the response of labor supply to changes in the wage rate does not exist for slave labor, the accompanying marginal cost of labor curve also does not exist. Therefore, the slaveowner could not have determined the profit-maximizing quantity of slaves by setting the marginal revenue product of labor equal to the marginal cost of labor associated with the free labor supply curve. Moreover, the slave "wage" actually paid could not have been derived from the labor supply curve at the given quantity of labor.

The slaveholder regarded slave labor as a capital good in determining the profit-maximizing quantity of slave labor to employ.[9] The slaveowner primarily had a stock of slave labor, and this stock was expanded either by purchases of additional slaves in the slave market or by the progeneration of his current slave population. A capital-investment model is much more appropriate for the theoretical analysis of the slaveholder's decision-making process. However, an analysis of the slaveowner's capital-investment decision with regard to the ownership of slaves does not assess the extent to which slaves were exploited under the institution of slavery. It is inappropriate to analyze the costs and benefits of a slave labor system purely from the viewpoint of the slaveowner when the professed goal is to evaluate the degree of slave exploitation. It is vitally necessary to incorporate the condition of freedom as the appropriate point of comparison and to shift the perspective to that of the slave.

The application of the neoclassical model of labor markets to such an appraisal would require the postulation of the position of the appropriate labor supply curve indicating the wage rates necessary to entice various quantities of free workers to voluntarily choose to commit their own and their progeny's labor to the occupation of slave, given that each individual worker is assumed to make an assessment of both the pecuniary and the nonpecuniary aspects of each employment opportunity and he or she pursues the maximization of his or her own well-being. Knowledge of such a labor supply curve would be required in order to accurately evaluate the extent of labor exploitation within the neoclassical paradigm. Yet, it is impossible for such a labor supply curve to exist because it would require the individual worker to be free to compare the net advantage of employment as a slave with the net advantage of alternative opportunities. This assumption of the supreme volition of the individual worker is totally inconsistent with the fundamentally coercive framework of the institution of slavery.

In addition, as indicated by Paul A. David and Peter Temin (1976, p. 229), even if the "luring wage" could be determined from the appropriate labor supply curve, it is unlikely that a slaveholder would be willing to pay a gross wage in a free labor market that would sufficiently offset the assuredly significant negative value of the disadvantages of employment as a slave for the worker, such that the net advantage of employment as a slave would compare favorably with the net advantage of other job opportunities. The slaveowner would find it profitable to employ alternative "types" of labor (free labor), and there would be no slave agricultural workers.

CONCLUSIONS

The neoclassical monopsony model underlies all of the previously estimated rates of slave labor exploitation. However, it has been shown that the basic assumptions of that theoretical model are fundamentally inconsistent with the characteristics of the situation under analysis; namely, slavery is an involuntary, compulsory institution, and the neoclassical model pivotally assumes that all participants in an economic system possess the freedom to pursue their own individual self-interests and thus have the freedom of choice. It can therefore be concluded that the neoclassical monopsony model is an inappropriate theoretical guide to the assessment of the extent to which slaveholders benefited and slaves suffered as a result of the exploitation of slave labor. Consequently, an alternative theoretical paradigm must be developed in order to accurately appraise the degree of slave exploitation during the antebellum period.

NOTES

1. An alternative definition of labor exploitation is based on the theories of Karl Marx. However, all of the previous estimates of the rates of slave exploitation have been applications

of the neoclassical definition of labor exploitation. Therefore, the neoclassical definition will be the focus of this appraisal of the previous estimates of slave exploitation rates.

2. Gordon F. Bloom (1941) differentiates between "deliberate" and "nondeliberate" exploitation. He categorizes exploitation due to monopsony (the employer facing an upward-sloping labor supply curve) as "nondeliberate" exploitation because the monopsonist cannot *profitably* pay labor its marginal revenue product. He also identifies an oligopolistic product market with a kinked product demand curve and price rigidity as another possible source of "nondeliberate" labor exploitation (wage less than labor's marginal revenue product). In addition, Bloom defines the deliberate exploitation of labor as taking place only when "the employer consciously attempts to pay labor less than its marginal revenue product, despite the fact that conditions are such that he could profitably pay the marginal revenue product if he so desired" (p. 437). In order for such deliberate exploitation to take place, Bloom states that it is necessary for the labor supply curve to be perfectly inelastic over the relevant range, the employer must be able to set the wage, and the product demand curve must be kinked at the prevailing price.

3. For additional discussions of the exploitation of labor due to monopsony, see Robinson (1933), Rima (1981, pp. 131–32), Marshall, Cartter, and King (1976, pp. 229–33), and Addison and Siebert (1979, pp. 48–52).

4. Fogel and Engerman cite two possible types of "offsetting services" which the slaves received: (1) the advantages of sharing in the lower costs of goods consumed because of the volume discounts gained on large plantation purchases and (2) the lower interest costs the slaves had as a result of "borrowing" from the master instead of in the open market. See Volume 1, pp. 153–57 and Volume 2, pp. 83 and 119–25 for the discussion of the procedures they employed in the estimation of the rate of slave exploitation.

5. Paul A. David and Peter Temin (1976) have advanced some serious criticisms of the techniques Fogel and Engerman employed to estimate the rate of slave exploitation. Most notably, they submit that Fogel and Engerman significantly understate the true rate of exploitation because they improperly discount the stream of future slave income and maintenance costs in deriving their estimate of the average rate of expropriation over a slaver's lifetime. In addition, David and Temin indicate that Fogel and Engerman's undiscounted estimate of the exploitation rate is also biased downward because: (1) Fogel and Engerman ignore the impact of the slaveowners' risk aversion on the market prices of slaves and (2) they overstate slave maintenance costs by assuming that the cost of feeding the slaves was proportional to the amount of calories the slaves consumed.

6. See Ransom and Sutch (1978, pp. 203–9) and Lee and Passell (1979), pp. 205–6 for these calculations.

7. See David and Temin (1976, pp. 223–30).

8. The substitution effect must dominate the income effect in order for the labor supply curve to be upward-sloping. For discussions of the theory of labor supply, see Addison and Siebert (1979, pp. 70–79), Rima (1981, Chapter 2), and Levitan, Mangum, and Marshall (1981, pp. 101–3).

9. See Anderson and Gallman (1977).

REFERENCES

Addison, John T., and Siebert, Stanley. *The Market for Labor: An Analytical Treatment.* Santa Monica, Calif.: Goodyear Publishing Co., 1979.

Anderson, Ralph V., and Gallman, Robert E. "Slaves as Fixed Capital: Slave Labor and Southern Economic Development." *Journal of American History* 64 (1977):24–46.

Bloom, Gordon F. "A Reconsideration of the Theory of Exploitation." *Quarterly Journal of Economics* 55 (1941):413–42.

David, Paul A., and Temin, Peter. "Slavery: The Progressive Institution?" In Paul A. David et al., *Reckoning with Slavery*. New York: Oxford University Press, 1976, pp. 165–230.

Fogel, Robert W., and Engerman, Stanley L. *Time on the Cross*. 2 vols. Boston: Little, Brown, 1974. Vol. 1, *The Economics of American Negro Slavery*; Vol. 2, *Evidence and Methods: A Supplement*.

Lee, Susan P., and Passell, Peter. *A New Economics View of American History*. New York: W. W. Norton, 1979.

Levitan, Sar A., Mangum, Garth L., and Marshall, Ray. *Human Resources and Labor Markets: Employment and Training in the American Economy*. 3d ed. New York: Harper & Row, 1981.

Marshall, F. Ray, Cartter, Allan M., and King, Allan G. *Labor Economics: Wages, Employment and Trade Unionism*. 3d ed. Homewood, Ill.: Richard D. Irwin, Inc., 1976.

Pigou, A. C. *The Economics of Welfare*. London: Macmillan, 1920.

Ransom, Roger L., and Sutch, Richard. *One Kind of Freedom: The Economic Consequences of Emancipation*. Cambridge, Eng.: Cambridge University Press, 1977.

Rima, Ingrid H. *Labor Markets, Wages and Employment*. New York: W. W. Norton, 1981.

Robinson, Joan. *The Economics of Imperfect Competition*. London: Macmillan, 1933.

Sutch, Richard. "The Treatment Received by American Slaves: A Critical Review of the Evidence Presented in *Time on the Cross*." *Explorations in Economics History* 12 (1975):335–438.

Vedder, Richard K. "The Slave Exploitation (Expropriation) Rate." *Explorations in Economic History* 12 (1975):453–57.

PART III

Slavery and the Economics of Discrimination

In this section, Warren C. Whatley and Gavin Wright establish the difficulty of understanding complex historical processes. Current discussions of race tend to gloss over the subtleties and overriding economic realities that influenced decision makers during slavery. But we should be clear that the purpose of this book is not to affix blame to the perpetrators of discrimination, but, rather, to identify the classes of direct and indirect beneficiaries, currently.

Next, Larry Neal and James Marketti attempt to show how we can get a feel for the magnitude of the benefits. Following these two chapters are two others by Vedder, Gallaway, and Klingaman and by Feiner and Roberts which analyze, from very different perspectives, how exploitation operated and how difficult it is to obtain a consensus on the full consequences of exploitation, however defined.

5.

Black Labor in the American Economy since Emancipation: What Are the Legacies of History?

Warren C. Whatley and
Gavin Wright

Approaching this topic with lead questions like "Who benefits from discrimination?" and "What happened to the benefits?" gives the inquiry a breath of scandal. The underlying premise is that racial discrimination has unjustly redistributed income in the past, that these benefits have been conserved and cumulated through historical time, and that some classes today are therefore receiving "a kind of unjust enrichment" which should rightfully be returned. In this chapter we take a different view. We agree that the present status of blacks in the American economy is very much a legacy of the past. But there is little consensus about the mechanisms through which discrimination has operated, and still less about processes of cumulation and intergenerational transfer. As we see it, most of today's discrimination models share an absence of history, a sense of how the black experience relates to the broader evolution of the American economy. Surely it is premature to calculate a reparations bill until we have an "economics of discrimination" that comes to grips with basic historical facts.

But our objection runs deeper. We argue that there has not in reality been a single persistent structure of discrimination through the past century of American history, but instead a series of regimes with very different properties and implications. Often, labor market structures have changed, for reasons having little directly to do with blacks or discrimination. We need to understand this history better, but the simple model of redistributive discrimination does not help us do so.

Above all, history is a learning process. The literature has placed heavy emphasis on only one kind of learning, formal education. But as we will argue, other kinds of learning have been at least as important: by employers, by white workers, and by black workers on and off the job. The most stubborn legacies of history are the things whites have "learned" about blacks and blacks have "learned" about themselves, learning that has in turn shaped the realities of economic life. From this standpoint, we have to be careful that the remedies we propose do not reinforce the very lessons which today need to be unlearned.

CONCEPTIONS OF DISCRIMINATION

There are enough surveys of discrimination models to satisfy anyone's appetite, and we do not propose to add to the list.[1] Some models emphasize prejudicial attitudes by employers or workers, barriers to entry, statistical discrimination, collusion and bargaining among factions, or state intervention.[2] A major distinction among models, and indeed the central concern to most theorists in this area, is whether a basis for discrimination exists in long-run competitive equilibrium, or whether, alternatively, discrimination can only be maintained in the long run by noncompetitive constraints or nonmarket institutions. From any standpoint, it is premature to set about measuring discrimination in history until we can determine which of these models is appropriate. The models do, however, have one feature in common: Virtually without exception, they have no historical context. This is not to say that every theoretical article ought to be a treatise in history as well, but only that it is not unreasonable to ask a theorist to specify whether the premises of the model are thought to prevail only in certain historical circumstances, and if so, which these might be.

Because the abstract models are not located explicitly in history, they are not reliable guides to historical (empirical) studies. In recent years a lively debate has persisted about the extent of changes in labor market discrimination, over the role of federal policies in suppressing or eliminating discrimination, and over the degree of permanence of black economic gains.[3] One reason why this discussion has been inconclusive is that there has never been a clear understanding of exactly what process of discrimination characterized earlier periods of U.S. history, nor indeed whether labor market discrimination per se has historically been a significant factor. For most economists, the world before about 1960 is a kind of never-never land in which blacks were too obviously oppressed for economic analysis to be relevant. Or at most, that era is now thought to be too remote to affect policy choices today. The result of this thinking is that we have no real perspective on what has happened, and hence little basis for knowing whether recent policies have been causal initiators or merely facilitators of a longer run historical process.

Rather than offer a tedious list of unhistorical examples, it is more constructive and more helpful to take note of the exceptions. Several economists have conducted historical studies of the supply-side impact of public discrimination in the provision of black educational facilities. Richard Freeman and Finis Welch have argued that the quantity and quality of black education have improved since the turn of the century and that the passage of various antidiscrimination policies has increased the economic return to such investments made by blacks.[4] While the documentation of racial differences in educational opportunities is very valuable, this debate contains very little analysis of wage or job discrimination as a historical phenomenon.

Among theorists, however, one can find various acknowledgments that labor market discrimination may be a phenomenon where history matters. Kenneth Arrow is perhaps the most explicit in identifying job segregation as a case for which nonconvexity is likely to prevail, promoting tendencies not toward the middle but toward extremes. He observes: "Obviously, in a situation like this, where there are costs to change, history matters a good deal."[5] The possibility that particular "initial conditions" may have created a self-reinforcing pattern of inequality is all the more reason for giving these models a concrete historical setting. Yet, among empirical labor economists virtually the only attempt at examining job discrimination as a long-term historical phenomenon is the Wharton School project on Racial Policies of American Industry, directed by Herbert Northrup and several associates between 1967 and 1974.[6] These studies tend to confirm the importance of exactly the kind of industry-specific factors that Arrow suggested (segregation systems, date of industry origin, patterns of training, promotion, and supervision). Because the Wharton studies were resolutely institutional, however, they did not provide a labor-market interpretation of the origins or impact of the various segregation systems they described.

Recently, some economists have moved to fill this vacuum, through longer term analysis of trends in black incomes and education. Most prominent is the work of James P. Smith and Finis Welch, who argue that a properly constructed time series on black education can explain (with a lag) the long delay in relative income convergence, as well as the progress since 1950.[7] Their evidence and interpretation have been subjected to serious criticism.[8] Most fundamentally, however, this research does not illuminate the phenomenon of discrimination. Smith and Welch assume that an occupational index is a sufficient proxy for income, and they equate "human capital" with schooling. In effect, they assume that the labor market has been a purely passive ratifier of the quality of black labor through time. Although the factors they emphasize are undoubtedly important, their approach seems to be driven by an urge for extreme simplification, by locating the major historical forces outside of the economic system.

A more balanced and complex view is presented by Robert Higgs.[9] In a rare historical labor market study, Higgs found that outright wage discrimination was in fact unusual, even in the segregated South of the early twentieth century. The significance of this result remains uncertain, however, until we know more about the basis for job assignments and promotions, and until we determine the nature and implications of job segregation itself. Higgs tends to argue that governmental discrimination has been more damaging and persistent than labor market discrimination. But this view of things may have more validity for some historical eras than for others.

It is tempting to bypass the issue that is central to writers like Smith, Welch, and Higgs (market versus premarket discrimination) and to argue that one way or another, long-term income differences must be due to discrimination. This is the view of Udinsky, Chechere, and America (in this volume), who argue that it is unlikely that "cultural and other factors" explaining the income gap would persist over long periods in an "open market, equal opportunity environment." Such a conclusion is not nearly as self-evident as it may appear. Black economic progress was set back by disfranchisement and the turn-of-the-century assault on black schools in the South, but it was no less damaged by the collapse of cotton demand after 1920 and the mechanization of Southern agriculture after World War II. Were these discriminatory moves? Was it discrimination when the New Deal doubled wage rates in tobacco manufacturing, triggering a mechanization program that reduced black employment by half within thirty years? Has discrimination been the cause of economic decline in the black-majority industrial cities of the Northeast? To be sure, in all of these examples racial discrimination *has* been involved, albeit indirectly. The economic impact, however, has come from the interaction between the economic structure and historical circumstances. Our object is not to downplay or minimize discrimination in American history, but to argue that it does not enhance understanding of the present situation to treat all income differences as part of a grand historical expropriation from blacks by whites.

The issue of culture is particularly critical. Udinsky, Chechere, and America assume that an "open market" environment would be one in which cultural differences between races tend to disappear. Perhaps if employers, lenders, landlords, and fellow workers took no notice of race whatever, cultural differences would diminish over time. But such a statement is a near-tautology, because initial differences in culture could not be very large if no one took any notice of them. As we argue, however, it is in the very nature of labor and capital markets to make distinctions among people, and it is in the nature of rational economic behavior to take note of preexisting differences. This is the essence of "statistical discrimination," emphasized by Stanley Masters, and developed theoretically by Edmund Phelps and Dennis J. Aigner, and Glen G. Cain.[10] The most powerful models go further, suggesting that a racially conscious market environment may in turn shape the incentives of the system, so that race consciousness comes to seem appropriate rather than discriminatory. This is the setting identified by Arrow as one in which nonconvexity is likely to prevail, promoting tendencies not toward the middle but toward the extremes.[11] The persistence of cultural differences between races is much more plausible, if those differences have been reinforced by the demands of the market. True, this scenario does not describe an "equal opportunity" environment; but if it is an environment likely to be fostered by market forces, then it is not best remedied by deifying the competitive market as the relevant ethical norm.

Recent theoretical treatments underscore this point. "Initial differences" between races, such as "language" (which may mean dialect or levels of education), will lead to maximal segregation in a competitive labor market.[12] But treating individuals according to group characteristics will in turn exacerbate the initial disparity. The resulting pattern will not necessarily be efficient, but like the QWERTY typewriter keyboard, it may be extremely persistent, difficult for any one employer to change.[13] This outcome will be adverse for blacks, but the direct transfer may be far less important than the perverse incentives established for blacks and whites alike.

Rather than belabor these points at this level, we proceed in the remainder of this chapter to argue by example and illustration. Our approach is historical. We do not begin by positing a set of motives and attitudes, but try instead to build up some "stylized facts" which an analytical interpretation ought to come to grips with. Our supporting evidence is mainly illustrative, and models are only sketched. But we hope to convince the reader that it is more relevant to identify the process than to finger the culprits.

SOUTHERN AND NATIONAL LABOR MARKETS, 1870–1914

The first basic historical fact is that for three-quarters of a century after the Civil War, American blacks were located predominantly in the South. Southern per capita income during this period was only half the national average, and black per capita income was no more than about two-thirds of the Southern average.[14] The obvious question is why Southern blacks did not migrate northward, and the equally obvious answer which has suggested itself is discrimination that effectively reduced the Northern wage available to blacks. Writers as diverse as Brinley Thomas, Jay Mandle, and Robert Higgs have all endorsed the proposition that pre-1914 regional outmigration was deterred by *Northern* prejudice against blacks.[15] Thomas writes: "If by a miracle there had been racial tolerance, the black workers from the South could have played their full part, in common with immigrants from Europe, in meeting the labor requirements of the rapidly growing cities of the North after the Civil War" (*Migration and Economic Growth*, p. xxvi).

The prejudice is attributed partly to potential employers, but largely to the immigrant workers who were keenly competing for industrial jobs. By this interpretation, the barriers to black migration were removed with the disruption of foreign immigration in 1914, and the strong wartime demand for labor which induced employers to overcome their own prejudice against hiring blacks. According to Higgs, the channels that opened during wartime continued to operate afterward: "By the late 1920's, a large and steady movement of blacks to the North had, like the weevil, become institutionalized . . . an established fact of American social life" ("The Boll Weevil," p. 335).

One aspect of this account is undeniably correct: that major Northern employers discriminated against blacks. Studies of cities, states, and industries in the North all show that the blacks who were there were systematically denied access to all but menial jobs with no advancement prospects.[16] In this situation the persistence of discrimination is not difficult to explain. The cost to a Northern employer for discriminating against blacks was probably not very great precisely because black workers represented such a small fraction of the total Northern labor force. But from the standpoint of a potential black migrant the available Northern wage may have been low enough to deter the kind of supply response needed to push racial wages and job assignments toward equality.

There are two troublesome facts that are difficult to reconcile with the Higgs-Mandle-Thomas scenario. First, research has revealed that by and large the Southern unskilled white wage was not substantially different from the wage available for Southern blacks. Using USDA surveys of farm wages by race, Higgs has shown that differences between black and white levels were small, averaging 8 percent in Southern states between 1899 and 1902.[17] Southern manufacturing wages were closely linked to these farm wage rates, at least before World War I. The evidence we have on racial-age patterns in industry suggests that the same pattern prevails.[18]

Figure 5.1 shows racial wage distributions for a set of industries in Virginia in 1907, the same data source used by Higgs. The correspondence of the model (peak) wage for blacks and whites is evident, as is the contrast in the right-hand tail. If we interpret the mode as the wage paid to "common labor," then this evidence goes even further than Higgs in documenting the effectiveness of the market in equilibrating wage rates by race.

The second disturbing fact is that the wage level of Southern *white* unskilled labor was also well below national standards. This was true in the cotton mills, and it was true for farm labor. Contrary to much casual commentary, in both cases there is clear evidence of high labor mobility and frequent turnover; in short, there is an operating labor market. It was a regional market, however, and not a branch of the national labor market. Labor moved from east to west and from low-wage to high-wage areas, just as in the North; but labor did not move from South to North in any appreciable volume before 1914. What we are driven to is the idea that the central phenomenon of this era was the isolation of Southern from national labor markets, for whites as well as for blacks. This isolation had something to do with race but was not exactly "racial discrimination." As Gavin Wright has previously argued, these patterns of labor market geography may be understood in terms of the "network

Figure 5.1
Racial Wage Distributions in Virginia, All Industry, 1907

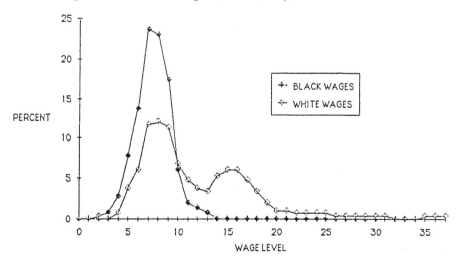

externalities" associated with the mobility of unskilled labor, particularly its dependence on informal channels for information, advice, and assistance with transition costs.[19] If we insist on considering all deviations from national norms "discrimination," then we have to allow that many Southern whites were also victims. If we insist on identifying the "gainers," the finger will point to Southern employers of unskilled labor; but these were not necessarily the perpetrators of "discrimination" against blacks!

At the same time, Figures 5.1 and 5.2 do suggest another kind of inequity within the South that is of more importance than wage discrimination: the blocking of black progress out of unskilled levels into higher paying jobs. This was the dimension of "segregation" which was not at all innocuous in its labor market impact, and it was also the form of discrimination that may have been least vulnerable to competitive pressures. This may be an example of the situation envisioned by Arrow, in which an initially arbitrary segregation line comes to have a self-ratifying discriminatory character over time. In the early Southern textiles industry, for example, beginning workers could not make more than blacks could earn as farm laborers. But the lily-white labor system that shut blacks out of any skill-enhancing positions also shut them out of any share of productivity gains over time. Employers in the industry expressed what seem to have been sincere skepticism that blacks would have any aptitude or capacity for that kind of work.[20]

It is easy enough to determine that the main immediate beneficiaries of the missing right-hand tail were the white workers who advanced into higher paying positions faster than they would have under a color-blind regime. They got a particularly high return for this, because relative skill premiums were much higher in the South than elsewhere (which is another way of saying that North-South differentials were

Figure 5.2
Racial Wage Distributions in Selected Southern Industries, 1907

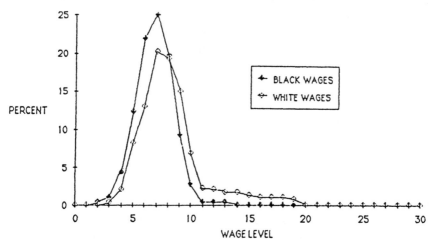

significantly lower for skilled labor categories). We should be cautious, however, about the simple identification of Southern skilled workers, a relatively small group, as the direct beneficiaries and perpetuators of this form of discrimination. The verdict must be qualified for several reasons. First, it would be difficult to distinguish between barriers that were "purely" discriminatory, in the sense that blacks were equally qualified but not chosen, and barriers that had some "justification" in the inferior levels of education and training among blacks. The second factor would locate the problem much more broadly in the white political structure where the allocation of public funds away from the provision of educational facilities for blacks reflects weak black political power.[21] But for this era of history, where industrial skills were gained primarily on the job, we are inclined to give the "pure" discrimination effect most emphasis. Yet even here the distinction is blurred by the possibility that many black workers, seeing the futility of pursuing industrial "skills" of some sort as a means of advancement, gave them low personal priority and hence were "unqualified."

A second qualification emanates from the fact that in essence the behavior of Southern skilled workers was not different from that of skilled workers elsewhere in the country. Craft unions in general sought to protect the economic status of their members by restricting access to certain skill-enhancing positions and lines of progression, enforcing preferential hirings and layoffs, and controlling crucial job designs.[22] The relatively high skill premiums in the South may reflect the additional market power of a white skilled worker there, but it is not at all clear that these higher skill premiums were actually the *creation* of restrictiveness, rather than a reflection of the paucity of skills in the South and the underdeveloped character of the Southern economy going back to the slave era.

Identifying the ultimate beneficiaries is still less certain when we allow that barriers to black industrial progress might be viewed as part of a broad coalition of interests between white industrial labor and white landlord classes. If the Southern labor market was regional and low wage, and if discrimination occurred primarily in promotion from unskilled industrial jobs, then blacks were "crowded" into agriculture. Hence, we do not really escape the ambiguities involved in measuring the benefits of discrimination by narrowing in on industrial skills, promotion rules, seniority systems, and the like. The Southern landlords may well have been the least discriminatory class and yet the major beneficiaries of discrimination.

STRUCTURAL CHANGE IN THE SOUTH AFTER 1914

Having pressed the crucial role of regionalism and ice-breaking costs in labor markets, it might seem that it was all downhill after 1914. All that was needed was for outmigration to "get a start and become a pattern" (in Myrdal's phrase), with World War I providing the initial spark. Once Southern workers came to understand that there was an "outside" demand for their labor, class relations in the South could never be the same. This is all logical, but a look at the wage data tells us that this is not quite the right story. Table 5.1 reveals the remarkable fact that in almost

Table 5.1
Farm Wage Rates (Daily Without Board)
Deflated by Williamson's COL Series for Unskilled Labor

	Va	NC	SC	GA	Ala	Miss	Ark	La	Texas	TN
1889-90	.82	.68	.69	.80	.81	.87	1.02	.97	1.07	.78
1899	.86	.73	.62	.72	.76	.85	.95	.95	1.10	.87
1902	.87	.78	.65	.76	.85	.88	1.09	1.11	1.18	.87
1906	1.15	1.03	.91	1.10	1.11	1.30	1.27	1.30	1.37	1.10
1909	1.05	.98	.78	1.00	.96	1.05	1.15	1.10	1.27	1.01
1910	1.07	1.03	.96	1.01	1.12	1.17	1.28	1.09	1.40	1.09
1911	1.07	1.04	.93	1.08	1.04	1.06	1.23	1.12	1.34	1.06
1912	1.08	1.06	.93	1.05	1.07	1.07	1.23	1.11	1.36	1.04
1913	1.17	1.08	.93	1.06	1.06	1.10	1.20	1.12	1.36	1.05
1914	1.09	1.02	.82	.94	.95	.98	1.12	1.04	1.34	1.00
1915	1.09	1.00	.74	.91	.92	.96	1.08	1.04	1.32	.96
1916	1.08	.96	.76	.87	.84	.90	1.04	1.02	1.22	.92
1917	1.20	1.09	.84	.95	.91	.92	1.14	1.01	1.20	.98
1918	1.35	1.18	.84	1.09	1.05	1.10	1.28	1.20	1.26	1.05
1919	1.27	1.32	1.11	1.13	1.10	1.22	1.29	1.27	1.66	1.12
1920	1.49	1.49	1.20	1.26	1.26	1.39	1.44	1.44	1.70	1.23
1921	1.07	.95	.69	.71	.74	.80	.89	.85	1.05	.87
1922	1.07	1.07	.66	.68	.79	.88	.93	.98	1.01	.85
1923	1.12	1.04	.66	.68	.78	.83	.90	.85	1.07	.90
1924	1.26	1.12	.79	.75	.85	.90	.97	.90	1.21	.95
1925	1.17	1.19	.79	.75	.82	.88	.95	.88	1.08	.87
1926	1.18	1.10	.77	.80	.85	.91	.93	.97	1.13	.90
1927	1.26	1.09	.78	.80	.87	.92	.95	.93	1.09	.90
1928	1.26	1.12	.77	.80	.86	.93	.93	.90	1.12	.88
1929	1.19	1.07	.72	.77	.86	.92	.95	.91	1.11	.90

Sources: Jeffrey G. Williamson and Peter Lindert, *American Inequality* (New York: Academic Press, 1980), pp. 319-20. Nominal wages taken from *Crops and Markets*, Vol. 19, no. 5 and Vol. 18, no. 11.

every Southern state, real farm wages *declined* between 1910 and 1916, by as much as 20 to 25 percent in Deep Southern states like South Carolina, Georgia, Alabama, and Mississippi. It is true enough that real wages soared during 1917-1920, but thereafter we find that they fell even further than they had before, and the rebound in the late 1920s was extremely modest. If we take the deflater literally, we would have to say that across the Deep South from South Carolina to Texas, real wages of farm labor were no higher in 1929 than they had been in 1890. The wage figures for the lumber industry (Table 5.2), another heavy consumer of black and white unskilled labor, show the same picture. At the same time the Northern wage for unskilled labor was increasing. Table 5.3 reports an index of the wage gap between Northern unskilled and Southern farm labor for 1914-1929. The 1914 gap is the

Table 5.2
Southern Lumber Wage Deflated by Williamson's COL Series (1914 = 100)

	Laborers	Doggers	Setters	Edgermen	Sawyers, Head Band
1912	.146	.163	.226	.236	.568
1913	.150	.168	.234	.245	.572
1915	.136	.152	.213	.221	.519
1919	.147	.188	.196	.197	.331
1921	.114	.136	.180	.196	.437
1923	.136	.164	.220	.227	.489
1925	.136	.159	.216	.221	.489
1928	.136	.163	.227	.223	.496

Source: Abraham Berglund, George T. Starnes, and Frank T. de Vyver, *Labor in the Industrial South* (Charlottesville, Va., 1930), p. 41.

base. Across the board we find that the gap *increased* at the very time historians have told us that national labor markets had begun to penetrate the region for the first time. The trend remains even when corrections are made for regional differences in the cost of living.

We infer that even before mechanization in cotton, supply-side developments within the South were an important part of the twentieth-century story of how the older regional structure broke down. (To be sure, the "push" factors of the boll weevil and a stagnant cotton demand have always had a place in the historical literature.) The demand-side breakthrough of World War I is surely important, but its impact was apparently quite selective geographically. Covariance analysis does show that some Southern labor markets were more attuned to national labor markets during the 1920s than before, but the effect is geographically specific to agricultural areas in economic distress, not part of a general process of national labor market integration.

Although state-level decennial migration data are less than ideal, a discernible pattern does emerge. The more Western delta states experienced substantial boll weevil and flood damage during the war decade and lost substantially more black population during that decade than previously (see Table 5.4). As the boll weevil moved eastward into Georgia and South Carolina in the early 1920s, crop destruction coincided with the postwar price deflation and created severe agricultural distress. Analyses of mortgage foreclosures and bank failures show that Georgia and South Carolina experienced far more extensive economic disruption during the 1920s than the delta states had experienced during the war boom.[23] Those states never regained their prewar cotton acreage, and the intercensal rate of black outmigration rose above 20 percent. Northern labor recruiters were particularly successful in these distressed cotton areas, offering travel packages and "justice tickets,"

Table 5.3
Indices of the North-South Wage Gap: Southern Farm Wage/Urban Unskilled Wage (1914 gap = 100)

	Va	NC	SC	Ga	Ala	Miss	Ark	La	Tx	Tn
1899	84.0	76.3	80.5	81.6	85.2	92.3	90.3	97.2	87.4	92.6
1914	100.0	100.0	100.0	100.0	100.0	100.0	100.0	100.0	100.0	100.0
1915	98.0	96.1	73.5	94.1	94.9	96.1	94.5	98.0	96.6	94.1
1916	100.3	95.2	75.4	93.7	89.5	92.9	94.0	92.2	92.1	93.1
1917	112.2	109.0	83.6	103.1	97.7	95.7	103.8	91.8	91.3	100.0
1918	110.2	102.9	73.3	103.2	98.3	99.8	101.7	95.3	83.6	93.4
1919	106.7	118.5	99.6	109.9	106.0	114.0	105.4	103.8	113.5	102.6
1920	116.9	125.0	100.6	114.6	113.4	121.3	109.5	110.0	108.6	105.2
1921	95.3	90.4	65.6	73.3	75.6	79.2	77.2	73.7	76.1	84.5
1922	95.8	102.4	63.2	76.6	81.3	87.7	81.1	85.4	73.6	83.0
1923	90.9	90.2	57.2	63.9	72.6	74.9	71.1	67.1	70.6	79.6
1924	100.0	95.0	67.0	69.0	77.3	79.4	77.5	69.6	78.1	82.2
1925	94.9	103.2	68.5	70.6	76.3	79.4	75.0	69.5	71.3	76.9
1926	93.2	92.8	65.0	73.2	77.0	79.9	71.4	74.5	72.5	77.5
1927	96.3	89.1	63.8	70.9	76.3	78.3	70.7	69.2	67.8	75.0
1928	93.8	89.1	61.3	69.1	73.5	77.0	67.4	65.3	67.9	71.4
1929	87.5	84.1	56.6	65.6	72.5	75.2	67.9	65.1	66.3	72.1

Corrected for Regional Cost-of-Living Differences

	Va	NC	SC	Ga	Ala	Miss	Ark	La	Tx	Tn
1899	86.7	80.2	85.1	85.9	94.1	103.4	103.8	110.5	100.4	101.7
1920	116.7	126.1	102.1	115.9	116.9	125.9	117.4	115.8	114.6	108.0
1929	94.0	95.8	67.1	67.1	88.8	86.9	85.8	72.4	76.4	83.2

Sources: See Table 5.1. Urban unskilled wage taken from Jeffrey Williamson and Peter Lindert, *American Inequality* (New York: Academic Press, 1980), pp. 319–20.

Table 5.4
Intercensal Rates of Net Black Outmigration, 1890–1970

	1890–1900	1900–1910	1910–1920	1920–1930	1930–1940	1940–1950	1950–1960	1960–1970
NC	8.68	4.55	4.14	2.06	6.56	12.98	16.53	15.68
SC	9.51	9.21	.10	23.62	11.89	19.53	22.00	23.76
Ga	3.18	1.57	6.36	21.56	8.43	17.62	15.53	13.71
Ala	.25	2.67	7.80	9.05	10.67	16.83	19.55	23.57
Miss	1.40	3.40	12.84	7.36	5.76	24.00	26.77	30.46
Ark	2.56	6.13	.23	9.81	6.97	24.04	25.43	28.79
La	3.86	2.47	7.17	3.64	1.08	13.40	7.51	15.69

Source: See Table 5.2.

and dispatching special railroad cars to carry the "Boll Weevil Negro" directly to Northern work camps.[24]

The persistent importance of geography within the South again cautions us about the dangers of concentrating on straightforward processes of discrimination. It was the very power of labor market forces which located blacks disproportionately on the best agricultural land and the higher wage areas within the South (at least in terms of broad regional divisions). But these were areas in which little progress occurred and with little protection against agricultural disasters. When these disasters set in, blacks were particularly vulnerable. Of course, state-level census data hide much of the complexity, but it appears that the beginnings of national labor market integration coincided with a worsening of the relative and absolute economic position of many blacks, and the intensity of Northern demand factors was to a large extent conditioned by these changes.[25]

A striking example of what we are talking about is presented by the racial employment practice of several major U.S. corporations from the beginning of World War I to the end of World War II. A random sample of 300 white and 300 black workers from the Ford Motor Company in Detroit, the Pullman Railroad Manufacturing Company in Chicago, and the A.M. Byers Steel Company in Pittsburgh, shows strikingly similar patterns.[26] While the war periods provided favorable stimuli to the employment of blacks, as expected, the most consistent feature is a sharp spike in the employment of blacks in the year 1923. At Ford there was not much experience with blacks during World War I. During World War II, 1943 represents the peak, when Ford hired 10.2 percent of its black workers during the period in question. But in 1923 Ford made 19.4 percent of its black hires for the period and, by contrast, only 9.7 percent of its white hires for the period.

The same pattern is repeated at Byers. Byers hired blacks earlier than Ford, as did many steel firms. During World War I Byers' employment of blacks peaked at 21 percent of the period's hires in 1918. Whites were 12.6 percent. Yet even this figure was surpassed in 1923, when Byers made 23.1 percent of its black hires. The corresponding figure for whites was 4.7 percent. World War II was not particularly good for blacks or whites, peaking at 3 percent and 1.6 percent, respectively, in 1945.

At Pullman the pattern is repeated again. The World War I peak is 1916 with 11 percent of the black hires and 6.6 percent of the white hires. But in 1923 the company made 17.6 percent of its black hires and only 8.0 percent of its white hires. The year 1943 represents the World War II peak of 8.6 percent for blacks and 15.7 percent for whites.

It should be emphasized that these firms are in different cities, different industries, and at different points in their life cycle, which explains much of the difference in wartime employment patterns. Yet each firm had a similar experience in 1923, hiring large numbers of blacks, far out of proportion to the number of whites. Why?

We believe the primary development was on the supply side. The boll weevil damage, coupled with the financial crisis, economic recession, and price collapse between 1920 and 1922, forced many blacks out of the agrarian South and into major industrial centers. Certainly, union concerns were high, and the economy was recovering from a recession, but these demand-side pressures should have peaked long before 1923.

Another structural change occurred in Southern labor markets after World War I, a change that has so far escaped notice: the emergence for the first time of large racial wage differentials at the unskilled level in the South. One reason why the histories of discrimination have been so erratic is that observers looking back from the 1930s assumed that the wage gaps they saw had always been there. Charles S. Johnson, for example, wrote that the racial wage differentials were "now so well established in custom that they are frequently maintained where work is identical. . . . Separate wage rates for Negroes are thus in a sense a fixed tradition." Edna Bonacich reproduced tables of Birmingham wage rates from the influential 1930 book by Sterling Spero and Abram L. Harris, implying that black and white wage distributions were virtually disjointed.[27]

Now it is certainly possible that these comments, so different from our assertions in the previous section, simply reflect variety in wage practices in different industries and localities. The scarcity of continuous wage series with racial information makes it hard to be sure. But it is difficult to find convincing documentation on racial wage differentials for the prewar period, and we are therefore inclined to hypothesize that there really was a structural change in labor markets in the wake of the wartime and immediate postwar boom and depression. One case is now well documented. In cotton textiles the link between the industry wage scale and farm wages, which had been very close until the war, was broken in the 1920s, giving way to dualism with a 30 to 40 percent wage gap in the Piedmont.[28] This case, however, must be considered only an implicit racial wage differential, because blacks had never been employed as operatives in that industry.

Figure 5.3 displays racial wage distributions for Virginia industry in 1926, showing that a significant gap in the model wage had emerged by that year. Whereas earlier one could say that there was no genuine "race differential" but only a "skill differential," by the 1920s it appears that racial distinctions had become routine even at the entry level. This tendency is confirmed more broadly in a survey of entrance rates for common laborers as of July 1937. Nearly 60 percent reported hiring only whites or only blacks; those hiring only blacks paid wages fully one-third lower than those hiring only whites. Of those that hired both blacks and whites, nearly 30 percent paid blacks a lower starting wage. This figure must be regarded as a lower bound.[29]

Why did this happen? We do not have a well-established explanation, but certain conjectures are possible. The emerging wage gap may be plausibly viewed as a delayed effect of inequality in schooling expenditures, which became extreme after 1900. Most of the jobs under discussion, however, were those for which formal education was not intrinsically required. In industries in which a fixed pattern of job segregation had persisted long enough, its economic character may have changed over time, as employers found it easier to change the standards and expectations of the jobs to match the background of the workforce than to alter the segregation lines in response to market forces. If so, then a pattern of job segregation, which initially had an innocuous "horizontal" character, may have been transformed into a racial "barrier to entry" over time. This seems to describe the textile industry, in which a number of unsuccessful experiments with black labor in the late 1890s had convinced employers that blacks were unsuited to the work. The episode of strong up-

Figure 5.3
Racial Wage Distributions in Selected Virginia Industries, 1926

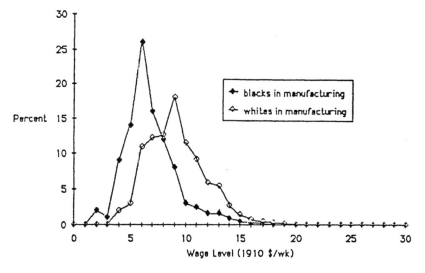

ward pressure on nominal and real wages during 1916–1920, followed by sharp declines in nominal prices and wages during 1920–1921, may have affected segregated groups differently. We conjecture that workers in "white" jobs, having built up job-specific experience over the years, were in a better position to resist wage cuts after the boom.

The important development was that labor market classifications had come to be crystallized along racial lines, a development that inevitably influenced the subsequent behavior of all parties involved. Without minimizing the importance of educational discrimination, it is equally important to remember that the causation was mutual. The gap in wages seemed now to *justify* the inequality in educational opportunity, to confirm the planters' belief that investing in black schools was throwing money away. As the historian of Southern education Louis Harlan observed: "Educational inequality came to seem part of the normal scheme of things when Negroes lacked equality in virtually every phase of opportunity."[30] Furthermore, the widening racial split within the Southern working class encouraged a different political coalition, between rural planters and white industrial workers, strengthening the economic basis for segregationist politics. The growing isolation of Southern blacks in low-wage jobs made them increasingly vulnerable to the elimination of those jobs under pressure from the federal government, which was a central tendency beginning in the 1930s.[31]

THE ENTRY OF BLACKS INTO NORTHERN LABOR MARKETS

Little is known about the early black experience in the North. World War I is often taken to be the watershed. When events during the war cut off the supply of unskilled European workers, many Northern employers looked South, sending recruiters to seek black replacements. It is estimated that 400,000 to 500,000 blacks migrated North during the war, most settling in the cities along the Northern industrial belt stretching from New York to Chicago.[32]

Race was often a factor in the workplace. Whites would work with and alongside blacks, but they often resisted working beneath them. The chances of black advancement were small when the possibility of a black outranking a white existed. Black workers openly complained about this situation, and more often than about any other kind of discrimination. In postwar Chicago, for example, about 10 percent of the black workers surveyed complained of promotion discrimination, with most complaints directed at abusive and discriminatory treatment by foremen. By contrast, no workers complained of wage discrimination for identical work. Promotion ceilings were sometimes reached within six months, and often because whites refused to work under blacks.[33] Price Fishback found the same evidence in the coal industry, and Donald Dewey found it so often in the South that he called it a "law."[34]

Many informed observers thought this racial prejudice among workers was a "fad" that would slowly wither away in the face of competitive pressures, and managers determined to employ the lower cost blacks. Myrdal, for example, expressing great faith in the "American Creed," believed that contact between the races was enough. This is his situation of "indifferent equilibrium" where "There are tremendous elements of inertia which resist the introduction of Negro labor where there had previously been none. If they get in, however, they will have better chance of staying. . . . If they (white workers) actually work together with Negro workers, they come to like them better, or dislike them less than they expected."[35]

W. L. Bulkley's earlier description of New York is similar: "The Northern employer is too prone to turn off the colored applicant with the bland assurance that he himself would have no objection, but his white workmen would disrupt the business if a black competitor were forced upon them. . . . This intolerant attitude against the Negro workman is largely a matter of fad and fancy. Upon a show of firmness on the part of the employer it would soon vanish away."[36]

It may have been true that racial attitudes were flexible during the early period of contact, but in reality most foremen did not feel the pressure to test them. An economist would immediately ask about competitive pressures. If blacks were segregated into lower level jobs because of their race, then skills were not being matched to jobs. In the long run competition in labor and product markets would penalize discriminators and drive firms toward racial integration or innocuous segregation patterns where all workers fully utilized their skills, regardless of race.

The problem with this scenario is that many firms did not initially view blacks as a long-run substitute for Europeans. Many viewed the cutoff of Europeans as temporary; this feeling was confirmed when, as expected, postwar immigration from Europe surged, climbing from 24,627 in 1919 to 246,295 in 1920 and 652,364 in 1921.[37] Immigration restrictions ultimately placed the 1925–1929 quota at 165,667 per year, and firms may have changed their strategies during this period. But this was a small window of opportunity, as the depression and massive unemployment of the 1930s relieved any pressure in labor markets.

The view that blacks were only temporary replacements for Europeans certainly impeded the labor market's ability to penalize discriminators. The initial cost of racially integrating workers was substantial. Shop floor disruptions from mixing antagonistic groups and new management policies used resources that would not have been required if the labor groups had remained segregated.[38] Racially segregated firms, however, were inefficient, and the losses accumulated over time. If blacks were viewed as permanent replacements, then employers would tend to pay the initial cost of integration to escape the inefficiencies later on. However, if black workers were viewed as temporary replacements, as they were during World War I and the early 1920s, then racial segregation would be the cost-minimizing arrangement.

These initial conditions may have had a lasting impact. As firms employed workers in racially segregated patterns, then any learning-on-the job reduced the cost of implementing similar racial job structures in other firms. The initial learning experience tended to generate a distribution of skills in the black labor force that reinforced the racial segregation of jobs. Even those firms that did not have prejudicial workforces (that is, those firms that were supposed to put pressure on the prejudicial firms and either drive them out or force them to change) would tend to hire workers along established racial lines because only those skills would be readily available in the market. The initial prejudices tend to become "institutionalized" or "reified" as racial job hierarchies that last long after the originating attitudes have changed.

The creation of job pyramids along racial lines was part of a larger tendency in early twentieth-century America to create clearly delineated job ladders in the workplace. During the half century before World War I, technological advances like the open-hearth furnace, the sewing machine, the Bosnack cigarette machine, and many other chemical and technological breakthroughs eliminated many jobs that required craft-training or brute physical strength.[39] Most jobs came to require semi-skilled operatives who learned their job from experience on the shop floor. Turnovers became costly because training was occurring in the firm and involved a larger portion of the workforce. At the same time the rate of turnovers accelerated because the lower average training and easier substitutability of factory workers reduced the cost of changing jobs.[40]

Firms tended to counter this state of affairs by adopting clearly delineated job ladders, where workers knew which jobs in the plant their experiences made available to them. Thus, workers had an incentive to stay with the firm as long as they faced a favorable job ladder, and as long as some of their training was firm-specific.[41] In the middle were blacks, integrating into firms in which whites preferred not to work beneath them. As the job ladders were formulated, they came to crystallize around these preferences and continued to operate long after the preferences themselves had changed.

This period witnessed still another structural change that was unfavorable to blacks. The years between 1914 and 1940 saw the triumph of what might be called "high wage" thinking in American labor relations, which we understand not merely as a labor union ideology or a reformer's naive conception of how to improve the lot of workers, but as a culmination of long-term trends in social thinking, legislation, industrial demography, and employer strategy. The notion that high wages would "pay for themselves" through improved morale, reduced turnover, and greater efficiency prevailed very widely in the 1920s. Many employers actively pursued such a labor market strategy on their own initiative, instituting personnel departments, internal promotion schemes, shop committees, promises of job security, and other such measures.[42] A second class of employers was induced to move in some of these directions by the threat of unionism. A third class was only pushed by legislation and industry pressure emanating from the first two groups in alliance with reform and labor organizations. The best evidence that businessmen themselves believed and actively implemented these measures may be found in the business-dominated National Industrial Recovery Act (NIRA) of 1933. In the process of creating industrial self-regulatory cartels backed by the authority of the federal government, the NIRA effected a massive wage increase (at the bottom of the depression!) for virtually all nonagricultural workers.[43] This was a collective "minimum wage" far more drastic in extent and comprehensive in coverage than any which labor has since pushed through.

This whole process had beneficiaries and losers, and it would be no easy task to identify and measure the gains and losses. There may be deep ambiguities in cases of women and older teenagers, who might be viewed as individuals or as members of households. But adult black male workers were probably among the chief losers, though the changes were not primarily directed at them. It was a poor time to try to crack Northern industrial labor markets as an unskilled worker. Those who did so found themselves at the bottom of the seniority line during a period of severe business fluctuations, now characterized by layoffs on a first-hired, first-fired basis. Just when the traditional means for accumulation as "good Negroes" in Southern agriculture were collapsing, the rising unskilled wage and increased selectivity in industrial employment put blacks at a disadvantage for entry. It is as though one class of discrimination models was ushered out, only to have a new class welcomed in.

BREAKUP OF THE PLANTATION AND INTEGRATION OF REGIONAL LABOR MARKETS

In our view, the decisive break with regionalism in the labor market occurred not during World War I but World War II. The stage was set, however, by structural changes in Southern agriculture, which occurred during the 1930s. The plantation area had long maintained a balance between relatively secure annual labor supplies obtained through local markets in tenancy and sharecropping on the one hand, and longer distance (though still Southern) markets in seasonal wage labor to satisfy peak period labor demands.[44] This balance was disrupted by the federal farm programs of the 1930s. The subsidy schemes of the AAA and its successors established incentives for planters both to contract cotton acreage and to substitute wage labor for tenancies. This trend, plus the depression itself, so increased the availability of wage labor that planters could do away with the annual tenancy arrangements and rely on the market to supply labor when needed.[45] This new flexibility opened the door to mechanization of preharvest operations, which had long been technically feasible but paradoxically accelerated only in the midst of the deepest depression in history. The effective demise of traditional channels of black advancement, however, meant that there was nothing to keep blacks in the South when outside job opportunities did open up during the war. The renewed Southern cries of "labor shortage" in the 1940s, coupled with the continued expansion of cotton acreage in areas outside the "traditional" South, created pressures for a technological solution to the remaining labor bottleneck, the cotton harvest. The real breakthrough finally came in the late 1940s when International Harvester began marketing the first commercially viable mechanical picker. The subsequent mechanization of cotton production severed the last remaining tie that many blacks had with Southern agriculture.[46]

Harvest mechanization was also accelerated by political agitation. The mechanical harvester became available in the late 1940s, but the Southeastern region did not begin to use it until the early 1960s. When the region did mechanize, it did not take long for the machine to sweep through the entire cotton industry. Within one decade all cotton grown was mechanically harvested.[47] Factor price movements do not explain this acceleration, nor do developments in complementary technologies.[48] A feasible explanation is the pressure of the civil rights movement. By 1960 student sit-in protests had brought demands for political change to almost every community.[49] With the election of President Kennedy in 1960, it was certain that the future was uncertain, and most likely the past was gone. Shifting from a dependence on a system of cheap labor, propped up by the very social structure being attacked, dependence on inanimate machinery seemed the obvious choice to anyone wanting to continue producing cotton. With this choice came the end of an era in Southern history.

A number of other channels were available through which national labor market integration was promoted. Some of these include national labor union pressure, corporate wage policies, and increases in the level and coverage of the national minimum wage.[50] In each of these three examples, it appears that nonmarket pressures for *wage* equalization preceded labor *market* integration, and wage equalization may indeed be considered part of the cause of labor market integration, not the reverse. Many of these processes worked severe hardships on blacks precisely because of their position in the prewar regionalism. For example, the rise in the unskilled wage in tobacco manufacturing set in motion a process of mechanization in tobacco processing (the "black" jobs) which caused the proportion of blacks to decline from 60 percent black in 1930 to 26 percent in 1960.[51] A recent paper by John Cogan shows that the disappearance of low-wage employment opportunities for black teenagers in the South was directly linked to the rise of black teenage unemployment in Northern cities.[52] More broadly, the *timing* of black migration was unfortunate in many respects. The long delay in the South meant that blacks missed crucial formative phases of unionization, and they were poorly educated at a time when employers were increasingly relying on educational credentials. They came to live in urban ghettos when job opportunities were dispersing.

But how much of this was discrimination? The impact of national wage equalization was actively debated by black leaders in the 1930s, and while there were at least two sides to the issue, the majority supported the New Deal policy.[53] The migration from the South inflicted hardships, but also produced the single most rapid period of black economic gains. And there was another lasting gain that emerged indirectly. The demise of the plantation system and the equalization of wages removed the class interest in protecting a cheap Southern labor pool, shifting the political economy of the South into an enthusiastic campaign to attract outside capital—in other words, traditional American boosterism. One casualty of this integration of national *capital* markets (plus national political pressure, to be sure) was the abolition of segregation practices, not just in social and educational areas, but in job segregation systems as well, with all that they had come to imply for racial inequality.[54]

CONCLUSIONS

The historical perspective ought to be part of everyone's thinking on labor market discrimination and its remedies. Such a historical perspective should not be content with paying quick lip-service to the possibility of discrimination as a labor market phenomenon in the "long run" in an introduction to an analysis of its seemingly more obvious public sector component. Many and perhaps all of the available models of discrimination had had their moments on stage, but the really decisive changes have involved structural changes (in the econometric sense of that term), and often for historical reasons not directly associated with black workers at all.

Is this the chicken crossing the road when the truck happened to be coming? It may appear that way, but there are some common threads. Migration from the rural South is the most characteristic feature of the twentieth-century black experience. But the migration did not occur spontaneously, even though there was a substantial wage gap between the North and the South. We do not yet know exactly what held the agrarian structure together in the South in the face of higher entry-level wages in the North. Low education levels certainly reduced information effects, and there were periods of income growth in the rural South that kept alive the hope of "making it" at home. Nonetheless, within this system the South was never able to solve its problem of creating an acceptable standard of living for its people. From this perspective, any change that induced a movement out of the rural South was positive. These include mechanization, the world wars, the decline in cotton demand, the Agricultural Adjustment Acts, the rise of unionism, the minimum wage, and high wage thinking in general.

The important point, however, is not that these national developments hurt blacks more often than they helped them. We would expect that to be the case because during times of economic crisis and change groups often use political power to protect or enrich themselves, and through much of this period blacks were politically ineffective. The important point is that America has been a racist society for a long time. We can debate the degree to which prejudice and discrimination still exist, but the more important point is that out of whatever changes that have occurred new institutions have emerged that tend to reflect the initial conditions. We study these changes not to identify the culprits, but to understand how these institutions continue to reinforce outcomes for which no one is willing to be held responsible.

NOTES

1. See Michael Reich, *Racial Inequality* (Princeton, N.J.: Princeton University Press, 1981), pp. 76–108; F. Ray Marshall, "The Economics of Racial Discrimination: A Survey," *Journal of Economic Literature* 12 (September 1974); Stanley Masters, *Black-White Income Differentials* (New York: Academic Press, 1975).

2. Recent additions include Marvin Smith, "Towards a General Equilibrium Theory of Racial Wage Discrimination," *Southern Economic Journal* 45 (October 1978); David H. Swinton, "A Labor Force Competition Model of Racial Discrimination in the Labor Market," *Review of Black Political Economy* (Fall 1978).

3. Richard Freeman, "Decline of Labor Market Discrimination and Economic Analysis," *American Economic Review* 63 (May 1973); James P. Smith and Finis Welch, "Race Differences in Earnings: A Survey and New Evidence," in Peter Lieszkowski and Mahlon Straszhein, eds., *Current Issues in Urban Economics* (Baltimore: Johns Hopkins University Press, 1979); Edward Lazear, "The Narrowing of Black-White Wage Differentials Is Illusory," *American Economic Review* 69 (September 1979); William A. Darity, Jr., "Illusions of Black Economic Progress," *Review of Black Political Economy* 10 (Summer 1980); Richard F. Kamalich and Solomon Polachek, "Discrimination: Fact or Fiction?" *Southern Economic Journal* 49 (October 1982).

4. Richard Freeman, "Alternative Theories of Labor Market Discrimination: Individual and Collective Behavior," in George M. von Furstenberg et al., eds., *Patterns of Racial Discrimination*, Vol. 2 (Lexington, Mass.: D. C. Heath, 1974); Finis Welch, "Education and Racial Discrimination," in Orley Ashenfelter and Albert Rees, eds., *Discrimination in Labor Markets* (Princeton, N.J.: Princeton University Press, 1973).

5. Kenneth Arrow, "The Theory of Discrimination," in Ashenfelter and Rees, eds., *Discrimination in Labor Markets*, p. 22. See also Glenn Loury, "A Dynamic Theory of Racial Income Differences," in Phyllis Wallace, ed., *Women, Minorities, and Employment Discrimination* (Lexington, Mass.: D. C. Heath, 1977) for a model in which "initial conditions" determine convergence or continued racial inequality (not discrimination).

6. Industry studies are collected in Herbert Northrup and Richard Rowan, eds., *Negro Employment in Southern Industry* (Philadelphia, 1970) and Northrup et al., *Negro Employment in Basic Industry* (Philadelphia, 1970).

7. James P. Smith, "Race and Human Capital," *American Economic Review* 74 (September 1984); James P. Smith and Finis Welch, *Closing the Gap: Forty Years of Economic Progress for Blacks*, Rand Publication Series, Santa Monica, Calif., 1986.

8. Robert A. Margo, "Race Educational Attainment and the 1940 Census," *Journal of Economic History* (March 1986); Robert A. Margo, "Race and Human Capital: Comment," *American Economic Review* (December 1986); David Keifer and Peter Phillips, "Doubts Regarding the Human Capital Theory of Racial Inequality," *Industrial Relations* (forthcoming).

9. Robert Higgs, "Firm-Specific Evidence on Racial Wage Differentials and Work-Force Segregation," *American Economic Review* 67 (March 1977). A more general treatment appears in Robert Higgs, *Competition and Coercion: Blacks in the American Economy, 1865–1914* (Chicago: University of Chicago Press, 1980; originally published in 1977).

10. Edmund Phelps, "The Statistical Theory of Racism and Sexism," *American Economic Review* 62 (September 1972). Dennis J. Aigner and Glen G. Cain, "Statistical Theories of Discrimination in the Labor Market," *Industrial and Labor Relations Review* 30 (January 1977).

11. Arrow, "The Theory of Discrimination," in Ashenfelter and Rees, eds., *Discrimination in Labor Markets*; Kenneth Arrow, "Some Mathematical Models of Racial Discrimination in the Labor Market," in Anthony Pascal, ed., *Racial Discrimination in Economic Life* (Lexington, Mass.: D. C. Heath, 1972).

12. Kevin Land, "A Language Theory of Discrimination," *Quarterly Journal of Economics* 101 (May 1986).

13. Steward Schwab, "Is Statistical Discrimination Efficient?" *American Economic Review* 76 (March 1986); Shelley Lundberg and Richard Startz, "Private Discrimination and Social Intervention in Competitive Labor Markets," *American Economic Review* 73 (June 1983).

14. Higgs, *Competition and Coercion*, p. 146.

15. Brinley Thomas, *Migration and Economic Growth*, 2d ed. (New York: Cambridge University Press, 1973), Ch. 18; Jay Mandle, *The Roots of Black Poverty: The Southern Plantation Economy After the Civil War* (Durham, N.C.: Duke University Press, 1978); Higgs, "The Boll Weevil, the Cotton Economy and Black Migration, 1910-1930," *Agricultural History* 50 (April 1976). See also the analysis of W. Arthur Lewis: "It was racial discrimination in the United States that kept the price of cotton so low; or to turn this around, given the racial discrimination, American blacks earned so little because of the large amounts of cotton that would have flowed out of Asia and Africa and Latin America at a higher cotton price." *The Evolution of the International Economic Order* (Princeton, N.J.: Princeton University Press, 1978), p. 17.

16. Representative conclusions may be found in Elizabeth Pleck, *Black Migration and Poverty* (New York: Academic Press, 1979), Ch. 5; David Gerber, *Black Ohio and the Color Line 1860-1915* (Urbana: University of Illinois Press, 1976), Chs. 4, 11.

17. "Did Southern Farmers Discriminate?" *Agricultural History* 46 (April 1972); *Competition and Coercion*, pp. 63-66.

18. We disagree, therefore, with Stephen J. DeCanio's assertion (citing Robert Mellman) that "Southern manufacturing wages were similar to Northern manufacturing wages" ("Accumulation and Discrimination in the Postbellum South," *Explorations in Economic History* 16 [April 1979], p. 183). Mellman has shown no such thing. Southern textile wages (primarily in the Southeast) were 30 to 50 percent below Northern levels in unskilled textile occupations, while iron industry wages for unskilled labor (principally Alabama-Tennessee) were 20 to 30 percent below those of their Northern counterparts.

19. Gavin Wright, "Postbellum Southern Labor Markets," in Peter Kilby, ed., *Quantity and Quiddity: Essays in Honor of Stanley Lebergott* (Middletown, Conn.: Wesleyan University Press, 1989).

20. For discussion, see Leonard Carlson, "Labor Supply, the Acquisition of Skills and the Location of Southern Textile Mills, 1880-1900," *Journal of Economic History* 41 (March 1981); Gavin Wright, "Black and White Labor in the Old New South," in Fred Bateman, ed., *Business in the New South* (Sewanee, Tenn.: University Press, 1981).

21. Robert A. Margo, "Race Difference in Pubic School Expenditures: Disfranchisement and School Finance in Louisiana, 1890-1910," *Social Science History* 6 (Winter 1982).

22. Cf. Sumner H. Slicter, *Union Policy and Industrial Management* (New York: Arno Press, 1969); Mancur Olson, *The Logic of Collective Action* (Cambridge, Mass.: Harvard University Press, 1965).

23. Lawrence Jones and David Durand, *Mortgage Lending Experience in Agriculture* (Princeton, N.J.: Princeton University Press, 1954); A. E. Nielson, *Production Credit for Southern Cotton Growers* (New York: Kings Crown Press, 1946), pp. 31-35.

24. Cf. U.S. Department of Labor, *Negro Migration in 1916-1917* (Washington, D.C.: GPO, 1919); Louise Kennedy, *The Negro Peasant Turns Cityward* (New York: Columbia University Press, 1930).

25. The only known study that uses county-level data to analyze black population movements during this period was conducted by Edward Lewis who found a correlation between variation in cotton acreage and yields and population movements. See Lewis, *The Mobility of the Negro* (New York: Columbia University Press, 1931). Also see Arthur Raper, *Preface to Peasantry* (Chapel Hill: University of North Carolina Press, 1936), Ch. 11.

26. Larger samples have been drawn and are being prepared for analysis as part of the larger project, *Race and Industrial Labor Markets Before 1950* conducted by Warren C. Whatley and Gavin Wright.

27. Charles S. Johnson, *Patterns of Negro Segregation* (New York: Harper and Row, 1943), p. 90; Edna Bonacich, "Advanced Capitalism and Black-White Relations in the U.S.: A Split Labor Market Interpretation," *American Sociological Review* 81 (November 1976); Sterling Spero and Abram L. Harris, *The Black Worker* (New York: Columbia University Press, 1931), pp. 168–78.

28. Gavin Wright, "Cheap Labor and Southern Textiles, 1880–1930," *Quarterly Journal of Economics* (November 1981):622–28.

29. Jacob Perlman and Edward R. Frazier, "Entrance Rates of Common Laborers in 20 Industries, July 1937," *Monthly Labor Review* 45 (December 1937):1497–98

30. Louis Harlan, *Separate and Unequal: Public School Campaigns and Racism in the Southern Seaboard States, 1901–1915* (Chapel Hill: University of North Carolina Press, 1958).

31. See Gavin Wright, *Old South, New South* (New York: Basic Books, 1986); John Cogan, "The Decline of Black Teenage Employment, 1950–70," *American Economic Review* 72 (September 1982).

32. See George E. Haynes, *The Negro at Work During the War and Reconstruction* (Washington, D. C.: GPO, 1921). Also see Flora Gill, "The Economics of the Black Exodus," Ph.D. diss., Stanford University, 1974; Higgs, "The Boll Weevil"; William Vickery, "The Economics of the Negro Migration, 1900–1960," Ph.D. diss., University of Chicago, 1969.

33. See Chicago Race Commission, *The Negro in Chicago* (Chicago: University of Chicago Press, 1922), pp. 365–91.

34. Price Fishback, "Segregation in Job Hierarchies: West Virginia Coal Mining, 1906–1932," *Journal of Economic History* 44 (September 1984); Donald Dewey, "Negro Employment in Southern Industry," *Journal of Political Economy* 60 (August 1952).

35. Myrdal, *An American Dilemma*, pp. 392–93.

36. W. L. Bulkley, "The Industrial Conditions of the Negro in New York City," *Annals of the American Academy* 27 (1906). For similar statements, see Louise Kennedy, *The Negro Peasant Turns Cityward* (New York: Columbia University Press, 1930), Ch. 5; and Abram Epstein, *Negro Migrants in Pittsburgh* (Pittsburgh, 1918).

37. U.S. Bureau of the Census, *Historical Statistics of the United States* (Washington, D.C.: GPO, 1979), p. 105.

38. For elaborate discussions of the costs of integration, see Dwight Forham, "Negroes as a Source of Industrial Labor," *Industrial Management* (1918); Chicago Race Commission, *The Negro in Chicago*; J. O. Houze, "Negro Labor and the Industries," *Opportunity* (1923); J. W. Knapp, "An Experiment with Negro Labor," *Opportunity* (1922); and Edward S. McClelland, "Negro Labor in the Westinghouse Electric and Manufacturing Corporation," *Opportunity* (1921).

39. See Alfred Chandler, *The Visible Hand* (Cambridge, Mass.: Harvard University Press, 1977); John A. James, "Structural Change in American Manufacturing, 1850–1890," *Journal of Economic History* 43 (June 1983); Jeremy Atack, "Industrial Structure and the Emergence of the Modern Industrial Corporation," *Explorations in Economic History* 22 (1982).

40. Sanford Jacoby, "Industrial Labor Mobility in Historical Perspective," *Industrial Relations* 22 (Spring 1983); Sumner Slichter, *The Turnover of Factory Labor* (New York: Appleton, 1919); Paul F. Brissenden, "Occupational Incidence of Labor Mobility," *Journal of the American Statistical Association* 18 (December 1923).

41. A classic in this area is Katherine Stone, "The Origins of Job Structures in the Steel Industry," *Review of Radical Political Economy* (Summer 1974).

42. Sumner Slichter, "The Current Labor Policies of American Industries," *Quarterly Journal of Economics* 43 (May 1929).

43. Michael Weinstein, *Recovery and Redistribution under the NIRA* (Amsterdam: North-Holland, 1980).

44. Warren C. Whatley, "A History of Mechanization in the Cotton South: The Institutional Hypothesis," *Quarterly Journal of Economics* (December 1985).

45. Warren C. Whatley, "Labor for the Picking: The New Deal in the South," *Journal of Economic History* 43 (December 1983).

46. See Richard Day, "The Economics of Technological Change and the Demise of the Sharecropper," *American Economic Review* 57 (1967); Warren C. Whatley, "Mechanization in the Cotton South: Historical Legacy vs. Natural Environment," unpublished mimeo, Department of Economics, University of Michigan (March 1988); James Street, *The New Revolution in the Cotton Economy* (Chapel Hill: University of North Carolina Press, 1957).

47. U.S. Department of Agriculture, *Statistics on Cotton and Related Data, 1920–73* (Washington, D.C.: Economic Research Service, 1974), p. 86.

48. Whatley, "Mechanization in the Cotton South."

49. Aldon Morris, *The Origins of the Civil Rights Movement* (London: Free Press, 1984); Horvord Sitkoff, *The Struggle for Black Equality, 1954–1980* (New York: Hill & Wang, 1980).

50. Martin Segal, "Regional Wage Differences in Manufacturing in the Postwar Period," *Review of Economics and Statistics* 43 (May 1961).

51. Herbert Northrup, "The Negro in the Tobacco Industry," *Racial Policies of American Industry*, Report No. 13 (Philadelphia: University of Pennsylvania, Wharton School, Industrial Research Center Studies, 1970), pp. 29, 31.

52. John Cogan, "The Decline of Black Teenage Employment, 1950–70," *American Economic Review* 72 (September 1982): 621–38.

53. Raymond Walters, *Negroes and the Great Depression* (Westport, Conn.: Greenwood Press, 1970).

54. The best sources here are James C. Cobb, *The Selling of the South* (Baton Rouge, La.: LSU Press, 1982) and Stanley Greenberg, *Race and State in Capitalist Development* (New Haven, Conn.: Yale University Press, 1980), Ch. 10.

6.

A Calculation and Comparison of the Current Benefits of Slavery and an Analysis of Who Benefits

Larry Neal

The existence of an active and expanding slave market in the United States up to the Emancipation Proclamation in 1863 creates unusual problems of analysis for the economic historian (Fogel and Engerman, 1974; David et al., 1976; Wright, 1980). It also creates unusual opportunities for quantification of the economic role which this distinctive part of our early labor force played in the country's development. Slaves were taxed, and so records of numbers were kept with relatively good detail for the time. Slaves were traded, and so prices were recorded. Slaves were an economic investment from the viewpoint of their owners, and so business accounts were kept on the costs of raising and maintaining them. To date, these data have been used primarily to understand the internal logic and operation of the economic system of slavery. Only recently have efforts begun to take the consensual facts and use them to compare the costs and benefits of slavery as the distinguishing characteristic of the Southern economy with the costs and benefits of free labor and family farming in the North. This chapter tries to take another step in this direction. It draws heavily on the work done previously by this author on the benefits of slavery (Simon and Neal, 1974) and on the benefits of immigration (Neal and Uselding, 1972). In the section "Concepts," this chapter develops the concepts needed to aggregate and compound the benefits slaves conferred on the American economy (seen as a transfer of the value of the slave's labor to others in the economy). The actual calculations are then made and presented in the section "Calculations." Finally, these results are compared with comparable results made for immigrants in the nineteenth century (seen as a transfer of the costs of producing adult labor from the U.S. economy to foreign economies) in the section "Comparisons."

CONCEPTS

The quantity sought in the following calculations is the difference between (1) what the black slaves' labor would have been worth in the Southern economy if they had been free, and (2) what was expended on their upkeep and consumption by their owners. That is, we seek to estimate the difference between what slaveowners would have had to pay free black men and women for the same tasks in the same economy, and what they actually spent on their slaves. This sounds more difficult than it is in practice, since the market price of slaves was precisely this. It was the estimate made by the slave buyers as a group of the present value of all the future gains that would be captured by the owner of a slave—that is, the expected value of a slave's marginal product less his upkeep costs in each year of his future work life, discounted back to the present. If a slave had been raised to maturity by an owner resident in the United States, then the present value at time of sale of these past costs of rearing would have to be deducted to determine the net transfer of value from slaves to masters. (Wright, p. 140, has a useful diagram to illustrate this idea.) Of course, if a slave had been raised to maturity abroad and then imported to the United States, no such deduction has to be made from the viewpoint of the U.S. economy. The import of slaves was outlawed at the end of 1807, and thereafter nearly all of the American slave population was the result of natural increase. Even before this date, a good part of the increase in American slaveholdings came from natural increase in sharp contrast to the typical case in the Caribbean Islands. And so some part of the present value of rearing costs has to be deducted from slave prices even before 1807.

No account is taken here of any indirect economic damage to slaves and their offspring owing to the cultural impoverishment of slavery, both because any such account is extraordinarily speculative and because it is contrary to the practice of American courts in according damages. Nor is any accounting made for mental and physical suffering owing to slavery and its aftermath. Furthermore, no attempt is made to allow for loss of potential productivity gains from lower rates of technological progress that may have been made under slavery, both because economic historians have not agreed on it and because productivity gains seemed to have kept pace on average with those in the North until the Civil War. It is of no concern here whether this was due to luck or to the logic of market forces.

It is more questionable but equally necessary to assume that only the private profitability of slavery to slaveholders is involved. Economic historians generally agree that slavery was quite profitable to slaveholders during the entire antebellum period. Moreover, reasonably good estimates can be made of the actual amount of profits made by slaveholders (e.g., Conrad and Meyer, 1964; Gray, 1933; Phillips 1929; and Yasuba, 1971).

The social profitability of slavery is much more problematic. Slaveholders were the ruling class of the antebellum South, and their private profits would, if anything, be larger than the profits obtained by the entire nonslave portion of Southern society. Eugene Genovese has restated arguments made even during the Civil War that a system of slavery necessarily generated social costs that reduced its social profitability below its private profitability. Foremost among these costs were the social costs of enforcing property rights in slaves and maintaining an "appropriable surplus" for the planter with his investment in human capital.

These social costs stemmed from the lack of an educational system or a transportation system, and the expense of maintaining a police state under such conditions. They were maintained by the unwillingness of the planter class to equip slaves with expensive capital equipment, including livestock. The Southern planters as a class apparently had a high propensity to consume rather than to invest their proceeds from slaveholding. Social affairs and luxurious living combined with a desire for display of martial skills meant that the profits of the Southern planters were not reinvested into the Southern economy but rather into the Northern and English economies.

Still, even with these social costs of the slavery system, the Southern economy remained viable and economically efficient as a whole as long as fertile cotton lands remained some place within its political domain. Fogel and Engerman have calculated that the rate of growth per capita income, the economist's best measure for the progress of economic efficiency in an economy, was roughly the same in the slaveholding South as in the North from 1840 to 1860.

This growth was based primarily on the development of the rich cotton lands of the Southwest where per capita income was more than double that in the old South. It is clear that this growth of economic efficiency, derived from the labor-gang exploitation of the rich cotton lands of the Southwest, was due to the effort of the enslaved blacks transported from the Old South. It is extremely doubtful that the South would have maintained this growth of economic efficiency with the growing problem of soil exhaustion in the Old South (Craven, 1926; Phillips, 1929) and the reaching of the geographical limits to the new cotton lands (Ramsdell, 1929). But the Civil War intervened long before the effects of these constraints could be felt in the Southern economy. Note that, in any event, had these constraints eventually come into play they would not have meant an end to slavery but rather a change in its form and location. It is still a matter of dispute whether or not the increased use of slaves in industry, for example, could have maintained the previous growth of economic efficiency. In sum, there is no solid quantitative historical evidence on which to build a case that the social rate of return to slavery was significantly lower than the private return, at least up to the Civil War. In the absence of such evidence, we should concentrate on the value of the initial and direct appropriation of slave labor surplus.

This is a partial model which assumes that wages and prices would have been the same if the slaves had been free. It may be thought that such an assumption leads to an overestimate of the free labor market wage because the addition of freed slaves to the pool of free labor would tend to drive down the market wage. But if all blacks had been free they could have acquired the education and skill denied them while in servile status. This would have increased their marginal product and hence their market wage. Moreover, the desire of slaveowners to minimize the net burden to them of childrearing may have meant greater use of child labor under slavery than under free labor.

These effects of freedom on the marginal product would have been enhanced by the ability of free blacks to acquire land and to become independent farmers. It was the prevalence of the family farm that limited labor supplies in the North and maintained high wages there. The same forces would have kept blacks from the labor market in the South even in the absence of slavery. Our use of the actual market evaluation of blacks' wages under antebellum conditions may, therefore, represent an underestimate of the appropriate wage. (Offsetting this may be an element of expected capital gain in the market price of slaves, but all scholars seem to agree that this element of slave pricing became important only during the 1850s.)

CALCULATIONS

The empirical work involves three steps. The first estimates the market value of the unpaid net wages of slaves who lived at various times before emancipation. The calculations will be made as present-value sums at a single point in time—the points being the eighteenth year of the slaves. The second estimates the number of slaves who labored without fair pay. Slaves will be counted in the years they turned 18 years of age. The third multiplies the amounts by the number of slaves, finds their value as of the present, and aggregates them.

Unpaid Wages of Slaves in Various Years

The market price of a slave at the age of 18 may be considered to be the present value in that year of the expected stream of future earnings less upkeep costs. We may reasonably assume that this sum was appraised accurately by the slave market.

Slave-price data are conveniently available in Conrad and Meyer (1964, ch. 3), Bean (1975), and Kotlikoff (1979). To estimate the overall lifetime net unpaid wages of a slave, however, one must also take into account the costs of raising slaves to age 18, and the revenues from their labor before age 18, such childhood expenditures and revenues being compounded to age 18. The necessary data are in Conrad and Meyer. Letting

V_t = value of slave at age 18 in year t

P_t = market price of slave at age 18 in year t

$L_{t\text{-}s}$ = value of labor performed by slave at s years under age 18

$M_{t\text{-}s}$ = maintenance costs of slave at s years under age 18

we can summarize this algorithm by the formula:

$$V_t = P_t = [L_{t\text{-}s} - M_{t\text{-}s}) (1 + r)^s].$$

L is zero until the child is six years old; that is, from $s = 13$ to $s = 18$. In the first year of life the maintenance costs include nursery costs and the value of the mother's lost time in the fields, in addition to the normal maintenance costs of food, clothing, and housing. The rate of interest obviously has great effect on the final estimate when considering the present value of the sums as of 1983. But the calculations of the value as of age 18 are not much affected by the rate of interest. Suffice it for now that since it does not affect the order of magnitude of the final sum for our purposes here, we will (1) note Conrad and Meyer's reasoning and judgment that 7 percent is appropriate, and work with that rate, and (2) also calculate using a 3 percent rate.

Table 6.1 shows estimates of pre-18 slaveholder's expenses and revenues as of 1840 based on Conrad and Meyer's data (pp. 62–65). One must take into account that some slave children died at ages young enough that they represented net losses to the slaveholders. As an adjustment we used the crude expedient of doubling all costs and revenues that occurred in the first 9 years in our 1974 calculations (Simon and Neal, 1974, p. 79). Since then, however, Richard Steckel has made detailed analyses of slave demographic data. His latest data (Steckel, 1983) show that, while in 1840 half of the babies born to slaves in that year could be expected to have died by age 9, the heaviest mortality was in ages 0 to 3. The calculations in columns 7 and 8, therefore, increase the numbers in columns 5 and 6 by 1.857 for ages 0 to 1 (25 percent of all births died by age 1), by 1.389 for ages 1 to 3 (30 percent of all one year olds died by age 3), by 1.144 for ages 3 to 6 (7 percent of all 3 year olds died by age 6), and by 1.03 for ages 6 to 11 (6 percent of all 6 year olds died by age 11). These adjustments assume that deaths occurred linearly over each age interval. These new calculations substantially reduce the net outlay of slaveowners in raising a slave to age 18 (from $355 to $179).

Now we add the adjusted pre-18 total to the value of the slave at age 18. In the 1974 study, we used Conrad and Meyer's interpretation of Phillips' estimate of market prices for a male slave of $925, and for a female slave $825. We then averaged the two ($875). In this study we have used Kotlikoff's calculations of slave prices in the New Orleans market. These lie well below Phillips' figures, especially in the 1820s, so this revision tends to decrease the net value of slaves at age 18 from our earlier calculations. For the years 1640 to 1770, we now have the detailed series of slave prices in British America compiled by Richard Bean. (See the calculations in the Appendix for the method of converting Bean's figures from current pounds sterling to 1840 American dollars.) During the transition period of 1780 and 1790, the slave prices shown are pure guesses. If we assume that the war reduced slave prices, the 1780 figure is placed slightly below the 1770 one. It is assumed then that a strong rebound in prices began with the opening up of trade to European markets on increasingly favorable terms and that this continued until 1800.

No estimates are made for slaves who reached maturity after 1840, on the ground that the work years after 1863 of slaves who matured in or before 1840 provide some balance to the work lives before 1863 of slaves who matured after 1840.

Table 6.1
Costs and Revenues Associated with Raising a Slave to Age 18

Expense or Wage Revenue	Year	n	Net in Dollars	3%	Value Age 18 7%
Nursery Costs	0-1=t-18	18	-50	-85	-169
Mother's time lost	0-1=t-18	18	-16	-27	-54
Maintenance	0-1=t-18	18	-10	-17	-34
Maintenance	1-2=t-17	17	-10	-17	-32
Maintenance	2-3=t-16	16	-10	-16	-30
Maintenance	3-4=t-15	15	-10	-16	-28
Maintenance	4-5=t-14	14	-10	-15	-26
Maintenance	5-6=t-13	13	-10	-15	-24
Imputed Wages	6-7=t-12	12	5	7	11
Maintenance	6-7=t-12	12	-10	-14	-23
Imputed Wages	7-8=t-11	11	10	14	21
Maintenance	7-8=t-11	11	-15	-21	-32
Imputed Wages	8-9=t-10	10	15	20	30
Maintenance	8-9=t-10	10	-15	-20	-30
Imputed Wages	9-10=t-9	9	20	26	37
Maintenance	9-10=t-9	9	-15	-20	-28
Imputed Wages	10-11=t-8	8	30	38	52
Maintenance	10-11=t-8	8	-15	-19	-26
Imputed Wages	11-12=t-7	7	40	49	64
Maintenance	11-12=t-7	7	-15	-18	-24
Imputed Wages	12-13=t-6	6	50	60	75
Maintenance	12-13=t-6	6	-15	-18	-23
Imputed Wages	13-14=t-5	5	60	70	84
Maintenance	13-14=t-5	5	-18	-21	-25
Imputed Wages	14-15=t-4	4	70	79	92
Maintenance	14-15=t-4	4	-18	-20	-24
Imputed Wages	15-16=t-3	3	80	87	98
Maintenance	15-16=t-3	3	-20	-22	-25
Imputed Wages	16-17=t-2	2	90	95	103
Maintenance	16-17=t-2	2	-20	-21	-23
Imputed Wages	17-18=t-1	1	100	103	107
Maintenance	17-18=t-1	1	-20	-21	-21
TOTALS				206	77

Expense or Wage Revenue	Year	n	Value at age 18 Adjusted for Mortality 3%	7%
Nursery Costs	0-1=t-18	18	-170	-338
Mother's time lost	0-1=t-18	18	-54	-108
Maintenance	0-1=t-18	18	-34	-68
Maintenance	1-2=t-17	17	-33	-63
Maintenance	2-3=t-16	16	-32	-59
Maintenance	3-4=t-15	15	-31	-55

Table 6.1 (continued)

Expense or Wage Revenue	Year	n	Value at age 18 Adjusted for Mortality	
			3%	7%
Maintenance	4-5=t-14	14	-30	-52
Maintenance	5-6=t-13	13	-29	-48
Imputed Wages	6-7=t-12	12	14	23
Maintenance	6-7=t-12	12	-29	-45
Imputed Wages	7-8=t-11	11	28	42
Maintenance	7-8=t-11	11	-42	-63
Imputed Wages	8-9=t-10	10	40	59
Maintenance	8-9=t-10	10	-40	-59
Imputed Wages	9-10=t-9	9	26	37
Maintenance	9-10=t-9	9	-20	-28
Imputed Wages	10-11=t-8	8	38	52
Maintenance	10-11=t-8	8	-19	-26
Imputed Wages	11-12=t-7	7	49	64
Maintenance	11-12=t-7	7	-18	-24
Imputed Wages	12-13=t-6	6	60	75
Maintenance	12-13=t-6	6	-18	-23
Imputed Wages	13-14=t-5	5	70	84
Maintenance	13-14=t-5	5	-21	-25
Imputed Wages	14-15=t-4	4	79	92
Maintenance	14-15=t-4	4	-20	-24
Imputed Wages	15-16=t-3	3	87	98
Maintenance	15-16=t-3	3	-22	-25
Imputed Wages	16-17=t-2	2	95	103
Maintenance	16-17=t-2	2	-21	-23
Imputed Wages	17-18=t-1	1	103	107
Maintenance	17-18=t-1	1	-21	-21
TOTALS			-15	-341

Slaves Coming to Age 18 in Various Years

Good censuses of slaves were not made. (Nor were censuses with modern detail made for nonslaves either, of course.) Therefore, rough approximations are necessary. The source for data unless otherwise mentioned is the *U.S. Historical Statistics.* Columns 2 and 3 of Table 6.2 give available age distributions from censuses in 1820 to 1840. Linear interpolations over the intervals yield estimates of the number aged 18 (col. 4). Because age 18 is above the middle of the 10 to 23 interval, the linear interpolations for 1830 and 1840 are scaled downward slightly as in column 5. The estimate for 1820 is similarly scaled upward for the same reason.

We may now estimate the proportions (age 18/total population), which are approximately 2.2 percent in 1840, 1830, and 1820. This proportion may be applied backward to the 1810, 1800, 1790 and on back estimates of total slave population to get the remaining estimates in column 5, Table 6.2.

Table 6.2
The Present Value of the Appropriate Surplus of Slaves Aged 18

Year	Total Slaves (000)	Slaves 10-23 (000)	Slaves 14-25 (000)	Slaves 18 (est.) (000)
	(1)	(2)	(3)	(4)
1840	2487	781	--	55.78
1830	2009	621	--	44.35
1820	1538	--	404	33.67
1810	1191	--	--	--
1800	894	--	--	--
1790	698	--	--	--
1780	575			
1770	460			
1760	326			
1750	236			
1740	150			
1730	91			
1720	69			
1710	45			
1700	28			
1690	17			
1680	7			
1670	5			
1660	3			
1650	2			
1640	1			
1630	0			
1620	0			

Year	Adjusted Estimates for Age 18	Net Value for Age 18 Slaves @ 7%	Total Value of Slaves Age 18 ($000)	Decadal Values Compounded to 1983 @ 3% ($000)
	(5)	(6)	(7)	(8)
1840	55	520	28600	17384212
1830	44	345	15180	16174745
1820	34	445	15130	15419213
1810	26	245	6370	11401992
1800	20	273	5460	10433591
1790	15	173	2595	6124800
1780	13	73	923	4078049
1770	10	81	820	4651713
1760	7	92	660	4718474
1750	5	88	457	4131047
1740	3	82	271	3210893
1730	2	75	150	2458463

Table 6.2 (continued)

Year	Adjusted Estimates for Age 18	Net Value for Age 18 Slaves @ 7%	Total Value of Slaves Age 18 ($000)	Decadal Values Compounded to 1983 @ 3% ($000)
	(5)	(6)	(7)	(8)
1720	2	59	90	1739314
1710	1	37	37	1089281
1700	1	36	22	1054799
1690	0	54	20	850831
1680	0	34	5	472809
1670	0	48	5	406772
1660	0	22	1	346580
1650	0	64	3	468176
1640	0	67	1	216183
1630	0	64	0	0
1620	0	79	0	0
			Sum =	106831939

The above estimates are confused by the fact that no account was taken of the "free colored" population which in 1820, for example, accounted for 113,000 of a total of 899,000 black males. (The age estimates above exclude "free colored.") As long as the market price reflected the possibility that the slave might become free, however, no problem should occur. But this matter prevents us from working backward from the black population in, say, 1880 to check our earlier estimates.

Aggregation and Present Value as of 1983

Now we must first multiply the number of slaves age 18 by their net values (col. 6). This is done for the decennial dates in column 7 of Table 6.2. For years in between, linear interpolations can now be made. This calculation gives us in principle a series of amounts for each year from 1620 to 1840. But for the present study, a further interpolation was made. The average value of slaves aged 18 over each decade was assumed to hold in each year of the decade. Compounding was then done from the midpoint of each decade. When this technique was compared to the results originally found in Simon and Neal when each annual figure was compounded forward to the present, an accumulated error of only 1 percent was found.

The only remaining problem is to decide on the appropriate interest rate to compound the sums to 1983. This decision is unexpectedly easy. It is quite clear that no interest rate below 3 percent makes any economic sense. Since 1880, and very likely since 1820, the U.S. economy has been growing at a rate of approximately 3 percent annually. In the eighteenth century, Adam Smith's observation that the American population tended to double every twenty-five years also implies a 3 percent growth rate if per capita income remained constant. Any asset that fails to yield this rate of return is unprofitable and must be replaced by another that yields at least the 3 percent. So we begin by computing the present value at this rate, which comes to $155.5 billion as of 1983.

This amount is in terms of antebellum dollars and should be inflated by the rise in the general price level which has occurred since then. The GNP deflator in 1983 was roughly nine times its 1860 level. Using this scale factor, we see that the result in 1983 dollars would be roughly $1.4 trillion—a very large sum indeed.

COMPARISONS

This kind of sums, created by a combination of compound interest and inflation rates over a very long period of time, are beyond the intuitive grasp of most of us. Some kind of reference point is needed against which we can gauge the significance of these sums in their historical context. Such a reference is conveniently at hand in the calculations performed by Larry Neal and Paul Uselding for the net benefits conferred on the American economy in the period 1790–1912 by the importation of free immigrant labor, primarily from Europe (Neal and Uselding, 1972). The argument there also relied on the human capital approach used here. But the sum transferred to the benefit of others in the American economy in the case of immigrants was the present value of the expenses of rearing the immigrants to working age. This is a net addition to the U.S. economy in the case of free immigrants, but not in the case of imported slaves. The purchase price of imported slaves is remitted abroad and is a net loss to the U.S. economy. Since immigrants work in a free labor market, however, there is no expropriable surplus from their future work efforts that needs to be capitalized. Two quite different kinds of benefits are being conferred on the American economy in each case. Nevertheless, if the same kind of quantitative calculation is made for each, a direct comparison of their relative sizes is possible.

Table 6.3 presents the calculations for the total net value of slaves coming to age 18 over each of the six decades starting in 1790 and ending in 1850 (col. 1). For this exercise, we have also included the slave population coming of age in the decade of the 1840s. This decade includes a large surge of immigrants, as a consequence of which, especially with the dip in slave prices that also occurred in the 1840s, our results tend to be biased in favor of the immigrants. The net values for each decade are then compounded only to 1914 and only at the rate of 3 percent (col. 2). The sum of benefits in that year from slavery in just the national period was $17 billion. By comparison, the resource pool calculated from the importation of immigrants in each of these six decades is given in column 3 (Neal and Uselding, p. 85, Table V, col. 1). This is very minor in comparison to the totals calculated for slavery until the decade of the 1840s. Even so, the compounded sum by 1914 is only a bit over one-third that for slaves ($6.4 billion). Adjustment for changes in price levels would increase both figures, but their relative sizes would remain the same.

Table 6.3

Comparison of Slave and Immigrant Benefits to 1914

Year	Decadal Value of Slaves ($000)	Total Value to Compounded 1914 @ 3%	Decadal Value of Immigrants ($000)	Total Value to Compounded 1914 @ 3%
	(1)	(2)	(3)	(4)
1850	346266.72	2661823.52	410800.00	3157904.12
1840	220484.30	2277814.81	197000.00	2035199.46
1830	152904.17	2122913.58	49000.00	506217.12
1820	108358.76	2021851.49	32400.00	334723.16
1810	59430.51	1490276.83	16100.00	166328.48
1800	40406.22	1361689.11	15400.00	159096.81
1790				
	SUM =	11936369.33	SUM =	6359469.15

These calculations confirm our historical sense of the relative importance of slavery and immigration for the American economy in the antebellum period. But note that, while slavery's benefits were nearly triple the size of those derived from immigration, they were conferred primarily in the South, which had only half the population of the North. Viewed this way, the proportional importance of slavery to the Southern economy was six times that of immigration to the Northern economy.

Yet by 1914 the Southern regional economy was markedly behind that of the rest of the country by any measure—per capita income, proportion of rural population, relative importance of agriculture, banking services, and so on. What had happened in the meantime? Clearly, the Civil War and the Reconstruction era that followed devastated the Southern economy even while the North accelerated its process of industrialization. Were the accumulated benefits that accrued to the slaveowners dissipated entirely by war, expropriation, and reconstruction? Were they transferred to the Northern industrialists? Or were they transferred abroad to the British industrialists by dint of the low cotton prices prevailing after the Civil War? Happily, resolution of these questions lies beyond the scope of this chapter. One thing seems clear: The accrued benefits of slavery were not transferred to the freedmen.

REFERENCES

Bean, Richard Nelson. *The British Trans-Atlantic Slave Trade, 1650–1775*. New York: Arno Press, 1975.

Cairnes, J. E. *The Slave Power*. London: Macmillan, 1862.

Conrad, Alfred H., and Meyer, John R. *The Economics of Slavery*. Chicago: Aldine Publishing Co., 1964.

Craven, Alfred. *Soil Exhaustion as a Factor in the Agricultural History of Virginia and Maryland, 1601–1860.* Urbana: University of Illinois Press, 1926.

David, Paul A.; Gutman, Herbert, G.; Sutch, Richard; Temin, Peter; and Wright, Gavin. *Reckoning with Slavery: A Critical Study in the Quantitative History of American Negro Slavery.* New York: Oxford University Press, 1976.

Fogel, Robert W., and Engerman, Stanley L. *The Reinterpretation of American Economic History.* New York: Harper & Row, 1971.

———. *Time on the Cross.* 2 vols. Boston: Little, Brown, & Co., 1974.

Genovese, Eugene. *The Political Economy of Slavery: Studies in the Economy and Society of the Slave South.* New York: Vintage, 1967.

Gray, Lewis Cecil. *History of Agriculture in the Southern United States to 1860.* Washington, D.C.: Carnegie Institute, 1933.

Kotlikoff, Lawrence J. "The Structure of Slave Prices in New Orleans, 1804 to 1862." *Economic Inquiry* 27 (October 1979):496–518.

Mitchell, B. R., and Deane, Phyllis. *Abstract of British Historical Statistics.* Cambridge, Eng.: Cambridge University Press, 1962.

Neal, Larry, and Uselding, Paul. "Immigration, A Neglected Source of American Economic Growth: 1790 to 1912." *Oxford Economic Papers* 24 (March 1972):68–88.

Phillips, Ulrich B. "The Economic Cost of Slaveholding in the Cotton Belt." *Political Science Quarterly* 20 (June 1905).

———. *American Negro Slavery.* New York: D. Appleton & Co., 1918.

———. *Life and Labor in the Old South.* Boston: Little, Brown & Co., 1929.

Ramsdell, Charles. "The Natural Limits of Slavery Expansion." *Mississippi Valley Historical Review* 16 (September 1929):6.

Simon, Julian, and Neal, Larry. "A Calculation of the Black Reparations Bill." *The Review of Black Political Economy* 4 (Winter 1974):75–86.

Steckel, Richard. "Adversity and Diversity: The Nutrition, Health, and Mortality of American Slaves from Conception to Adult Maturity." Unpublished paper, Ohio State University, November 1983.

U.S. Department of Commerce, Bureau of the Census, *Long-Term Economic Growth, 1860–1965.* Washington, D.C.: GPO, 1966.

———. *Historical Statistics of the United States, Colonial Times to 1970.* Bicentennial ed., 2 vols. Washington, D.C.: GPO, 1975

Wright, Gavin. *The Political Economy of the Cotton South: Households, Markets and Wealth in the Nineteenth Century.* New York: W. W. Norton, 1978.

Yasuba, Yasuki. "Profitability and Viability of Slavery in the Ante-Bellum South." In Robert Fogel and Stanley Engerman, eds., *The Reinterpretation of American Economic History.* New York: Harper & Row, 1971.

APPENDIX: DETAILED CALCULATIONS
OF SLAVEOWNERS' BENEFITS

Year	British Wheat Prices	British Pindex 1697=100	British Pindex 1701=100
	(1)	(2)	(3)
1840			
1830			
1820			162.40
1810			213.20
1800			184.40
1790			121.00
1780			113.80
1770			106.20
1760			98.40
1750			93.60
1740			97.40
1730			95.00
1720			96.80
1710			111.40
1700			114.80
1690		81.60	99.55
1680	36.32	91.60	111.75
1670	37.50	92.40	112.73
1660	48.09	111.00	135.42
1650	46.85	108.14	131.93
1640	39.86	92.00	112.24
1630	39.69	91.60	111.75
1620	35.38	81.67	99.63

Note: All figures are centered five year averages.

Year	British P index 1821-25=100	British Pindex 1838-42=1.0	Slave Prices in Current #	Slave Prices in 1840 #
	(4)	(5)	(6)	(7)
1840	106.20	1.00		
1830	101.66	0.96		
1820	113.98	1.07		
1810	154.00	1.45		
1800	132.14	1.24		
1790	84.92	0.80		
1780	82.20	0.77		
1770	76.10	0.72	38.00	53.03
1760	69.06	0.65	36.00	55.36
1750	67.61	0.64	27.00	42.41
1740	69.80	0.66	27.00	41.08
1730	66.68	0.63	25.00	39.82
1720	69.92	0.66	24.00	36.45
1710	79.83	0.75	24.00	31.93
1700	80.57	0.76	24.00	31.63
1690	71.91	0.68	24.00	35.44
1680	80.08	0.75	19.00	25.20
1670	79.12	0.74	21.00	28.19
1660	97.82	0.92	21.00	22.80
1650	94.54	0.89	28.00	31.45
1640	78.77	0.74	17.00	22.92
1630	80.72	0.76	17.00	22.37
1620	71.40	0.67	17.00	25.29

Year	Prices in 1840 $	Net Values in 1840 $	Total Slaves ('000)	Slaves aged 18 estimated ('000)
	(8)	(9)	(10)	(11)
1840	875.00	520.00	2487.00	55.21
1830	700.00	345.00	2009.00	44.60
1820	800.00	445.00	1538.00	34.14
1810	600.00	245.00	1191.00	26.44
1800	450.00	272.50	894.00	19.85
1790	350.00	172.50	698.00	15.50
1780	250.00	72.50	575.00	12.77
1770	258.04	80.54	460.00	10.21
1760	269.38	91.88	326.00	7.24
1750	206.37	88.04	236.00	5.24
1740	199.91	81.57	150.00	3.33
1730	193.76	75.43	91.00	2.02
1720	177.38	59.04	69.00	1.53
1710	155.36	37.03	45.00	1.00
1700	153.93	35.60	28.00	0.62
1690	172.47	54.14	17.00	0.38
1680	122.61	33.86	7.00	0.16
1670	137.16	48.41	5.00	0.11
1660	110.94	22.19	3.00	0.07
1650	153.05	64.30	2.00	0.04
1640	111.53	67.15	1.00	0.02
1630	108.83	64.46	0.00	0.00
1620	123.05	78.67	0.00	0.00

Year	Number of Slaves Aged 18 x Value ($000)	Decadal Average Total Value Compounded to 1983 @ 3%
	(12)	(13)
1840	28709.93	17510031.07
1830	15386.93	16319273.42
1820	15193.90	15542388.38
1810	6477.85	11456064.62
1800	5408.25	10467584.34
1790	2672.99	6264066.95
1780	925.46	4089134.55
1770	822.45	4676355.57
1760	664.94	4758482.88
1750	461.25	4161694.09
1740	271.64	3235870.42
1730	152.38	2490407.95
1720	90.44	1756479.39
1710	36.99	1095100.47
1700	22.13	1059471.50
1690	20.43	859611.58
1680	5.26	478188.81
1670	5.37	414026.32
1660	1.48	351868.09
1650	2.86	474266.19
1640	1.49	218638.00
1630	0.00	0.00
1620	0.00	0.00

107679004.59

APPENDIX (continued)

Note: All figures are centered five-year averages. Notes on detailed calculations:

1. Five-year averages centered on the decade year of English wheat prices. Eton College prices for 1620, Exeter prices for 1630 on.
   Source: Mitchell and Deane, 1962, p. 486.
2. Five-year averages centered on the decade years 1670–1690 of Schumpeter-Gilboy price index for consumers' goods (1697=100) and extended back to 1620 on basis of col. 1.
   Source: Mitchell and Deane, 1962, p. 468.
3. Five-year averages centered on the decade years 1700–1820 of Schumpeter-Gilboy price index for consumers' goods (1701 = 100) and extended back to 1620 on basis of col. 2 $\times$ (1.22), the ratio of the two indexes in the year 1697.
   Source: Mitchell and Deane, 1962, pp. 468-69.
4. Five-year averages centered on the decade years 1800–1840 of the Gayer-Rostow-Schwartz price index for domestic commodities (1821–1825 = 100) and extended back to 1620 on basis of col. 3 $\times$ (col. 4/col. 3)$_{t+2}$.
   Source: Mitchell and Deane, 1962, p. 470.
5. Shift of col. 4 to five-year average centered on 1840 (col. 4/106) and set to 1838–1842 = 1.0.
6. Five-year averages of British-American slave prices centered on decade year from 1640–1770 in current British pounds sterling per slave.
   Source: Historical Statistics, p. 1174 (Series Z 166).
7. British-American slave prices in 1840 British prices (col. 6/col. 5).
8. American slave prices in 1840 dollars.
   1800–1840: Kotlikoff, 1979, p. 498. (Price at each decade year read from chart.)
   1780–1790: Backward linear extrapolation from 1800, assuming depressed market prices for slaves.
   1620–1770: col. 7 $\times$ 4.866 (par rate of British pound sterling in terms of dollars in 1840).
9. Net values of American slaves in 1840 dollars.
   1810–1840: Market price (col. 8) less $179 (assuming all slaves were raised in the United States).
   1760–1800: Market price (col. 8) less $179/2 (assuming only one-half of slaves were raised in the United States).
   1690–1750: Market price (col. 8) less $179/3 (assuming only one-third of slaves were raised in the United States).
   1650–1680: Market price (col. 8) less $179/4 (assuming only one-fourth of slaves were raised in the United States).
   1620–1640: Market price (col. 8) less $179/8 (assuming only one-eighth of slaves were raised in the United States).
10. Total number of slaves in decade year.
    Source: 1790–1840: *Historical Statistics*, p. 14, n. 1 to Series A 91-104.
    1620–1780: *Historical Statistics*, p. 1168, Series Z 1 (Negro). These include freedmen as well but are also judged to be underestimates (p. 1152).
11. Total number of slaves 18 years of age in decade year. Calculated by taking 2.22 percent of total population (col. 10 $\times$ 0.0222).
12. Total value of 18-year-old slaves at decade year. (col. 11 $\times$ col. 9)
13. Estimate of decade average total value of 18-year-old slaves compounded to 1983 at 3 percent annual growth rate.
    (col. 12)$_t$, (col. 12)$_{t-1}$)/2)*10*1.03$^{1983-t-5}$).

    The "bottom line" number, $155,451,738,350, is the current estimated transferred value to the American economy of all past slaves in 1840 prices.

7.

Estimated Present Value of Income Diverted during Slavery

James Marketti

At a crucial point in the development of the industrial United States, large amounts of free labor were deployed, from which surplus was extracted and filtered through various exchange mechanisms to nearly every budding industrial enterprise in the nation.[1] In this chapter, an attempt is made to estimate income exploited during slavery. Using tools of capital theory and historical data on slave population and prices, we estimate the diverted income and its value compounded through 1983. The 1983 present value estimate, in current dollars, ranges from $2.1 to $4.7 trillion. We also present the methodology used for making the estimate. The approach is only partial. That is, exploitation is considered for the period 1790 to 1860; exploitation in the colonial period, the post–Civil War period, and outside the slave sector is not included.

DEFINITION

Robert Evans notes that the slave industry consisted of two types of firms. One owned or rented the capital goods (slaves) and used them as factors of production to produce a marketable commodity (labor services) or combined them with other factors to produce marketable commodities (cotton, railroad services, gold, and so on). The other type of firm owned those capital goods (female slaves) used to produce new capital goods (slaves). Some firms, usually plantations, engaged in all three, producing labor services, agricultural products, and slaves.[2]

All capital investments, including those in human capital, are made on the same basis: "[assets are] capitalized by the price bids of buyers and sellers in the market place at the present discounted value of all its future net receipts."[3] The human capital concept applied to investments in slave capital is well grounded in the literature on the economics of slavery.

As early as 1905 Ulrich B. Phillips wrote, "From an economic point of view the American system of slavery was a system of . . . capitalizing the prospective value of labor of each workingman for the whole of his life."[4] In 1933 Lewis C. Gray wrote, "the prospective series of annual incomes from the ownership of a slave were capitalized on the same principle as a terminable annuity or any other terminable use-bearer."[5] Evans concurs in the view: "The slave market performed for the ante-bellum South some of the same functions now performed by the New York Stock Exchange, such as it served in the eyes of the public as a sensitive reflector of current and future business prospects."[6]

The net income stream on slave capital was returned to slaveholders. A possible measure of the present value of the net income stream is the price of a slave. Extensive aggregate data are available for 1790 to 1860 on the number of slaves from census data and the price of slaves from various historical sources. Those data can be used to find the aggregate present value of net incomes exploited from slaves at several points in the 1790–1860 period. From those stock values, an implicit net income flow can be considered (the value exploited), and from those we can derive the present value.

The usefulness of the price-quantity relationship in deriving net income generated by slave investments can be demonstrated by, first, considering the case of a single slave or a cohort of slaves. The more complicated case using the entire slave population, 1790 to 1860, is considered later. The present discounted value of slave income (V_t)—conceptualized as the price of a slave or the average price of a cohort, multiplied by the number of slaves in a cohort—includes three implied calculations made by slave investors: (1) the annual net income return (V_k) on the investment, (2) the time period (n) during which income would be returned, and (3) the discount rate (i) or rate of expected return.

The relationship is

$$V_t = \sum_{k=1}^{n} V_k \, (1 + i)^{-k} \tag{1}$$

By assuming that annual net income returns (V_k) are constant, we can solve for (V_k).[7]

$$V_k = \frac{V_t}{\sum_{k=1}^{n} (1 + i)^{-k}} \tag{2}$$

The present value of the exploited or diverted stream (V_n) is defined as the accumulated annual net incomes,

$$\sum_{k=1}^{n} (V_k)$$

with interest compounded. Interest is compounded because, unlike net annual incomes to slaveholders, slaves did not have the option of consuming or investing the returns. The calculation is:

$$V_n = \sum_{k=1}^{n} V_k (1 + i)^{n - k + x} \tag{3}$$

where $(X) = N - n$ and N is years beyond the expected lifetime of a slave (n) $(N \geq n)$. (V_n) can also be derived directly from (V_t).[8]

$$\sum_{k=1}^{n} V_k (1 + i)^{n - k + x} = V_k \sum_{k=1}^{n} (1 + i)^{n - k + x} = \tag{4}$$

$$\frac{V_t}{\sum_{k=1}^{n} (1 + i)^{-k}} \sum_{k=1}^{n} (1 + i)^{n - k + x} =$$

$$\frac{V_t}{\sum_{k=1}^{n} (1 + i)^{-k}} \sum_{k=1}^{n} (1 + i)^{n + x} (1 + 1)^{-k} =$$

$$\frac{V_t}{\sum_{k=1}^{n} (1 + i)^{-k}} (1 + i)^{n + x} \sum_{k=1}^{n} (1 + i)^{-k} =$$

$$V_t (1 + i)^{n + x} = V_t (1 + i)^{-N}$$

The fact that income diverted can be computed directly from the price-quantity relationship (V_t) rather than first finding (V_k), with which the income derived is conceptually defined, is laborsaving. The usefulness of this approach will be seen in operationalizing the model for the entire slave population, 1790 through 1860, to which we now turn.

PRICE

To find the price-quantity relationship between number of slaves and prices it would be simple to multiply the number of slaves at each census by average price. Rather than assume homogeneity of slaves, however, we distinguish in Tables 7.1 to 7.3 among cohorts of slaves on three variables: two *geographical*, two *sex*, and four *age* classifications. The geographical variables are (1) the lower South, including Alabama, Arkansas, Florida, Georgia, Louisiana, Mississippi, and Texas and (2) the upper South, border, and Northern states, including North Carolina, South Carolina, and Virginia. The large variation in prices between the upper and lower South reflect the large difference in slave productivity based on how they were used in the two regions.[9]

The lower South is in the fertile black belt. Settled in 1790–1860, this area was well suited for high-yield agricultural production, primarily cotton. In the upper South, border, and Northern states, slaves were allocated to small farms or engaged in domestic services. Virginia and North and South Carolina slaves, while employed on marginal cotton and tobacco plantations, were just as likely to be domestics or to be hired out as handymen, harvest hands, or railroad laborers. Toward the end of the period, slaves in the upper South were employed primarily for breeding, the offspring being sent at maturity to the more productive lower South.[10]

Age is also a reflection of productivity. Differential prices reflect expected net income returns at various stages of life. The four age intervals are (1) children, under fifteen, (2) prime, fifteen to forty-five, (3) past prime, forty-five to seventy, and (4) old, seventy and over. We would expect that prime slaves would bring the largest price since they worked at peak productivity, and income returns were fairly immediate. Past prime reflects reduced productivity. While children had earnings potential, the high mortality rate and reluctance to separate them from the family before they were full grown made them a risky and low-priced asset. Old slaves had estimated negative expected net income (gross income below maintenance costs).

Sixteen price-quantity calculations, one for each cohort, are computed for each decade, 1790 and 1860. The sum of those sixteen products is the present discounted value of slave income by decade (V_t). It is, therefore, a weighted average of the present discounted value of slave income in the sixteen cohorts.

$$V_t = \sum_{c=1}^{16} (p \cdot q)_c \qquad\qquad (5)$$

t = decade
p = price
q = quantity (slaves per cohort)
c = one of sixteen cohorts

The present discounted value of slave income in each decade contains some double- and overcounting. Otherwise we could sum them

$$\sum_{t=1790}^{N} V_t (1 + i)^{N - t} = V_n \qquad (6)$$

to determine the present value of income derived at any point (N).[11] (V_n) contains the accumulated annual net incomes with interest compounded through (N). (V_n) is found directly from (V_t) as was shown in Eq. (4).

The present-value calculation in each decade after 1790, however, contains four implicit expected net income elements, some of which should be added to the 1790 calculation of (V_t) and some of which should not. These are:

1. Some living in period $(t - 10)$ are also included in period (t) and are, therefore, in two (V_t) calculations.
2. The present value of changes in net expected income of the cohort in decade $(t - 10)$ resulting from
   a. movement from one age cohort to another, and
   b. movement from one location cohort to another.
3. The present value of new expected net income to be generated by additions to the population from
   a. births between period $(t - 10)$ and (t) and
   b. inmigration during the same period.
4. The present value of changes in the market price of slaves reflecting both
   a. effects of changes in the real value of money and
   b. changing expectations about the return on slave investments.

The money/real value effect in (4a) can be handled by appropriate deflators. It is the double-counting in (1) that creates difficulty, and while these four implicit elements are not directly separable in finding (V_t), sources of double-counting attributable to (1) above can be separated out by adding in each decade after 1790 only changes in the present value of slave income.[12] The computation thus becomes

$$V_t = 1790 (1 + i)^{N - t} + \sum_{t=1800}^{t=1860 \text{ by decade}} (V_t - V_{t - 10}) (1 + i)^{N - t} \qquad (7)$$

The overcount results from the fact that expected net incomes for slaves living beyond 1860 never materialized because of emancipation. The magnitude of unrealized additions to diverted income, it is argued, is simply $V_t = 1860$, the present value of expected net income returns of the entire 1860 population. When the emancipation overcount is considered, the model is

$$V_n = V_{t\,=\,1790}(1 + i)^{N-t} + \sum_{t=1800}^{1860\text{ by decade}}(V_t - V_{t-10})$$

$$(1 + i)^{N-t} - V_{t\,=\,1860}(1 + i)^{N-t}$$

where

$$V_t = \sum_{c=1}^{16}(p \cdot q)_c \text{ in any decade } (t) \text{ (see Eq. 5)} \tag{8}$$

t = decade
V_n = present value of income diverted as of year (N)
N = year in which is computed
i = rate of expected return on slave investments

As shown in Eq. (8), (N) is the translation of $(n + x)$ in Eq. (4) into a specific year. Let us recall that (n) is the expected lifetime of a slave investment, with the initial period designated $(k = 1)$. (x) is the period between the end of that lifetime and (N), the point at which the present value of diverted income calculated $(x = N - n)$. By setting (t) equal to the year in which the present value of an expected income stream is evaluated, (N) is then the year in which present value is computed. (N) remains constant regardless of the values of (t). For example, to compute the present value of income diverted through 1860, $N = 1860$ and $N - t = 70$ where $t = 1790$, $N - t = 60$ where $t = 1800$, and so on; when subtracting out the emancipation overcount, we use $V_t = 1860$ since $(1 + i)^{1860-1860} = 1$.[13]

The model can also be simplified to show that after 1860 we are only accumulating interest on the 1790 through 1860 income streams.

$$V_n = [V_{t\,=\,1790}(1 + i)^{1860-t} + \sum_{t=1800}^{1860\text{ by decade}}(V_t - V_{t-10})$$

$$(1 + i)^{1860-t} - V_t = 1860](1 + i)^{N-1860} \tag{9}$$

where N = any year after 1860.

We have not discussed the appropriate value of (i), the rate of return on slave investments. Several values of (i) will be employed. Using positive values of (i) begs the question concerning the profitability of slavery. The price-quantity relationship between number of slaves and price will measure an actual future net income stream only insofar as absolute certainty existed in slave markets. However, one advantage of the model is that it does in some sense test the profitability assumption by providing a decade by decade reevaluation of future income prospects.

Those who argue that slavery was unprofitable have implicitly, if not explicitly, made absolute certainty central to their argument. Slaveholders, they maintain, overcapitalized their investments in slaves. Slave prices were far beyond levels that would ensure a profitable return on investment; at the same time slaveholders were locked in—damned if they stayed in by unprofitability, damned if they got out by presumed social consequences. Against this view of Southern investors is contrary economic logic:

> Slavery must have been profitable, it could be argued, otherwise planters would not have continued to invest their money in it. Indeed, they could not, in the long run, continue to invest in a system in which they regularly lost money. Certainly planters were aware of investment opportunities and profit margins in other businesses. It would seem that they would quickly have foregone a losing enterprise in favor of profitable investment. Hence, the very persistence of the institution would appear to be adequate evidence of its profitability.[14]

Contrary to being reluctant buyers of slaves, we find that investment increased approximately 5 percent per year. If slavery was unprofitable, the value that slaveholders put on slave capital inputs did little to reflect the fact. Analysts of the "profitability" question have had the curious habit of treating the question as economists on some occasions and as accountants on others. If the profitability of slavery is an economic question, slaveholders clearly received both pecuniary and nonpecuniary returns. Part of the nonpecuniary return was the psychic income slaveholders derived by insuring that their sociopolitical system and culture remained intact.

PRESENT VALUE

Tables 7.1 to 7.3 show slave cohorts by decade, prices, and the present discounted value of slave income by decade 1790 through 1860. In some instances population cohorts were estimated since population figures for slaves were not returned by sex or age until 1820, and age distinctions were not entirely consistent after 1820. Price data were also estimated from various sources. (The estimating procedures are included with the tables.) Table 7.3 shows the price–quantity relationship for the slave population disaggregated into cohorts for the 1790–1860 period. The sum in each decade is simply (V_t).

Table 7.4 summarizes the weighted averages of present discounted value of slave income in each decade (V_t), shows the decade change in those averages ($V_t - V_{t-10}$), and reports in both current and adjusted prices. Note that, held in constant dollars, prospects declined only in the decade 1790–1800. The observation corresponds with Ulrich Phillips' viewpoint: "Thus in 1790–95, slave prices reached the bottom of a twenty years' decline. . . . Till 1815 'colonial' conditions prevailed, and the market for slave labor was relatively quiet and steady. In 1815 began the antebellum regime."[15] Between 1800 and 1860, the real present value of expected income grew steadily, approximating 7 percent annually for the entire period.

Table 7.1
Slave Population by Decade, 1790–1860

Upper South–Northern States	1790	1800	1810	1820	1830	1840	1850	1860
Male								
Under 15 (Child)	159,135	197,575	246,187	295,351	340,866	349,139	412,093	448,388
15–Under 45 (Prime)	148,437	184,293	229,636	276,400	322,901	338,398	372,261	405,366
45–Under 70 (Past Prime)	24,739	30,715	38,273	46,135	57,135	59,941	90,606	99,150
70 and Over (Old)	10,029	12,452	15,516	18,210	22,564	24,655	13,625	12,764
Female								
Under 15 (Child)	149,774	185,953	231,705	278,583	335,092	346,970	412,654	447,492
15–Under 45 (Prime)	144,425	179,312	223,430	268,278	321,273	339,841	372,843	406,020
45–Under 70 (Past Prime)	22,734	28,225	35,170	42,520	55,631	59,693	90,427	98,927
70 and Over (Old)	9,361	11,622	14,482	17,621	23,105	24,927	15,442	14,581
Lower South								
Male								
Under 15 (Child)	6,497	13,962	34,846	65,357	116,821	203,847	315,638	437,996
15–Under 45 (Prime)	7,287	15,660	39,085	73,555	127,410	226,646	323,379	458,748
45–Under 70 (Past Prime)	995	2,138	5,337	10,051	19,863	33,575	67,326	97,241
70 and Over (Old)	293	629	1,570	2,969	5,881	10,316	7,317	22,963
Female								
Under 15 (Child)	6,204	13,333	33,277	62,564	115,506	204,534	315,389	436,487
15–Under 45 (Prime)	6,965	14,969	37,358	70,048	123,394	225,944	324,629	455,503
45–Under 70 (Past Prime)	790	1,698	4,238	8,032	17,034	30,110	63,295	90,625
70 and Over	234	503	1,256	2,454	5,195	8,818	6,811	21,498
Total	697,899	893,039	1,191,366	1,538,128	2,009,753	2,487,354	3,203,735	3,953,749

Table 7.2
Slave Prices by Decade, 1790–1860

Upper South—Northern States	1790	1800	1810	1820	1830	1840	1850	1860
Male								
Under 15 (Child)	$ 80	$ 80	$ 80	$ 112	$ 184	$ 304	$ 300	$ 640
15–Under 45 (Prime)	200	200	200	275	463	763	750	1,600
45–Under 70 (Past Prime)	100	100	100	138	232	382	375	800
70 and Over	-20	-20	-20	-28	-46	-76	-75	-160
Female								
Under 15 (Child)	68	68	68	92	152	252	248	532
15–Under 45 (Prime)	166	166	166	228	384	633	623	1,328
45–Under 70 (Past Prime)	83	83	83	114	192	317	312	664
70 and Over (Old)	-17	-17	-17	-23	-38	-63	-62	-133
Lower South								
Male								
Under 15 (Child)	122	180	232	320	300	380	420	720
15–Under 45 (Prime)	275	450	575	800	750	950	1,050	1,800
45–Under 70 (Past Prime)	138	225	288	400	375	475	525	900
70 and Over	-28	-45	-58	-80	-75	-95	-105	-180
Female								
Under 15 (Child)	92	148	192	264	248	316	348	596
15–Under 45 (Prime)	228	374	477	664	623	789	872	1,494
45–Under 70 (Past Prime)	114	187	239	332	312	395	436	747
70 and Over (Old)	-23	-37	-48	-66	-62	-79	-87	-149

Table 7.3
Present Discounted Value of Slave Income by Decade, 1790–1860

(thousands of dollars)

Upper South—Northern States	1790	1800	1810	1820	1830	1840	1850	1860
Male								
Under 15 (Child)	$12,731	$15,806	$19,695	$33,079	$62,719	$106,138	$123,628	$286,968
15–Under 45 (Prime)	29,687	36,859	45,927	76,010	149,503	258,198	279,196	648,586
45–Under 70 (Past Prime)	2,474	3,072	3,827	6,367	13,274	22,897	33,977	79,320
70 and Over (Old)	-201	-249	-310	-510	-1,038	-1,874	-1,022	-2,042
Female								
Under 15 (Child)	10,185	12,645	15,756	25,630	50,934	87,436	102,338	238,066
15–Under 45 (Prime)	23,975	29,766	37,089	61,167	123,369	215,119	232,281	539,195
45–Under 70 (Past Prime)	1,887	2,343	2,919	4,847	10,681	18,923	28,213	65,688
70 and Over (Old)	-159	-159	-246	-405	-878	-1,570	-957	-1,939
Lower South								
Male								
Under 15 (Child)	728	2,513	8,084	20,914	35,046	77,462	132,568	315,357
15–Under 45 (Prime)	2,004	7,047	22,474	58,844	95,558	215,314	339,548	825,746
45–Under 70 (Past Prime)	137	481	1,537	4,020	7,449	15,948	35,346	87,517
70 and Over (Old)	-8	-28	-91	-238	-441	-980	-768	-4,133
Female								
Under 15 (Child)	571	1,973	6,389	16,517	28,645	64,633	109,755	260,146
15–Under 45 (Prime)	1,588	5,598	17,820	46,512	76,874	178,270	283,076	680,521
45–Under 70 (Past Prime)	90	318	1,013	2,667	5,315	11,893	27,597	67,697
70 and Over	-5	-19	-60	-162	-322	-697	-593	-3,203
Total	$85,683	$117,926	$181,823	$355,260	$656,689	$1,267,111	$1,724,184	$4,083,489

Table 7.4
Present Discounted Value of Slave Income by Decade (V_t) and Decade Change in Current and Adjusted Prices

Year (t)	Current Prices		Adjusted Prices, 1957–59=100		
	Value (V_t) (nearest $100,000)	Decade Change ($V_t - V_{t-10}$)	Value (V_t) (nearest $100,000)	Decade Change ($V_t - V_{t-10}$)	Deflator[a]
1790	85,700,000	---	252,100,000	---	.34
1800	117,900,000	32,200,000	245,600,000	-6,500,000	.48
1810	181,800,000	63,900,000	371,000,000	125,400,000	.49
1820	355,300,000	173,500,000	888,300,000	517,300,000	.40
1830	656,700,000	301,400,000	1,931,500,000	1,043,200,000	.34
1840	1,267,100,000	610,400,000	3,519,200,000	1,587,700,000	.36
1850	1,724,200,000	457,100,000	5,561,900,000	2,042,700,000	.31
1860	4,083,500,000	2,359,300,000	11,667,100,000	6,105,200,000	.35

[a] U.S. Bureau of the Census, Historical Statistics of the United States: Colonial Times to 1957 (Washington, D.C.: GPO, 1960).

Wholesale Price Indexes, Series E1–12. Wholesale Price Indexes (Warren and Pearson), by Major Product Groups; 1749 to 1890, pp. 115–16.

U.S. Bureau of the Census, Historical Statistics of the United States, Colonial Times to 1957; Continued to 1962 and Revisions (Washington, D.C.: GPO, 1965).

Prices and Price Indexes, Chapter E. Wholesale Price Indexes (BLS), p. 17.

The Warren and Pearson Index uses as its base years 1912–1914=100. The BLS Index uses as its base years 1957–1959=100. The Warren and Pearson Index was modified by deflating it to conform to the BLS Index. The deflation factor used was 0.37.

Table 7.5 arrays six calculations of the present value through 1860. The array is based on the model in Eq. (8), using six rates of expected return from 2.5 to 6 percent. The model is slightly modified in that five years are added to the number of years on which the expected rates of return are computed for present values added $(V_t - V_{t-10})$. The additional five years make $(N - t)$ properly $(N - t + 5)$ and reflect the fact that values added accumulated steadily during the interdecade period.

Present value through 1860 ranges from \$7,060,500,000 to \$40,951,400,000, depending on the rate of return used. The appropriate rate of return is crucial, as the time period is lengthened. Nowhere is this more clear than in Table 7.6. This table shows twelve calculations of present value through 1983, in constant 1957–1959 prices based on the model in Eq. (9), using various combinations of rates of return (i and i'). The model is again slightly modified to reflect the interdecade accumulation of value added.

Aside from providing a range of possibilities, Table 7.6 also dramatically portrays the effect of long-term periods on the computations even when rates of return vary only slightly. Present value through 1983 (1957–1959 prices) ranges from \$147 billion to \$53.1 trillion, depending on the combinations of rates of return. Obviously, with such magnitudes of difference, as much care must be given to selecting the appropriate interest rate as to making the original calculations.

Rational grounds can no doubt be found for several of the models. Models 8 and 11 seem especially useful. Alfred H. Conrad and John R. Meyer, for example, conclude that the rate of return on slave capital in its best alternative would not have been much below 4.5 to 5 percent and could not have been expected to earn more than 8 percent.[16]

An interest rate of 5 percent in the pre-emancipation period seems a modest estimate of what slaves could have earned had they been allowed to hold property rights in themselves and to invest their income returns in other alternatives. Six percent is still a moderate estimate. Three percent was selected as an appropriate post-emancipation interest rate because it approximates the rate of growth of the U.S. gross national product from 1869 to 1980.[17] Using this logic, the present (1983) value of income diverted or expropriated during 1790 to 1860 ranges from \$0.7 billion to \$40 billion in 1957–1959 prices.[18] Adjustment to current dollars is made by multiplying by 3 for current estimates of \$2.1 to \$4.7 trillion.

NOTES

1. An overall view of the economics of slavery literature is in Harold D. Woodman, ed., *Slavery and the Southern Economy: Sources and Readings* (New York: N.p., 1966).

2. Robert Evans, Jr., "The Economics of American Negro Slavery, 1830–1860," *Aspects of Labor Economics* (Princeton, N.J.: National Bureau of Economic Research, 1962), pp. 185–243.

3. Paul Samuelson, *Economics* (New York: McGraw-Hill, 1967), p. 587.

4. Ulrich B. Phillips, "The Economic Cost of Slaveholding in the Cotton Belt," *Political Science Quarterly* 20 (1905): 260–61.

Table 7.5
Present Value of Income Diverted Through 1860

Year (t)	Present Value (V_t) (millions)	Present Value Added $(V_t V_{t-10})$ (millions)	Time Period $(N-t)$ (years)	Decade Contributions at Various Rates of Interest Through 1860					
				i=.025 (millions)	i=.03 (millions)	i=.035 (millions)	i=.04 (millions)	i=.05 (millions)	i=.06 (millions)
1790	$ 252.1	$ 245.6	70	$ 1,383.3	$ 1,944.1	$ 2,729.3	$ 3,826.7	$ 7,472.7	$14,509.1
1800	245.6	(-6.5)	—	—	—	—	—	—	—
1810	371.0	125.4	55	487.7	637.3	831.8	1,084.3	1,835.3	3,091.2
1820	888.3	517.3	45	1,571.5	1,956.2	2,432.5	3,021.6	4,647.9	7,120.4
1830	1,931.5	1,043.2	35	2,475.7	2,935.4	3,477.6	4,116.6	5,754.3	8,018.1
1840	3,519.2	1,587.7	25	2,943.5	3,324.3	3,752.1	4,232.5	5,376.5	6,814.2
1850	5,561.9	2,042.7	15	2,958.4	3,182.5	3,422.2	3,678.8	4,246.6	4,895.4
1860	11,667.1	6,105.2	5	6,907.5	7,077.6	7,251.1	7,427.9	7,792.0	8,170.1
Sub-total		11,667.1		$18,727.6	$21,057.4	$23,896.6	$27,388.4	$30,080.3	$52,618.5
Emancipation Overcount		11,667.1		11,667.1	11,667.1	11,667.1	11,667.1	11,667.1	11,667.1
PRESENT VALUE				$ 7,060.5	$ 9,390.3	$12,229.5	$15,721.3	$18,413.2	$40,951.4

Table 7.6
Present Value Through 1983

Model #	Pre-Emancipation Rate of Return (i)	Present Value Through 1860 (millions)	Post-Emancipation Rate of Return (i)	Present Value Through 1983 (millions)
1	.025	$ 7,060.5	.025	$ 147,187.4
2	.03	9,390.3	.03	356,170.3
3	.035	12,229.5	.035	841,533.9
4	.04	15,721.3	.025	327,735.7
5	.04	15,721.3	.03	596,302.6
6	.04	15,721.3	.04	1,956,992.1
7	.05	18,413.2	.025	383,852.6
8	.05	18,413.2	.03	698,405.3
9	.05	18,413.2	.05	7,437,260.3
10	.06	40,951.4	.025	353,697.5
11	.06	40,951.4	.03	1,553,270.2
12	.06	40,951.4	.06	53,075,021.8

5. Lewis C. Gray, *History of Agriculture in the Southern United States to 1860* (Washington, D.C.: Carnegie Institute, 1933) in Woodman, ed., *Slavery and the Southern Economy*, pp. 31–32.

6. Evans, "The Economics of American Negro Slavery," p. 197.

7. Annual net income returns (V_k) are not calculated in this chapter.

$\sum_{k=1}^{n} (V_k)$ can be considered the net income stream received by slaveholders.

(V_k) in the aggregate for the 1790–1860 period is the value exploited.

However, as shown later, the 1969 value can be computed directly and simply from (V_t).

8. We again assume (V_k) is constant over the lifetime of the investment. The assumption is no doubt unrealistic where one slave or a single slave cohort is concerned. However, as we will see later, the cohorts are aggregated and reevaluated each decade, making the effects of the assumption relatively negligible.

9. Evans, "The Economics of American Negro Slavery," Table 11, p. 202.

10. Alfred H. Conrad and John R. Meyer, "The Economics of Slavery in the Ante-Bellum South," *Journal of Political Economy* 66 (April 1958): 114.

11. N is any year $\geq t$ and is conceptually the same as N in Eq. (4), where $t = O$.

12. Actually, the addition of decade-to-decade change in the present discounted value of slave income to that computed in 1790 underestimates the exploited value of slave income for two reasons. First, the double-count is overestimated (1) because not all members of the population living in period (t) are not alive in period $(t + 10)$; and (2) because it is separated out at its value in period (t) while in period $(t + 10)$ it represents the present discounted value of an expected net income stream that accumulates for ten or fewer years. The result of overestimating the double-count is to underestimate the present value of the income diverted.

13. The model is designed to compute value in time periods after 1860. It could easily be adapted to calculations between 1790 and 1860.

14. Woodman, *Slavery and the Southern Economy*, p. 21.

15. Phillips, "The Economic Cost of Slaveholding," pp. 262–64.

16. Conrad and Meyer, "The Economics of Slavery in the Ante-Bellum South," p. 113.

17. John W. Kendrick, *Productivity Trends in the United States* (New York: National Bureau of Economic Research, 1959), Table A-111, p. A-110 and *Economic Report of the President* (Washington, D.C.: GPO, 1968), Table B-2, p. 210 and Table B-3, p. 212. The growth rate was calculated after adjusting to constant 1958 dollars. (U.S. Bureau of the Census, *Statistical Abstract of the U.S.*, 1081, Table 704, p. 423.)

18. The CPI All Items Index (1967 dollars) rose by a factor of 3.2 between 1956 and 1981. The GNP implicit price deflator (1972 dollars) rose by a factor of 2.6 between 1960 and 1980 (*Statistical Abstract*, 1981, Tables 779 and 776). The original article and tables were constructed in 1957–1959 dollars. While this updated gross estimate incorporates some error, it does not substantially alter the magnitude of the estimate.

REFERENCES

Becker, Gary S. *Human Capital*. Chicago: University of Chicago Press, 1983, Ch. 3.

Conrad, Alfred H., and Meyer, John R. "The Economics of Slavery in the Ante-Bellum South." *Journal of Political Economy* 66 (April 1958): 95–122.

Davidson, Ralph K., Smith, Vernon L., and Wiley, Jay W. "Investment Decisions Under Capitalism." In *Economics: An Analytical Approach*. Homewood, Ill.: N.p., 1962. Reprint of pp. 103–4, 106–8, and 110–11.

Economic Report of the President. Washington, D.C.: GPO, 1968.

Engerman, Stanley. "The Effects of Slavery upon the Southern Economy: A Review of the Recent Debate." *EEH Second Series* 4, no. 2. Madison, Wis.: Graduate Program in Economic History, University of Wisconsin, 1967.

Evans, Robert, Jr. "The Economics of American Negro Slavery, 1830–1860." *Aspects of Labor Economics*. Princeton, N.J.: National Bureau of Economic Research, 1962, pp. 185–243.

Kendrick, John W. *Productivity Trends in the United States*. New York: National Bureau of Economic Research, 1959.

Phillips, Ulrich B. "The Economic Cost of Slaveholding in the Cotton Belt." *Political Science Quarterly* 20 (1905): 257–275.

————, *American Negro Slavery*. Baton Rouge, La.: LSU Press, 1966.

Ramsdell, Charles W. "The Natural Limits of Slavery Expansion." *Mississippi Valley Historical Review* 16 (1929): 151–71.

Rose, Louis. "The Magnitude and Distribution of Southern Slaveholder Capital Losses Due to Emancipation." *Discussion Paper 6*. Los Angeles, Southern California Economic History Group, undated.

Samuelson, Paul. *Economics*. New York: McGraw-Hill, 1967, 7th ed.

U.S. Bureau of the Census. *Population of the United States* in 1790, the first census. Washington, D.C.: GPO, 1792); 1800, the second census; 1810, the third census; 1820, the fourth census; 1830, the fifth census; 1840, the sixth census; 1850, the seventh census; 1860, the eighth census.

U.S. Bureau of the Census. *A Century of Population Growth, 1790–1900*. Washington, D.C.: GPO, 1909.

————. *Negro Population in the United States, 1790–1915*. Washington, D.C.: GPO, 1918.

————. *Historical Statistics of the United States; Colonial Times to 1957*. Washington, D.C.: GPO, 1960.

U.S. Department of State. *Population of the United States in 1790–1915*. Washington, D.C.: GPO, 1792.

APPENDIX: METHODOLOGY USED FOR TABLE 7.1

Population censuses for slaves were not returned by sex and age until 1820; nor were age distinctions entirely consistent after 1820. The various census return classifications during the period are shown below.

1790–1810   Slaves by state only

1820   Slaves by state, by sex, and by the following age categories: under 14, 14 to under 26, 26 to under 45, and 45 and over.

1830–1840   Slaves by states, by sex, and by the following age categories: under 10, 10 to under 24, 24 to under 36, 36 to under 55, 55 to under 100, and 100 and over.

1850–1860   Slaves by state, by sex, and by the following age categories: under 1, 1 to under 5, 5 to under 10, 10 to under 15, 15 to under 20, 20 to under 30, 30 to under 40, 40 to under 50, 50 to under 60, 60 to under 70, 70 to under 80, 80 to under 90, 90 to under 100, 100 and over, and unknown.

Except for the 45 and over classification in 1820, linear interpolations were used between 1820 and 1860 to make the census figures conform to the classifications used here. The 45 and over class in 1820 was divided into past prime and prime classes on the basis of the percentage breakdown in 1830 between the two classes within the Male—upper South Male—lower South, Female—upper South and Female—lower South categories. Census population figures for 1790, 1800, and 1810 were divided by geographical location. The population percentages in each of eight cells in each geographical location in 1820 (two sex classifications by four age-interval classifications) were used to divide the population in those decades according to the criteria used here.

Using linear interpolations throughout the data and applying 1820 percentages to the 1790–1810 population serves to overestimate the number of children and old slaves at the expense of prime age slaves. If the age distribution of a population is normally distributed, we would expect frequencies to become asymptotic at both ends of the age scale. The linearity of the interpolations creates somewhat larger frequencies at the extremes.

Furthermore the unknown age classifications available in 1850 and 1860 were added in with the 70 and over group, based on the assumption that age information tends to be lost more often for the old. Finally, 70,000 slaves were imported between 1790 and 1808 (39,000 between 1790 and 1800, 31,000 between 1800 and 1808—U.S. Bureau of the Census, *A Century of Population Growth, 1790–1900* [Washington, D.C.: GPO, 1909], p. 36). We can safely assume that imported slaves were seldom old or even past prime age. However, subsumed as they are in the general population, they are distributed in the same proportions as existed in the general population during a period in which no inmigration occurred. The overall effect of these maladjustments is to underestimate the capitalized value of slave assets.

8.

Black Exploitation and White Benefits: The Civil War Income Revolution

RICHARD VEDDER,
LOWELL GALLAWAY, AND
DAVID C. KLINGAMAN

Most of the world's great revolutions have resulted at least in part from concerns over the distribution of income and wealth; the French and Russian Revolutions are but two good examples. By contrast, the American Revolution was far less an economic revolution. To the extent that it was one at all, it largely reflected the discontent of upper middle-class merchants and professionals over their taxes. It was a revolution of the "taxpayer's revolt" variety of more recent times as manifested in Proposition 13 and other protests. The Civil War was in a true sense America's *real* revolution, if by revolution one means a radical real change in the status of the population or a significant subset of it. While the Civil War was a somewhat unique revolution in that the prime benefactors of the revolutionary change, America's blacks, by necessity played a comparatively passive role, few other revolutions have achieved as profound an economic result.

This chapter makes four specific points. First, not only were American blacks heavily exploited under slavery, but also the rate of expropriation increased continuously over time. This provided added economic impetus to the moral arguments for emancipation and, at the margin, may have contributed to the outbreak of hostilities. Second, the war itself meant an immediate and extraordinary redistribution of wealth and income away from the white slaveowning class toward the newly freed blacks. This extraordinary redistribution was not so obvious at the time owing to the sharp fall in total Southern income resulting from the war, but it was real nonetheless. Third, the sharp relative improvement in Southern black economic status may have given rise to a sense of complacency, which manifested itself by the decision of many black Americans not to use their newly achieved freedom to move to the North. Fourth, this era of complacency apparently began to break down around World War I in part because of a "revolution of rising expectations" not dissimilar to that observed today in many less developed countries. Fifth, although black incomes relative to those of whites showed some positive changes after 1880, those gains were small relative to the gains associated with emancipation.

THE INCREASING EXPLOITATION OF BLACKS IN THE ANTEBELLUM PERIOD

Notwithstanding Fogel and Engerman, there is strong evidence that slaves were severely exploited on the eve of the Civil War.[1] There is some debate about the precise magnitudes of that exploitation, but there is little likelihood that slaves "earned" in a material sense more than half what they would have received had they been working as free persons, and they probably earned less than that.[2] Moreover, their freedom to spend these meager "earnings" was severely limited, further lowering the utility derived from their income.

In several papers published in the mid-seventies, we (working collectively or separately) statistically estimated the marginal product of slave labor and compared it with slave "wages" to estimate what Fogel and Engerman called a "Robinsonian" exploitation or appropriation rate.[3] The estimation involved statistically fitting a production function of the Cobb-Douglas variety. The rate of return calculations on slavery that we made gave us estimates that are consistent with most other studies and, in addition, permitted us to calculate the returns on agricultural land and capital, compute rates of exploitation, and so forth.

If one is willing to assume that the rate of return on slave labor for production (ignoring returns from breeding and capital gains) remained constant throughout the nineteenth century at the rate estimated by Vedder and Stockdale for 1859 (7.51 percent), it is possible to estimate the marginal product of slave labor and compare it with the "slave wage" in order to calculate a rate of expropriation. In making such a computation, we assume that the slave wage (received largely in the form of in-kind payments) remained constant, in a real sense, over time, although its money value changed with prices, as measured by the index of wholesale prices in New Orleans.[4] Use of alternative price indices would alter the numerical values of the findings but not the nature of the change in those magnitudes over time. Three-year averages of relevant data are used to reduce cyclical variations related to business conditions, crop failures, and so on.[5] Slave prices varied as shown in Table 8.2.

The results, detailed in Table 8.1, suggest that exploitation increased over time. Around 1820 slaves received about 50 percent of their marginal product, with the remaining 50 percent expropriated by slaveowners. This is a high rate of exploitation; by contrast, textile workers in early nineteenth-century New England suffered much less expropriation, indeed none in a statistically significant sense.[6] By 1860, however, slaves were receiving only about 32 percent of their marginal product, while some 68 percent was expropriated by their owners. Southern economic ex-

Table 8.1
Estimated Exploitation of Slaves, 1820–1860

Period	Estimated Marginal Revenue Product	Assumed Slave "Wage"*	Absolute Magnitude of Exploitation	Exploitation Rate**
1819–1821	$72.60	$36.55	$36.05	50%
1829–1831	$54.87	$24.30	$30.57	56%
1839–1841	$67.68	$28.48	$39.12	58%
1849–1851	$64.42	$25.82	$38.60	60%
1858–1860	$93.46	$30.00	$63.46	68%

Sources: The marginal revenue product is calculated by assuming a 7.51 percent rate of return, the slave wage shown above, and the slave prices of Table 8.2. The marginal revenue product estimate in current dollars is simply the rate of return times the slave price *plus the slave wage.*
* Assumed to have been constant at $30, 1858–1860 prices.
** The absolute magnitude of exploitation expressed as a percentage of marginal revenue product.

Table 8.2
Wealth Effects of Slavery

Period	Average Slave Price	Slave Population*	Total Wealth From Slavery**
1802–1804	$300	975,207	$ 292,562
1809–1811	$424	1,191,392	$ 505,138
1819–1821	$480	1,538,038	$ 738,258
1829–1831	$407	2,009,043	$ 814,368
1839–1841	$522	2,487,455	$1,298,452
1849–1851	$547	3,410,037	$1,752,759
1858–1860	$845	3,871,164	$3,271,218

Sources: U.S. Department of Commerce, *Historical Statistics of the United States, Colonial Times to 1970* (Washington, D.C.: 1975); John Meyer, "The Economics of Slavery in the Antebellum South," *Journal of Political Economy* (April 1958), drawing on U. B. Phillips, *Life and Labor in the Old South* (Boston: Little, Brown, 1935).
* In Southern states.
** In thousands of current dollars.

pansion was accompanied by increased exploitation and a decline in the relative economic status of Southern blacks.

Some sensitivity analysis was performed to see whether the trends observed in Table 8.1 held under differing assumptions. For example, it might be argued that the rate of return on slaves changed over time with interest rates and that the risk premium prevailing in 1860 should be added to the secure interest rate on bonds for earlier years to obtain an assumed rate of return on slaves. Doing that makes little difference, in part because interest rates (especially long-term) were remarkably stable.[7] Alternative calculations, based on various assumptions, yield the same basic conclusion: Exploitation rose substantially as the century progressed toward the Civil War.[8]

INCOME AND WEALTH DISTRIBUTIONAL EFFECTS

In equilibrium, the discounted present value of the stream of expected future expropriation of slave labor should equal the slave price. On the eve of the Civil War, it appears that equilibrium conditions existed.[9] We are not aware of any good evidence indicating that those conditions did not exist earlier. Slave prices, then, are an approximate measure of the benefits (or expected benefits) to slaveowners. Table 8.2 shows the present value of slave exploitation, assuming that the price of the "average" slave was equal to one-half the price of a male field hand, as compiled by Ulrich B. Phillips for different dates.[10]

These estimates present a dramatic picture of the growing inequalities and inequities associated with slavery. Slave-related wealth grew some elevenfold from the turn of the century to the Civil War and an astounding 4.41 percent a year over the period 1820–1860. This is a higher growth rate than that for annual output or income, which almost certainly were not much more than 4 percent a year over the entire period in the nation as a whole or the South by itself.[11] Slave wealth in 1860 was slightly under $500 per white person living in the South.[12] Using only a 6 percent interest rate, this implies about $30 in income for every white Southerner at a time when the national per capita income for free persons was about $144.[13] Americans probably receive a roughly equivalent proportion of their total income from ownership of all forms of property today as Southern property owners received from the ownership of slaves in 1860.[14] The ratio of wealth created by slavery to income in 1860 for all Southern whites (including nonslaveowners) was between 3 and 4 to 1. A recent accounting of total net worth of Americans showed that the ratio of net worth to personal income was also between 3 and 4 to 1. The wealth derived from slavery by slaveowners was roughly as high in relation to income as wealth from *all* sources (real estate, stocks, bonds, insurance policies, bank accounts, etc.) in contemporary America.[15]

In Table 8.3, an attempt is made to quantify by state the exploitation income derived from slavery in 1850. The second column shows the exploitation income per slaveowner, and the third column shows this income per white person. If the white per capita income of the Southern states was around $125 in 1850, roughly 25 per-

Table 8.3

Slaveowner and White Per Capita Income Derived from Slave Exploitation in 1850

(current dollars)

State	Slave-owner	White Person
Alabama	$439	$30
Georgia	$373	$27
Louisiana	$445	$36
Mississippi	$503	$39
North Carolina	$383	$20
South Carolina	$565	$53
Virginia	$322	$20

Sources: Total state slave exploitation income is found by multiplying the number of slaves in the state by $500 and then multiplying that figure by .0751. The number of slaves, slaveowners, and whites, by state, is from the 1850 census.

cent of such income was attributable to slave exploitation. There would be a variation among states, of course.

The income distributional effects of slavery and emancipation were marked. Given the quality of nineteenth-century income statistics and the necessity of making several assumptions to arrive at income estimates by race, our estimates should be interpreted cautiously. With that caveat, we have estimated Southern black-white income differentials for three dates: 1840, 1860, and 1880. The results are shown in Table 8.4. We assume that slaves earned an income that averaged $30 in 1860 and slightly less in 1840 (owing to somewhat lower prices in that year), that free Southern blacks earned an amount based on the estimated marginal revenue product of slaves in 1860, and that black property income was so small that it could be ignored for all dates (all nonlabor income was received by whites). For the 1880 estimates, there are two views on black exploitation during the Reconstruction era. The "optimistic" view, represented in the writings of such scholars as Robert Higgs, Stephen DeCanio, and Joseph Reid, argues that the newly freed blacks were able to obtain compensation roughly approximating their marginal productivity, and that sharecropping, debt peonage, and so on, did not lead to exploitation.[16] The "pessimistic" view, most articulately presented by Roger Ransom and Richard Sutch, implies that such factors as information costs and discrimination led to a significant amount of exploitation of blacks living in the South in the postbellum period.[17]

Although we are sympathetic to the "optimistic" view, believing the evidence for that argument to be more persuasive, we have chosen to adopt an intermediate

Table 8.4
Black and White Income Per Capita

(current dollars)

Year	Black	White	Black as % of White
1840	$30.74	$105	29
1860	$32.25	$150	22
1880	$59.22	$100.45	59

Sources: The 1840 and 1860 figures for blacks are the estimated slave maintenance wage. The 1880 figure for blacks is the 1860 marginal revenue product reduced by 20.8 percent for a per capita
commodity output decline in the South between 1860 and 1880 (see Engerman below), plus a
20 percent reduction for exploitation and discrimination. The 1840 and 1860 figures for whites
are from Robert Fogel and Stanley Engerman, *The Reinterpretation of American Economic
History* (New York: Harper & Row, 1971), p. 335. The 1880 figure for whites is the 1860 figure
lowered by 20.8 percent for the estimated decline in per capita commodity output in the South
(see "The Economic Impact of the Civil War," in Engerman, *Reinterpretation*, Table 2).

stance in this respect by assuming that by 1880 the emancipated slaves were earning
an amount 20 percent less than their marginal revenue product. We further assume
that average marginal product for blacks and whites fell by 20.8 percent from 1860
to 1880, the decline in commodity output per capita in the South, as estimated by
Robert E. Gallman.[18] Our income estimates for whites for 1840 and 1860 ultimately derive from the work of Richard A. Easterlin, although they reflect, in part,
modifications by Fogel and Engerman.[19] The 1880 estimates assume that income
per capita declined from 1860 to 1880 by the same amount as commodity output
per capita, and these estimates take into account the loss of exploitative income
earned from slavery.[20] The results of this arithmetic exercise are revealing: The
fruits of economic growth between 1840 and 1860 meant dramatic increases in
Southern white income while black income stagnated. The per capita income of
Southern blacks fell from 29 percent the average of whites in 1840 to just 22 percent
by 1860. By 1860, only a little more than one-tenth of total Southern income went
to provide for the region's black population. The Civil War meant a generalized
lowering of Southern income. More importantly, however, it also ushered in a substantial redistribution of income in favor of blacks. Black per capita income is estimated to have gone from 22 percent of the white level to 59 percent in just twenty
years, with blacks receiving nearly one-fourth of total Southern income by 1880, a
doubling of their 1860 share of total income. The improvement occurred for two
reasons: Black per capita income rose sharply after the War, and white per capita income fell significantly. This is not to say that blacks in 1880 were no longer poor or
that racial discrimination did not exist, but rather that the economic status of blacks
improved relative to what it had been a generation earlier.

POSTBELLUM BLACK BEHAVIOR: THE ERA OF "UNCLE TOM"

An essential aspect of slavery was the legal restriction on personal movement. The end of slavery, then, might have been expected to have led to a surge in black migration as the newly freed slaves sought to demonstrate their freedom. It is true that many historians have commented on a certain amount of postbellum experimentation with migration on the part of blacks.[21] On the whole, however, the evidence is clear that postbellum blacks were relatively immobile.[22] Robert Higgs summarized it succinctly when he said, "In 1910 the blacks lived, by and large, in the same areas they had inhabited in 1860."[23] Even the relatively few blacks who ventured into the North tended to come from states bordering that region rather than from the Cotton Belt. An early twentieth-century Census Bureau official observed that, "even as recently as 1910, 48 percent . . . of the southern-born Negroes living in the northern states came from two states—Virginia and Kentucky."[24]

Table 8.5 demonstrates the tepid nature of pre-1900 net black migration to the North. In light of the documented discrimination of the antebellum period, why did blacks act very similar to Southern whites after the Civil War, at least in terms of their migration behavior?

A possible answer to this question may be found in the data of Table 8.4. The Civil War brought about a dramatic improvement in the relative economic status of Southern blacks. Real incomes were rising, both absolutely and relative to those of whites. The black person living in the South in 1870 or 1880 had "never had it so good." To be sure, there were possible material gains to be obtained by moving to the North, but they were modest in relation to the gains already achieved and the risks involved. As Richard Easterlin has argued, utility is probably largely a function

Table 8.5
Net Migration from the South, 1870–1930

Decade	Negro*	Native White*
1870s	− 68	+ 91
1880s	− 88	−271
1890s	−185	− 30
1900s	−194	− 69
1910s	−555	−663
1920s	−903	−704

Source: Hope T. Eldridge and Dorothy S. Thomas, *Population Redistribution and Economic Growth, United States, 1870–1950*, Vol. 3 (Philadelphia: American Philosophical Society, 1964), p. 90.
* In thousands.

of one's income relative to what one expects.[25] The typical black living in, say, 1885, had an income far greater than any expected "target income" established twenty-five years earlier. This, in conjunction with the climatic and other amenities of Southern living, led Southern blacks to reject the use of their freedom to move north. Hence, the "Uncle Tom" complacency of postbellum blacks was an understandable, rational response. The added utility from expanding income still further through migration, or even by protesting any residual exploitation, was modest in relation to the costs. Comparatively happy people do not take risks that conceivably could jeopardize a status in life that exceeds expectations in childhood or as young adults.

THE EVOLUTION OF BLACK BEHAVIOR: THE GREAT MIGRATION NORTH

As Table 8.5 shows, net black migration to the North began increasing after 1890, and especially after 1910. There were a variety of "pull" factors (e.g., improving job opportunities in Northern manufacturing during World War I, when immigration was sharply reduced) and "push" factors (e.g., the impact of boll weevil infestations on cotton farming) that might be involved in this change in black behavior.[26] We suggest that a precondition for the surge in black movement to the North was the end of the era of black complacency. This, in turn, reflected the fact that the new generation of blacks, born after, say, 1885, had come to expect the income gains achieved by their grandparents, born in the antebellum period. The "optimistic," complacent, black living in 1880 might have thought, "My income is 50 percent higher than my father's was when he was my age and I am free to move and spend my money as I like." A "pessimist" might have interpreted the same circumstances differently: "My income is only half that of most white persons and it is not enough to provide me with the good things in life." By 1910 more and more blacks were "pessimists" who could not forecast a substantial improvement in their economic status relative to their parents or relative to whites. A "revolution of rising expectations" lowered the utility associated with existing income levels. World War I increased economic opportunities in the North, providing an economic differential beyond the narrowing threshold necessary to induce previously complacent blacks to give up the perceived amenities of remaining in place.

THE CHANGING ECONOMIC STATUS OF BLACKS AFTER 1900

The great gains that black Americans made in terms of their relative income in the years immediately following the Emancipation Proclamation were not duplicated in the twentieth century. Table 8.6 looks at black-white income differentials for a number of alternative dates using different data sources. The data suggest little or no further gain in the relative economic status of blacks since 1880, despite changes in the political environment following the New Deal of the 1930s and

Table 8.6
Black-White Family Income Differentials, 1907–1985

Year	Source	Black/White Income Ratio*
1907–09	Immigration Commission	60%
1935–36	An American Dilemma	15–51%
1947	Census; Current Population Reports	51%
1964	Census; Current Population Reports	54%
1985	Census; Current Population Reports	58%

Sources: See text; the 1947 numbers are for nonwhites; a black only figure, not available, would probably be less than 50 percent.

* The first two estimates are based on mean incomes, and the last three on median incomes; this may serve to bias down twentieth-century progress since black/white ratios using mean incomes are higher than when medians are used.

Brown v. *Board of Education* in 1954. It should be noted, however, that the 1880 data are confined to the South and based on mean incomes; the 1985 data are national and based on medians, so care should be used in making comparisons.

Data for 1907–1909 are based on a huge sampling (over 3.2 million persons) of the American population done by the Dillingham Commission (U.S. Immigration Commission).[27] The comparison includes black families relative to white families headed by native-born Americans; inclusion of immigrants would raise the ratio to the extent immigrant incomes were below the average of native whites. The black family data are based on just 124 families, and their geographic location is not known. Thus, the results should be interpreted cautiously.[28]

The data for the mid-1930s are those reported by Gunnar Myrdal et al. in his landmark study of black American life. Since they were collected in the midst of the Great Depression, and since they were confined to just six cities (excluding the important rural black population), they are somewhat suspect, particularly relative to other numbers in the table.

The figures for the last forty years suggest two things. First, on the eve of the civil rights revolution black income had not gained relative to white income since Reconstruction. Indeed, if the Immigration Commission results are reasonably accurate, the possibility exists that there was some measurable deterioration in black economic status beginning early in this century and continuing for several decades. Second, a substantial increase in government social programs and sensitivity to civil rights since World War II has been accompanied by some improvement in relative black economic progress, but the gains are small compared with the earlier gains associated with the end of slavery.

In making interracial comparisons in economic status, however, one needs to be careful about interpreting results, since they can vary considerably with the measure of central tendency used, as Table 8.7 illustrates. The average or mean black family income in 1985 was 69 percent the white average, while the *median* family income of blacks was only 58 percent the white figure. This reflects the fact that black incomes are more unequally distributed than white ones. Thus, not only are black incomes still relatively low, but also the wide dispersion in black incomes around the mean suggests that the lowest quintile of blacks is much worse off than the lowest quartile of whites or those of other races. The 1985 data suggest that the black family with income at the top of the lowest quintile (20 percent of families having lower income, 80 percent higher income) received about $6,750 a year, only 46.5 percent the income received ($14,528) by whites in similar circumstance.[29] In addition, the incomes of black people fare quite poorly relative to those of other nonwhites and even Hispanics.

CONCLUSIONS

The economic status of blacks deteriorated substantially in the late antebellum period as the fruits of economic progress brought about in part by black labor were captured exclusively by whites, particularly the slaveowners. The end of slavery

Table 8.7
Family Incomes for Various Groups, United States, 1985

Group	Measure of Central Tendency	Income	Income As % of Whites
Whites	Median	$29,152	100
Blacks	Median	$16,786	58
All Non-Whites	Median	$18,625	64
Hispanics	Median	$19,027	65
White	Mean	$34,375	100
Black	Mean	$21,359	62
All Non-Whites	Mean	$23,755	69
Non-Black, Non-Whites	Mean	$33,830	98
Hispanics	Mean	$23,152	67

Source: U.S. Bureau of the Census, *Money Income and Poverty Status of Families and Persons in the United States: 1985,* Current Population Reports, No. 154, p. 160.

brought about enormous income gains for blacks and significant income and wealth losses for whites. As noted earlier in this chapter, in a real sense the Civil War was "America's revolution" from an economic perspective. By contrast, the experience in the century since Reconstruction has been less revolutionary, with black incomes generally ranging between 50 or 60 percent the white standard, with little or no evidence of a strong upward trend. The gains in recent decades essentially offset some possible deterioration earlier in the century, although the tenuous nature of the data makes even that conclusion somewhat speculative. While blacks have undeniably shared in the nation's economic growth, their relative economic status is not dramatically different from what it was a century ago.

NOTES

1. See Susan Previant Lee and Peter Passell, A *New Economic View of American History* (New York: W. W. Norton, 1979), pp. 205–6, for a good discussion of slave exploitation. See also Robert W. Fogel and Stanley L. Engerman, *Time on the Cross* (Boston: Little, Brown, 1974); Roger Ransom and Richard Sutch, *One Kind of Freedom: The Economic Consequences of Emancipation* (Cambridge, Eng.: Cambridge University Press, 1977); and Richard Vedder, "The Slave Exploitation Rate," *Explorations in Economic History* (October 1975).

2. Vedder estimates that slave compensation amounted to only 35 percent of a competitive wage in 1859, while Ransom and Sutch have an estimate of 41 percent for large plantations and 46 percent for all slave farms.

3. See Richard K. Vedder, David C. Klingaman, and Lowell E. Gallaway, "The Profitability of Ante Bellum Agriculture in the Cotton Belt: Some New Evidence," *Atlantic Economic Journal* (November 1974); Richard Vedder and David Stockdale, "The Profitability of Slavery Revisited: A Different Approach," *Agricultural History* (April 1975); and Vedder, "The Slave Exploitation Rate."

4. See U.S. Bureau of the Census, *Historical Statistics of the United States, Colonial Times to 1970* (Washington, D.C.: GPO, 1975), Series E-118, p. 207. To our knowledge, no retail price index specific to the South exists for this period. Given the nature of slave consumption, it may well be that the wholesale price index is the more appropriate in any case. The use of the consumer price index (Series E-135) for the United States does not fundamentally alter the nature of the findings.

5. In some instances slave prices showed a sharp (e.g., 15 to 20 percent) change from one year to the next. The use of an abnormal single-year slave price could cause a significant distortion in the observed intertemporal trend in exploitation.

6. See Richard K. Vedder, Lowell E. Gallaway, and David Klingaman, "Discrimination and Exploitation in Antebellum American Cotton Textile Manufacturing," in Paul Uselding, ed., *Research in Economic History*, Vol. 3 (Greenwich, Conn.: JAI Press, 1978).

7. For example, in the fifteen years used to calculate the three-year averages reported in Table 8.1, the annual interest rate on New England municipal bonds varied from 4.77 percent in 1829 to 5.31 percent in 1849; on U.S. government bonds, the spread was from 4.32 percent to 5.90 percent. See Sidney Homer, A *History of Interest Rates*, 2d ed. (New Brunswick, N.J.: Rutgers University Press, 1977), pp. 286–87.

8. In addition, an attempt was made to calculate exploitation rates for the 1802–1804 and 1809–1811 periods. The results, in our judgment, are highly suspect and thus are not reported here. The reason is that the New Orleans price index used to calculate the "slave wage" for different time periods is incomplete; a discontinuity in the index for 1811–1815 (a period of significant price movement) necessitates the making of assumptions about the relative change in prices in New Orleans compared to other cities in that period.

9. Obviously, the actual (as opposed to expected) present value of slave expropriation in 1860 was very small, given slavery's abolition shortly thereafter. The estimated rate of return on slaves in 1859 was roughly in line with alternative investments of comparable *perceived* risk.

10. See Ulrich B. Phillips, *Life and Labor in the Old South* (Boston: Little, Brown, 1935), p. 177, and Alfred H. Conrad and John R. Meyer, *The Economics of Slavery* (Chicago: Aldine Publishing Co., 1964), p. 76.

11. Of course, there is some disagreement on the magnitude of per capita income growth. For three accounts, see Robert Gallman, "The Pace and Pattern of Economic Growth," in Lance Davis et al., *American Economic Growth: An Economist's History of the United States* (New York: Harper & Row, 1972); Paul David, "The Growth in Real Product in the United States to 1840," *Journal of Economic History* (June 1967); and Richard K. Vedder, *The American Economy in Historical Perspective* (Belmont, Calif.: Wadsworth Publishing Co., 1976), especially Chs. 1 and 4.

12. Calculated by dividing the total value of slaves (last column, Table 8.2) by the total Southern white population in 1860.

13. Robert Fogel and Stanley Engerman, eds., "The Economics of Slavery," *The Reinterpretation of American Economic History* (New York: Harper & Row, 1971), p. 335.

14. In 1981 interest, dividend, rental, and proprietors' income equaled 23.7 percent of personal income; since some of proprietors' income was for labor services, it is doubtful that "capital's share" exceeded 20 percent. If one accepts the income estimates in Table 8.4 and the $30 slave-related income figure, slave exploitation income amounted to about one-fifth of total Southern white income in 1860.

15. Contemporary wealth data are available in detail for recent years. Probably the best recent survey of wealth holding in the United States may be found in U.S. Department of Commerce, *Household Wealth and Asset Ownership: 1984* (Washington, D.C.: GPO, 1986). These data indicate that 86,790,000 households had total net worth of $7,498.8 billion, or $86,402 per household. Mean household income that year was $27,464. This indicates a wealth to income ratio of 3.15 to 1. This may be a minimal estimate of the wealth-income ratio. The Federal Reserve Board's balance sheet estimate of household wealth for 1984 shows total net worth of $8,122.9 billion. A 1983 wealth survey conducted by the Survey Research Center at the University of Michigan shows substantially greater amounts of wealth. However, the findings of that survey are quite suspect. For a detailed discussion of the problems with the 1983 survey, see Lowell Gallaway and Richard Vedder, *Poverty, Income Distribution, the Family and Public Policy*, Joint Economic Committee, Congress of the United States (Washington, D.C.: GPO, 1986), Chs. 15 and 16.

16. A sampling of their writings includes: Robert Higgs, *Competition and Coercion: Blacks in the American Economy, 1865–1914* (Cambridge, Eng.: Cambridge University Press, 1977), Stephen DeCanio, *Agriculture in the PostBellum South: The Economics of Production and Supply* (Cambridge, Mass.: MIT Press, 1974), and Joseph D. Reid, "Sharecropping as an Understandable Market Response—The Post-Bellum South," *Journal of Economic History* (March 1973).

17. See Ransom and Sutch, *One Kind of Freedom*.

18. Robert E. Gallman, "Commodity Output, 1839–1899," in *Trends in the American Economy in the Nineteenth Century*, National Bureau of Economic Research, Studies in Income and Wealth, Vol. 24 (Princeton, N.J.: Princeton University Press, 1960).

19. Richard A. Easterlin, "Interregional Differences in Per Capita Income, Population and Total Income, 1840–1950," in *Trends in the American Economy*, and Robert W. Fogel and Stanley Engerman, "The Economics of Slavery," in Fogel and Engerman, eds., *Reinterpretation of American Economic History*.

20. We calculated white nonslave-derived income in 1860 ($117.67 per capita) and assumed it fell, as black marginal revenue product (MRP) fell, by 20.8 percent (to $74.02 per capita for blacks and $93.19 per capita for whites). We assumed 20 percent of the black MRP was monopsonistically exploited by whites, reducing the black figure by $14.80 per capita and increasing the white figure by $7.26.

21. A representative study is Peter Kolchin, *First Freedom: The Responses of Alabama's Blacks to Emancipation and Reconstruction* (Westport, Conn.: Greenwood Press, 1972).

22. See Philip E. Graves, Robert L. Sexton, and Richard K. Vedder, "Slavery, Amenities and Factor Price Equalization: A Note on Migration and Freedom," *Explorations in Economic History* (March 1983). A more extended treatment of the black migration experience is provided in Richard Vedder, Lowell Gallaway, Philip E. Graves, and Robert Sexton, "Demonstrating Their Freedom: The Post-Emancipation Migration of Black Americans," in Paul Uselding, ed., *Research in Economy History*, Vol. 10 (Greenwich, Conn.: JAI Press, 1986), pp. 213–39.

23. Higgs, *Competition and Coercion*.

24. Joseph A. Hill, "Recent Northward Migration of the Negro," *Monthly Labor Review* (March 1924):5.

25. Richard Easterlin, "Does Economic Growth Improve the Human Lot? Some Empirical Evidence," in Paul David and Melvin Reder, eds., *Nations and Households in Economic Growth* (New York: Academic Press, 1981).

26. See the articles cited in note 22 for a fuller treatment of the possible sources of this change in migration patterns.

27. See *Report of the Immigration Commission*, 61st Congress, 3d session, Senate Document No. 747, Vol. 1.

28. Ibid., pp. 412–15.

29. U.S. Bureau of the Census, Current Population Reports, Series P-60, No. 154, *Money Income and Poverty Status of Families and Persons in the United States: 1985*, p. 11.

9.

Slave Exploitation in Neoclassical Economics: Criticism and an Alternative Direction

SUSAN F. FEINER AND
BRUCE B. ROBERTS

The chapters in Part III raise important issues of economic policy, theory, and history. As a practical matter, the calculations of the current actual value of past exploitation provide a foundation for public policies of income and wealth redistribution through the tax system and through policies aimed at labor market and educational equality as well. In commenting on these chapters we hope to bolster the claim that such income and wealth redistribution policies are justified on the basis of past, as well as present, inequities.

Three of the chapters (Neal; Marketti; Vedder, Gallaway, and Klingaman) attempt to calculate the present real value of the income transfers arising from the nineteenth-century exploitation of Afro-Americans under the slave regime. The magnitudes involved suggest that the relative impoverishment of Afro-Americans, and by extension other minorities and women, is in no way a "natural" phenomenon or one that follows inevitably from the (exogenously given) nature of preferences. In addition, the estimates of the dollar value of the coerced labor of Afro-Americans raise questions about claims that "Americans made it on their own" or "pulled themselves up by the bootstraps." Not all economic gains arise from losses imposed on some segment of society, but clearly some do, and an appreciation of the interdependence between "winners" and "losers" can enhance the quality of debate over current public policy issues.

This chapter, however, finds theoretical problems with the neoclassical manner in which these estimates have been generated. Marginalist equilibrium analysis is, by the very nature of the concepts it employs, poorly equipped to confront the fundamental conflicts of group interest that lie at the heart of the questions posed in this volume. Accordingly, we criticize the estimates derived on several levels. Section I draws on recent work in the theory of capital and distribution to criticize the theoretical basis ("marginal productivity") of the definitions of exploitation employed. Section II then questions whether the partial equilibrium approach in the chapters is fully consistent with their neoclassical posing of the problem. And in Section III we present an alternative conceptual approach, that of "classical/Marxian" economics, which reformulates and broadens the notion of exploitation, thereby opening up new avenues for further investigation. We hope this will demonstrate the strong explanatory power, the relevance, and the need to pose questions about slavery and discrimination in terms of a class analysis of the struggles over the economic surplus. Without such a category of surplus, the very notion of exploitation, and of redistributive policies to mitigate it, is undercut.

SECTION I

Despite their differences, the three chapters that estimate the magnitude of exploitation under slavery share a common theoretical foundation. Each treats exploitation as measured, in principle, by the difference between the value of the marginal product of slave labor and the value of the actual remuneration in kind received by slaves. Vedder, Gallaway, and Klingaman take an aggregate approach: They estimate an aggregate Cobb-Douglas production function and use the resulting figures on marginal productivity to derive their estimate of the "exploitation rate." In contrast, both Neal and Marketti build to an aggregate estimate from microeconomic roots: Each, in a slightly different fashion, uses the price of slaves as an expression for the present value of the gains which the slaveowner is to reap over the lifetime of the slave.

Each is a thoroughly neoclassical treatment of the issues, sharing the strengths as well as the weaknesses of that theoretical approach. It is on the weaknesses of this approach that we will focus, since the basis of the *theoretical* critique of neoclassical economics is not well known. Indeed, many economists and econometricians proceed as if the propositions of the supply and demand approach to the theory of capital and distribution are not products of theory at all, but instead an immediate appropriation of reality.

As stated, in each of the models, exploitation is conceived as the gap between the value of the actual in-kind income of slaves and an alternative equilibrium distribution of income which fulfills the usual marginal productivity conditions on factor rewards. In other words, the conception of exploitation embedded in these models takes for granted the possibility of defining a "nonexploitation equilibrium," which in turn depends on the existence and theoretical validity of a solution for general competitive equilibrium. The problem is this: Since P. Sraffa (1960), a growing modern literature has, at the very least, problematized (and, at most, utterly destroyed) the theoretical claims to validity of such an approach.[1] There is no satisfactory proof of the existence of a general position of supply and demand equality which meets the traditional criteria for long-run equilibrium. If the general equilibrium position does not exist, what are we to make of a notion of exploitation which takes that theoretical point as its premise?

A long-run equilibrium position is traditionally understood as one in which prices have adjusted to the point where (1) quantities supplied and demanded are equal in markets for produced goods and for the services of produced and nonproduced factors, and (2) there is a competitively equalized uniform rate of profit (interest) on the supply price of the capital deployed in each sphere of production. As J. Eatwell (1977) has argued, the neoclassical derivation of such an equilibrium takes as data (1) preferences (utility functions); (2) technology; (3) the size of the initial resource endowments; and (4) the initial distribution of those endowments.

The specification of resource endowments is at the root of the problems that then emerge; however one specifies the "capital" factor—as a scalar (a fund of "finance") or a vector (a list of heterogeneous capital goods)—difficulties of one sort or another follow.

If capital is treated as a scalar for purposes of specifying initial endowments (the "production function" approach taken by Paul Samuelson [1962]), then, with appropriate assumptions concerning the form of the various functions, a determinate solution emerges which embodies the usual neoclassical propositions. But the result is *not general*: A scalar magnitude of "capital" (the economists' traditional "K") in the same units as "output" means that the economy is effectively a "one-commodity world." More importantly, the result is *not generalizable*: The parable of the production function fails in that none of the conventional truths expressed by means of production functions holds, in general, in a world with more than one produced means of production. This is by no means a mere index-number problem, nor are the difficulties surmounted by pointing to the apparent success of empirical estimation efforts.[2] As P. Garegnani has shown, there *is no* production function in labor and "capital" outside of a one-commodity world; consequently, "no definition of 'capital' allows us to say that its marginal product is equal to the rate of interest" (Garegnani, 1972, p. 271).

The alternative to production function exercises is the full-scale "Walrasian" treatment of the capital endowment as a vector of heterogeneous capital goods used in production, such as that of G. Debreu (1959). Again, with appropriate assumptions, a solution exists which, on its own terms, is perfectly valid. Problems remain, however, since that solution does not generally fulfill *both* of the characteristics of long-run equilibrium already mentioned. The system can be solved for meaningful (nonnegative) values for market-clearing quantities and prices only if it is expressed in terms of inequalities, which means that in general the rate of interest earned on capital will not be uniform—a result incompatible with the long-run mobility of capital (Eatwell, 1983, p. 211). Moreover, one cannot simply impose the additional constraints necessary to guarantee such a single competitive rate of interest. Since the system was initially determinate, the imposition of additional constraints simply means it cannot solve. To avoid this indeterminacy requires in general a return to the specification of the capital endowment as a single quantity of value, an expedient that again reduces the model to the special and uninteresting case of a one-commodity world (Eatwell, 1982, p. 221). Eatwell (1983, p. 210) states the strong conclusion: "it is not logically possible to solve a neo-classical system for the determination of long-run equilibrium."

A discussion of the abstrusities of general equilibrium theory may seem unrelated to the concrete question faced by the papers that estimate exploitation in the antebellum economy, but the connection is direct and theoretically unavoidable. If, as in these chapters, exploitation is *defined* as an institutionally imposed deviation from the distributional outcome present in a long-run general equilibrium position, then the *theoretical nonexistence* of such a position effectively obliterates the terms on which the question is posed.

We should stress that a critique on these grounds has nothing to do with any issue of the realism of the assumptions required in an equilibrium model, and nothing to do with the historical question of whether or not the slave economy really was in equilibrium. The problem is more general: The neoclassical equilibrium model is itself logically inconsistent as a theoretical basis for empirical studies.

SECTION II

Here we set aside the general theoretical difficulties already considered in order to examine a more specific set of issues: whether the empirical estimates generated really conform to the problem as it must be defined within a neoclassical approach.

As already discussed, each of the estimates of slave exploitation is in its own way an attempt to measure the difference between the situation of slaves as it was and the situation if slaves instead had been "paid what they were worth" (the value of the marginal product of slave labor). In effect, then, exploitation defined in this way could be eliminated simply and solely by raising the remuneration to slaves to a level comparable to that of a perfectly competitive capitalism. Slavery, it would seem, is little more than a peculiarly institutionalized form of monopsony (Vedder, 1975), one with effects that can be quantified through a partial analysis of the affected markets.

However appealing this may be as a simplification, it is simply not adequate to the task at hand. To be rigorous, a neoclassical approach must define slavery as a social situation in which one set of agents is systematically excluded from the initial distribution of endowments. (Slaves are, in fact, a *part* of the resource endowments of others.) As a result, slaves as economic agents face a choice set so thoroughly constrained that their utility functions effectively do not "count" in determining, for example, their own consumption bundles, the duration (if not the intensity) of their labor, and so on. Hence, slaves are not merely "underpaid," but they are institutionally excluded from the role of economic chooser in most of those dimensions of choice that are economically important. Under these circumstances, any inquiry into the exploitative effects of this system requires the prior admission that none of the economic outcomes produced within the antebellum economy (e.g., the structure of prices, the composition of demand, the distribution of income, the choice of technique, the pattern of saving and accumulation) is independent of the particular social institutions that made that economy a slave economy.

Institutionally, then, for slaves to have actually been paid "what they were worth," they would have had to have been "not-slaves." Hence, a focus on the distribution of income which takes prices, quantities, and the like, as *given* is not theoretically appropriate. For a neoclassical economist interested in the magnitude of slave exploitation, the relevant comparison is between the different *general* equilibrium worlds of slavery and "not-slavery," rather than the admittedly more tractable question of a *partial* comparison between "low subsistence" slavery and a hypothetical "higher subsistence" slavery.

To illustrate, suppose we are confronted by data for, say, the returns to slaves and slaveowners in the year 1820. To determine the magnitude of exploitation embodied in these incomes, we would need to compare these data to the similar returns generated in a situation where the entire structure of initial resource endowments is different—where Afro-Americans *have* an endowment of their own labor time to choose to sell or not to sell, and so forth. Under these circumstances, with a different set of economic choosers and differently constituted units of production, a variety of effects would inevitably follow: More than likely there would be a different set of final demands, a different pattern of technical choices—in short, the entire set of equilibrium prices and quantities would change.

Neal (pp. 5–6) confronts at least an aspect of the problem which these differences imply, but he is compelled to dismiss the issue on the grounds that it is impossible to say a priori whether the "wages" of slaves would have risen or fallen in the presence of free labor markets. But the problem is not so easily dismissed: It is theoretically illegitimate, even if almost unavoidable at times in actual practice, to treat a general equilibrium comparison by means of a partial analysis. The difference between the situation faced by slaves and the relevant alternative for comparison is a *qualitative* difference between utterly dissimilar forms of social relations and economic institutions, a difference sufficiently encompassing that no *ceteris paribus* assumptions can reasonably be justified.

One can have sympathy for the problems of estimation involved in making such a comparison, but it is the logic of the neoclassical approach itself which demands this broader sort of comparison.[3] Indeed, it is ironic that, having previously criticized these chapters for their implicit use of a (questionable) general equilibrium framework, we now object that the use of that general equilibrium framework is not explicit enough.

SECTION III

The preceding sections of this chapter addressed some of our objections to the standpoint of neoclassical economics as a theoretical position from which to comprehend the complex issues of income distribution and exploitation. Many, if not most, economists will wonder if there is any "rigorous" alternative. The purpose of the discussion that follows is to sketch the implications of just such an alternative.

Conceptual conflicts are at the heart of the disputes that separate different paradigms, and how one conceives the meaning of a term like *exploitation* is clearly a question theoretically prior to any issue of empirical estimation. We will argue that the very narrow definitions of income and exploitation used in the mainstream approach lead to a potentially severe underestimation of the surplus labor of the antebellum slave population and that a "classical/Marxian" approach can provide a viable alternative.

We have stressed that in the neoclassical paradigm exemplified by these chapters, exploitation is estimated solely with reference to the gains realized by slaveowners due to their ownership of slaves. No other approach is possible within the conceptual boundaries of orthodox theory, in which any income generated *within* a production process accrues, in one way or another, *to* the factors of production involved in that process. It is a truism of supply and demand theory that the "worth" of a product is given by its price, which in turn is equal to the sum of the payments to the factors that produced it. Any income paid to those factors of production must have been (in the aggregate, at least) generated by them, and conversely, any income not paid to these factors as a whole could not, by definition, have been generated by them. What the slaves "lose" to exploitation, the slave's master, as the embodiment of "capital-and-land," gains.

In contrast to this view is the "classical/Marxian" approach. The fundamental premise of this approach is that every human society produces a surplus (an excess of output over that amount required to reproduce the performers of labor and the consumed means of production) which is then distributed to different groups or classes through mechanisms particular to the social organization of the society in question.[4] Moreover, the recipients of the social surplus are not necessarily classifiable as "factors of production" in the neoclassical sense.

One significant difference between these alternative frameworks of analysis can be illustrated by reference to the classical distinction, dating from Adam Smith (1954), between productive and unproductive labor.[5] In the classical tradition a variety of social activities are viewed as not, in themselves, productive. The distinction is a complex one involving numerous "gray areas," but, for our purposes here, unproductive activities are those which, however necessary they may be to the ongoing reproduction of the society as a whole, are not directly involved in the generation of the social surplus. Consequently, the incomes that accrue to the performers of unproductive labor must have originated in the surplus generated elsewhere by the performers of productive labor. Thus, in classical political economy, producing a surplus is only the beginning of the story, for once a surplus has been successfully produced, the answers to distributional questions—which groups/classes will receive what shares of the already produced surplus?—do not follow automatically from any a priori correspondence between the receipt of income and an implied contribution of productive services. The classical treatment of merchants' profits usefully illustrates the implications of this point.

Both antebellum observers and contemporary economic historians have commented on the importance of merchants in the cotton economy (Green, 1972;

Woodman, 1968). Merchants' income took the form of profits and was earned through a combination of interest, commission, and insurance charges. If one approaches merchanting as an unproductive activity (since the mere act of buying and reselling does not directly contribute to the material basis for social reproduction), then the profits realized by *unproductive* merchants must have had their origin in the surplus generated by *productive* slave labor. That is, some of the surplus produced by slave labor and appropriated by slaveowners did not accrue to the slaveholders as income, but instead was captured by merchants who controlled the selling channels through which plantation outputs moved (Feiner, 1982, 1986, and 1987).

Now, as already suggested, for a neoclassical approach, merchant profit is in no way relevant to the estimation of slave exploitation because merchants' incomes are viewed as payments for services rendered—services that are a priori productive in the neoclassical approach simply by virtue of commanding a payment and thereby receiving income. Yet in a classical (Marxian or Ricardian) approach, these types of distributions, out of the already produced surplus, are extremely relevant for two reasons.

First, recognizing the importance of the social arrangements under which surplus redistributions occur allows classical economists to construct sophisticated notions of class and class conflict (Resnick and Wolff, 1982). This view of redistribution underlies a particular reformulation of classical political economy in which class, and consequently class conflicts, are not limited to or bounded by the arena of "production." In this formulation explicit attention is paid to the possibility that the many unproductive agents in a society may compete with each other and with the direct appropriators over the terms of the redistribution of the already produced social surplus (Resnick and Wolff, 1982; 1987).[6] Of particular importance to the questions raised by these chapters is the possibility that some slaves may have been unproductive, and so, however exploited they may have been in terms of their freedoms and standard of living, they, along with the class of slaveowners, lived off the productive labor of the rest of the slave population (Feiner, 1982, 1986). Not only does this conceptualization carry significant implications for estimating the exploitation of slaves, but it also directs our attention to a variety of social sites at which conflict, and hence change, is likely.

Second, and even more directly relevant, the failure to consider the further socially enforced redistributions of the fruits of slave surplus labor leads to the underestimation of the exploitation of slaves. Without exception, these chapters calculate exploitation solely by estimating the extra income flowing to slaveholders as a result of imperfections in the "labor market." Nowhere do they consider, as part of the money value of slave exploitation to be capitalized into the future, the incomes flowing to, for example, the unproductive classes of merchants, religious personnel, bankers, state officials, school teachers, lawyers, and personal servants (Feiner, 1981, 1987). Thus, the concept of exploitation which is required in a classical analysis is much broader, and consequently its estimate would be far greater than that of neoclassical political economy.

An interesting example of the significance of these different conceptualizations of income in the classical and neoclassical worlds is provided by the large and growing literature on the topic of "unequal exchange."[7] The term *unequal exchange* describes a situation in which the surplus generated in one industry (or "nation") is effectively transferred to another through trade at the competitive prices established in international and interregional commodity markets. This is not an idle possibility. From a Marxian standpoint, it is quite likely that a major share of the surplus generated by slave exploitation was realized as income outside the antebellum South.[8] That is, British and New England textile manufacturers (and workers), as well as British and New England manufacturers (and workers) in the industries producing the various inputs to the slave-based production processes, probably received shares of the already produced slave surplus (Williams, 1966). A surplus transfer process such as this would be likely to occur owing both to the relatively greater labor intensity of slave monoculture vis-à-vis manufacturing and nonslave agriculture, and to the lower "wage" paid to slaves. When this possibility is considered, this further increases the value of the exploitation of slaves.

In the neoclassical conceptualization of exploitation, however, this basis for estimating the exploitation of slaves is ruled out. The neoclassical premise that voluntary exchange is by definition equal and mutually beneficial makes it impossible to conceive the exploitation of slaves as resulting in incomes realized by anyone other than the direct agent of exploitation: the slaveowner. From a non-neoclassical perspective, this again means that the estimates of that exploitation will tend to understate significantly the magnitude of the unpaid surplus labor of slaves because much of this surplus could quite easily have accrued to groups far removed from the planter class.

In contrast, a classical/Marxian analysis would approach the problem by attempting first to conceive and then to measure the size of the surplus derived from the exploitation of slaves, regardless of whether that surplus was realized as income to slaveholders or to others inside or outside the South. Only when *both* the unproductive incomes of some Southern classes and the unequal exchange mechanisms that transferred income out of the hands of the slaveholders are taken into consideration will estimates of the current value of the past exploitation of Afro-Americans under the slave regime be accurately calculable.

CONCLUSIONS

The critical stance of these comments is aimed not at the project of determining the magnitude of slave exploitation, but rather at the conceptual approach employed to carry out that project. We have focused on what we see as the most significant weaknesses of the neoclassical theoretical tradition, weaknesses that undermine both the logical coherence and the conceptual breadth of its application.

Disavowing mainstream economics is not, however, tantamount to abandoning economic science. Indeed, it is ironic to see questions about the exploitation of slaves, slave surplus labor, and the classes that benefited from slavery posed within the orthodox paradigm, since it is precisely the emphasis on these questions that distinguishes classical political economy, especially in its Marxian form, from neoclassical political economy. Any economist with even a passing familiarity with the Marxian tradition must know that the concepts of surplus labor, exploitation, and classes are the cornerstones of Marxian analysis. Thus, one is left to wonder why, when critiques of neoclassical economics have been so extensively developed, and when a rigorous alternative does exist, so many important social issues continue to be confronted almost exclusively within the orthodox framework.

Perhaps it is because the conclusions of neoclassical analyses (even those which, like these estimates, may suggest remedies such as racial restitution which clearly contradict market-determined outcomes) are still less threatening than those that follow from a legitimate class analysis. From the perspective we advocate, the point is that the social structure of property and power in the American economy, then *and* now, is itself the basis for a multileveled class process of surplus extraction, appropriation, and redistribution. The market distribution of rewards *already* embodies an effective redistribution of the surplus generated by productive black and white workers, so that the activities of government merely superimpose a further set of reinforcing or counteracting redistributions. The undeniable fact that blacks have historically been the biggest losers in this process should not be interpreted to mean that the remedy involves a restitution defined solely on racial lines. In our view the economic losses borne by blacks are largely the consequence of the *class* positions to which racism, among other factors, has consigned them. Thus, any lasting reversal of the pattern of racial gains and losses must be based on a broader class restructuring of the economy. Hence, it is not enough to suggest that "white Americans owe black Americans," or even that some white Americans do. Blacks, in common with other racially diverse groups subject to similar if less historically egregious exploitation, are deserving of, not merely restitution or greater wage equity, but more fundamentally a change in the rules of the game.

NOTES

1. See, among others, Robinson (1953), Symposium (1966), Garegnani (1972), and Eatwell (1983). A useful summary of the early phases of the capital theory debates is Harcourt (1972). Eatwell and Milgate (1983) contains several essays that bear on the critique which we summarize in the text.

2. The significance of estimates of aggregate production functions, such as that of Solow (1957), was called into question by the massive simulation experiments reported in Fisher (1971). Such estimation efforts were further undercut by Shaikh (1974), who showed that the "good fit" obtained by Solow was a result of *algebraic* necessity rather than a demonstration of the underlying nature of the production conditions.

3. Temin (1971) makes a somewhat similar point, arguing (p. 58) that "it has been hard to formulate the models needed for (certain "classic" problems in economic history) because

they are more complex than the standard Marshallian partial-equilibrium model we use so extensively."

4. For a discussion of this view, that all societies produce a surplus by means of an expenditure of (surplus) labor in excess of necessary labor, see Marx (1967), pp. 877–78, and Hindess and Hirst (1975), pp. 23–28.

5. Cf. also Marx's extensive discussions of the productive/unproductive distinction, especially Marx (1963), pp. 152–304, 393–413. A contemporary interpretation of this distinction, one to which we subscribe, can be found in Resnick and Wolff (1982).

6. This approach has been applied in Feiner (1982), Weiss (1982), and Jensen (1982).

7. The concept of unequal exchange was developed in the work of Emmanuel (1972) and has been carried forward by, among others, Amin (1977). Evans (1984) contains an exhaustive bibliography on this topic.

8. In order to demonstrate the possibility of such a process of surplus transfer, one must employ a concept of value, distinct from price and yet dimensionally the same, so that values and prices can be compared in common units. For a discussion and a demonstration that this is indeed possible, see Roberts (1981), as well as Wolff, Roberts, and Callari (1982, 1984).

REFERENCES

Amin, S. *Unequal Development*. New York: Monthly Review Press, 1977.

Debreu, G. *Theory of Value*. New Haven, Conn.: Yale University Press, 1959.

Eatwell, J. "The Irrelevance of Returns to Scale in Sraffa's Analysis." *Journal of Economic Literature* 15 (1977).

———. "Competition." In I. Bradley and M. Howard, eds., *Classical and Marxian Political Economy*. New York: St. Martin's Press, 1982.

———. "The Analytical Foundations of Monetarism. In J. Eatwell and M. Milgate, eds., *Keynes's Economics and the Theory of Value and Distribution*. New York: Oxford University Press, 1983.

———, and Milgate, M., eds. *Keynes's Economics and the Theory of Value and Distribution*. New York: Oxford University Press, 1983.

Emmanuel, A. *Unequal Exchange: A Study in the Imperialism of Trade*. New York: Monthly Review Press, 1972.

Evans, D. "A Critical Assessment of Some Neo-Marxian Trade Theories." *Journal of Development Studies* 20 (1984).

Feiner, S. "The Financial Structures and Banking Institutions of the Antebellum South: 1811 to 1832." Ph.D. diss., University of Massachusetts, Amherst, 1981.

———. "Factors, Bankers and Masters: Class Relations in the Antebellum South." *Journal of Economic History* 42 (1982).

———. "Property Relations and Class Relations in Genovese and the Modes of Production Controversy." *Cambridge Journal of Economics* 10 (1986).

———. Slavery, Accumulation and Classes in the Antebellum South. Unpublished mimeo, 1987.

Fisher, F. "Aggregate Production Functions and the Explanation of Wages: A Simulation Experiment." *Review of Economics and Statistics* 53 (1971).

Garegnani, P. "Heterogeneous Capital, the Production Function and the Theory of Distribution." In E. K. Hunt and J. Schwartz, eds., *A Critique of Economic Theory.* Harmondsworth, Eng.: Penguin Books, 1972.

Green, G. *Finance and Economic Development in the Old South. Louisiana Banking 1804–1861.* Palo Alto, Calif.: Stanford University Press, 1972.

Harcourt, G. *Some Cambridge Controversies in the Theory of Capital.* Cambridge, Eng.: Cambridge University Press, 1972.

Hindess, B., and Hirst, P. *Pre-Capitalist Modes of Production.* London: Routledge & Kegan Paul, 1975.

Jensen, R. "The Transition from Primitive Communism: The Wolof Social Formation." *Journal of Economic History* 42 (1982).

Marx, K. *Theories of Surplus Value I.* Moscow: Progress Publishers, 1963.

———. *Capital III.* New York: International Publishers, 1967.

Resnick, S., and Wolff, R. "Classes in Marxian Theory." *Review of Radical Political Economics* 13 (1982).

———. *Knowledge and Class: A Critique of Political Economy.* Chicago: University of Chicago Press, 1987.

Roberts, B. "Value Categories and Marxian Method: A Different View of the Value-Price Transformation." Ph.D. diss., University of Massachusetts, Amherst, 1981.

Robinson, J. "The Production Function and the Theory of Capital." *Review of Economic Studies* 21 (1953).

Samuelson, P. "Parable and Realism in Capital Theory: The Surrogate Production Function." *Review of Economic Studies* 29 (1962).

Shaikh, A. "Laws of Production and Laws of Algebra: The Humbug Production Function." *Review of Economics and Statistics* 56 (1974).

Smith, A. *The Wealth of Nations.* London: Irwin, 1954.

Solow, R. "Technical Change and the Aggregate Production Function." *Review of Economics and Statistics* 39 (1957).

Sraffa, P. *Production of Commodities by Means of Commodities,* Cambridge, Eng.: Cambridge University Press, 1960.

Symposium. "Symposium on Paradoxes in Capital Theory." *Quarterly Journal of Economics* 80 (1966).

Temin, P. "General Equilibrium Models in Economic History." *Journal of Economic History* 31 (1971).

Vedder, R. "The Slave Exploitation (Expropriation) Rate." *Explorations in Economic History* 12 (1975).

Weiss, R. "Primitive Accumulation in the United States: The Interaction Between Capitalist and Non-Capitalist Class Relations in 17th Century Massachusetts." *Journal of Economic History* 42 (1982).

Williams, E. *Capitalism and Slavery.* New York: Capricorn Books, 1966.

Wolff, R., Roberts, B., and Callari, A. "Marx's (not Ricardo's) 'Transformation Problem': A Radical Reconceptualization." *History of Political Economy* 14 (1982).

———. "A Marxian Alternative to the Traditional Transformation Problem." *Review of Radical Political Economics* 16 (1984).

Woodman, H. *King Cotton and His Retainers: Financing and Marketing the Cotton Crop of the South: 1800 to 1925.* Lexington: University of Kentucky Press, 1968.

PART IV

Achieving Racial Equality through Restitution

Part IV looks primarily at twentieth-century issues of labor market discrimination and remedial public policy. David H. Swinton focuses on the impact of past practices on African-American human capital. The following chapter is a summary of a long research paper that was originally completed at the University of California at Berkeley in 1972. In it, Gerald Udinsky and Bernadette Chachere estimated the present value of the benefits from labor market discrimination over four decades. Richard America has summarized the original paper, and adjusted for inflation through 1984.

Then, Sheldon Danziger and Peter Gottschalk review federal safety net programs for their redistributive effects, and Stanley H. Masters similarly asks whether certain affirmative action programs produce positive redistributive results.

Lynn C. Burbridge wraps up this section with a further reminder of the shortcomings of the present state of analytical comprehension of how past costs and benefits affect current wealth and income shares.

Robert S. Browne concludes the volume by suggesting that reparations theory is key to understanding most of the chronic domestic social problems that fill the headlines.

10.

Racial Inequality and Reparations

David H. Swinton

Reparation, n.
1. The act or process of repairing or the condition of being repaired.
2. The act of or process of making amends; expiation. 3. Some thing done or paid to amend or make up for; compensation. 3. Plural. Compensation or remuneration required from a defeated nation as indemnity for damages or injury during a war. (The American Heritage Dictionary of the English Language)

INTRODUCTION

The year 1984 marked the thirtieth anniversary of the *Brown* decision and the twentieth anniversary of the passage of the Civil Rights Act of 1964. These milestones mark the turning points in the fight against racial inequality and discrimination. They signaled the beginning of public policy commitment to eradicate the traditional subordination of black people in the United States. Yet from our vantage point today racial inequality is still a fact of economic life. Whether we measure wealth, income, employment, poverty, or welfare dependency, there are still widespread disparities between blacks and whites. Moreover, in the last ten years many disparities have grown.

Of greater consequence for the future of racial inequality, however, is the disillusionment with the policies of the civil rights era. Rightly or wrongly, many people believe these policies have failed. They are widely perceived, especially by neoconservatives, as at best expensive palliatives that waste taxpayers money and create economic inefficiencies. Even liberals sympathize with the belief that enough has been done for blacks and it is time to move to other social concerns. These changes in attitudes are due at least in part to the notion that since we have ended overt discrimination as a major barrier black failure to be as successful as whites must be their own fault. Blacks' failure to take advantage of opportunities opened up by the civil rights era is said to be due primarily to the "enemy within" the black community—low morals, crime, illegitimate babies, irresponsible males, and so on. Those who share this perspective believe that court decisions and legislation ended official tolerance or sanction of discriminatory behavior. Ending racist practices should have been sufficient. To these observers society has no other obligations.

In the sixties, civil rights activists and liberals did recognize a need to repair some historic damage done to the black community in order to provide a realistic chance to gain equality. For these observers a kind of reparations was called. Their efforts to increase equality in economic life resulted in new policies and programs during the sixties.

Thus, we have reached another watershed in the movement to complete racial equality. An important change in public policy is occurring. We are abandoning policies of the past two decades in favor of a do nothing or laissez-faire policy. Yet as indicated, we are still far from racial parity in economic life. Since we still profess the goal of equality, it would seem important to make sure that the new laissez-faire policy is adequate to achieve parity within a reasonable time.

In this chapter we explore these issues using the concept of reparations. At various points in our history, the concept has emerged as part of the effort to eradicate the legacy of slavery, segregation, and discrimination. It provides an appropriate framework for discussing the issues. Using the reparations concept, we can phrase the issue in terms of three questions. First, are reparations necessary to end inequality, or are civil rights laws and court decisions sufficient? Second, did the efforts of the sixties provide adequate reparations? Finally, would reparations be sufficient to end racial subordination in economic life?

ARE REPARATIONS NECESSARY TO ACHIEVE EQUALITY?

The operative terms in the definition of reparation given at the start of this chapter were to repair and to compensate. Specifically, the concept refers to repairing or compensating for damages done during slavery and subsequent periods of Jim Crow and discrimination. While there is dispute about how to measure these damages, there seems little question that the costs were large.

The cost during slavery not only included the value of appropriated labor services, but also the economic value of the lost freedom, as well as pain and suffering. The theoretically appropriate method of evaluating these costs would require determination of the amounts required to pay a free individual to submit to permanent slavery. Of course, no such price exists because, by definition, slaves made no such voluntary contracts in free markets. One can imagine, however, that the cost would be incalculably large.

The costs of Jim Crow, discrimination, and segregation to the black population are similar to the costs of enslavement. The economic component consists of lost value from denied opportunities, both capital and labor, in their highest and best uses. In addition, there is lost value from restricted opportunities to acquire human and physical capital on the same terms and the same conditions as whites. Again, however, the noneconomic costs of indignities, pain, and suffering caused by discrimination must be added to obtain a complete estimate. While these costs are probably smaller than similar costs under slavery, they are nonetheless significant.

In principle, the cost of slavery and discrimination can be estimated in a straightforward fashion. In each year of slavery and discrimination we would sum the components of cost. We represent this symbolically as

$$CS(t) = EL(t) + LC(t) + LF(t) + PS(t) \qquad (1)$$
$$CD(t) = RL(t) + RC(t) = LC(t) + PS(t) \qquad (2)$$

where:

CS = cost of slavery
CD = cost of Jim Crow, segregation, and discrimination
EL = value of labor expropriated
LC = value of lost opportunities to acquire capital
RL = reduced value of labor due to discrimination
RC = reduced value of capital due to discrimination
LF = value of lost freedom
PS = pain and suffering
t = year in which cost occurred

This would permit us to derive the present value of each year's cost and sum across all years. Assuming we can determine the appropriate interest rate, we can represent the present value symbolically as

$$PV(COST) = [(CS(t) + CD(t))](1 + 4)^t$$

where:

r = appropriate interest rate

As far as we know, no other estimates offer such a complete specification. Of course others researching the economics of slavery have estimated the value of slaves to slaveholders. These calculations provide minimal estimates of the value of expropriated labor, which is one component of the cost imposed on slaves. The value of the expropriated labor to slaves must be assumed to be at least as great as it is to slaveowners. However, these estimates do not include any value for the other costs of slavery.

Nonetheless, the magnitudes of this one component found in other chapters in this volume are so large that increasing these estimates by several orders of magnitude to account for the other components would have no practical consequences for our subsequent discussion. For example, estimates by Larry Neal suggest that the present 1983 value of the expropriated labor ranges from $963 billion to $97,074 billion, depending on whether a 3 percent or a 6 percent rate of interest is used. Neal figured the value of expropriated slave labor from 1620 until the end of slavery. James Marketti derived a 1983 present value for slave labor expropriated from 1790 to 1860, which ranged from $2.1 to $4.7 trillion.

Thus far, no attempts have been made to estimate what slavery and discrimination cost to the black population. There have been estimates of costs of the labor component in a particular year. Udinsky, Chachere, and America have provided a rough estimate of the benefits from labor market discrimination from 1929 to 1969. They put the 1972 value of the cost of labor market discrimination in 1972 prices at $363 billion. The 1983 value, compounding at a rate of 6 percent, is $689 billion in 1972 prices. Adjusting for inflation, we find that the present 1983 value of the benefits from discrimination in the labor market from 1929 to 1969 is $1,633 billion. Since this is only an estimate for parts of the period, and since some components of the cost of discrimination are omitted, it is clearly a conservative estimate of the present value of the benefits of discrimination to whites.

Although there may be some technical issues concerning the precise magnitude of the costs, these estimates leave little doubt that the costs were extremely large. To place these numbers in perspective, we note that the 1983 value of all private nonhuman capital assets in the United States was estimated to be $7.1 trillion. Thus, these estimates suggest that it could take more than the entire wealth of the United States to compensate blacks fully.

While at first blush these figures may seem ridiculous, they make more sense when one realizes that the large magnitudes result primarily from compounding the cost incurred in each year to the present time. When one considers that the wages expropriated during slavery, and denied by discrimination, were used to finance higher consumption levels, as well as higher investment levels, it is not surprising that the present value is so high.

The question that arises is whether it is necessary to compensate blacks for all these costs in order to achieve equality currently. The legacy of discrimination is its impact on current economic status. Much of the economic cost resulted in lost consumption. The pain and suffering cost, and the cost of lost freedom, while experienced in the actual events, pose no barriers to attainment of equality at present or in the future. While reparations as compensating or making amends might require payment for these costs, such payments would not be required to attain equality.

Reparations, in the sense of repairing damages, captures the essence of what would be required to attain equality. The legacy of discrimination and enslavement for the living black population is captured entirely in the impact that these historic processes have had on capital stocks, in the broadest sense, owned by living blacks and whites. Discrimination and racism reduced the historic accumulation capital by blacks and increased the accumulation by whites. The resulting disparities in ownership of capital are transmitted intergenerationally. These capital disparities would prevent attainment of racial equality even if current discrimination ended and blacks and whites had identical tastes and preferences. It would, therefore, be necessary to repair historic damage to the black capital stock in order to ensure attainment of equality.

This notion can be illustrated in a straightforward fashion using a simple model. First, assume that the income per capita received by blacks and whites is determined by the amounts of nonhuman and human capital that each group owns. Next, assume that a certain amount of the income of each group is invested in additional human and nonhuman capital. The new capital stock in the subsequent period will be increased by the net addition to the human and nonhuman capital stocks. The income in the new period is then determined by the new capital stocks. This model can be represented symbolically by the following recursive equations:

$$Y(t) \quad = aPK(t) + bHK(t) \qquad (1)$$
$$IPK(t) \quad = spY(t) \qquad (2)$$
$$IHK(t) \quad = shY(t)$$
$$PK(t + 1) = PK(t) + IPK(t) \qquad (3)$$
$$HK(t + 1) = HK(t) + IHK(t)$$
$$Y(t + 1) = aPK(t + 1) + bHK(t + 1) \qquad (4)$$

where:

Y = per capita income
PY = nonhuman capital per capita
HK = human capital per capita
I = net additions to per capita capital stock
t = year
a = rate of return to nonhuman capital
b = rate of return to human capital
sp = rate net investment in nonhuman capital
sh = rate of investment in human capital

This equation system may be readily solved to express income in any year as a function of the system parameters and the initial capital stocks. If B is used to represent black variables and W for whites, this yields:

$$YB(t) = [aPKB(0) + bHKB(0)] [1 + asp + bsh] \exp t \qquad (5)$$
$$YW(t) = [aPKW(0) + bHKH(0)] [1 + asp + bsh] \exp t$$

These equations imply that the absolute and relative differences in black and white per capita income at any future date t years from the initiation of equal opportunity would be

$$YW(t) - YB(t) = [a(PKW(0) - PKB(0)) + b(HKW(0) -$$

$$HKB(0))] [1 + asp + bsh] exp\ t \qquad (6)$$

and

$$\frac{YW(t)}{YB(t)} = \frac{aPKW(0) + bHKW(0)}{aPKB(0) + bHKB(0)} = \frac{YW(0)}{YB(0)} \qquad (7)$$

Equation (6) makes it quite clear that, under the assumptions of this model, any initial absolute gap in capital stocks that is not closed will result in a continuously increasing absolute gap in incomes. The absolute gap in black-white income at any future point will be determined by the initial gaps and the parameters of the system. Equation (7) implies that any relative gap in income would remain constant at the ratio of white-black income that existed in the initial year after discrimination ended. In other words, there would be a one-time gain in relative black income following the end of discrimination. However, after this gain, no additional gains could be expected unless the initial disparities in the capital stocks were repaired. Thus, it appears that reparations sufficient to repair the racial disparity in the ownership of capital stocks, which is the legacy of history, are required to ensure the achievement of equality.

DID THE EFFORTS OF THE LAST TWO DECADES PROVIDE ADEQUATE REPARATIONS?

The concept of reparations for the damages done to the capital stocks enables us to place the significance of the efforts made over the last two decades in better perspective. Our objective is not to thoroughly analyze these efforts, but rather to take a first rough look at the magnitude of this effort in light of this reparations concept. The calculations we will use in this exercise are illustrative. While more refined estimates would result in a more accurate appraisal, this would probably not alter the overall conclusions significantly.

There are no good studies on black wealth ownership or on the impact of racism and discrimination on the historical process of wealth accumulation. Nonetheless, it is well known that current black ownership of wealth, especially productive business wealth, is significantly below parity. For example, on the basis of black ownership of businesses and receipts from property income, it can be surmised that black wealth ownership per capita is much less than 20 percent of that required for parity. Estimates of the value of the human capital stock are rarer. However, if half the gap in black earnings from labor could be attributed to differences in human capital, then black human capital ownership would be roughly 85 percent of what is required for parity.

For ownership parity in private property, blacks would have to own roughly $820 billion in private assets. Using the above estimate of the gap in wealth ownership would imply a $656 billion gap in private wealth ownership in 1983. Since we have no good estimates of the value of human capital embodied in the workforce, we cannot make a similar estimate of the gaps in human capital ownership. However, in view of the much lower estimated disparities in human capital ownership, this would probably not change the basic order of magnitude of the estimate. Using an overall wealth gap number of $700 billion would probably adequately represent the approximate level of reparations required to repair the cost that discrimination has imposed on the living black population. While this figure is still relatively large, it is several orders of magnitude less than any reasonable estimate of the costs of slavery and discrimination.

Over the last two decades, as noted, there were increased social expenditures to assist the disadvantaged. These programs focused on human capital enhancement and income transfers to the poor. These programs can be viewed as a type of reparations to the extent that black participation exceeded parity. The question is the extent to which these programs adequately compensate for the damages of discrimination and slavery.

Although levels of cash and in-kind transfers have increased since the mid-1960s, it is reasonable to discount these payments as reparations in the sense of repairing damages to the capital stock. These payments are more like compensation for current damages experienced each year for failure to correct the historic damages. It is estimated that annual welfare and public assistance to blacks is ten times smaller than the annual loss due to racial inequality in labor earnings alone. However, even if all excess welfare payments to blacks since the mid-1960s were counted as reparations, the present value of these payments would amount to no more than $60 billion.

We have had personnel and training programs since the 1960s. Again, to the extent that blacks participated at a level greater than parity, one could interpret these expenditures as reparations. But the value of the human capital created by these programs was less than the dollar expenditures on the programs. Some programs were work programs, and the net value of the work would have to be subtracted from the cost to get the net investment made by the program. Other programs included a large transfer component in their cost. Moreover, whether the programs' net benefits actually enhance the earning power of participants has been questioned.

Since the 1960s blacks have participated at rates greater than their proportion in the labor force, the actual participation rates varying across programs and years. Overall, blacks may have participated at up to three times their presence in the labor force.

Between 1953 and 1983 expenditures on all employment and training programs totaled about $90 billion. By rough estimate $30 billion of this total was expended on blacks. This implies an excess expenditure of $20 billion through the entire period. Certainly, an estimate of $50 billion as the present value of excess personnel expenditures during the last two decades more than accounts for these programs. All other programs such as those involving minority business development and higher education could not add more than $40 billion in current value. Indeed, these programs may add nothing since blacks probably received less than a proportionate share of expenditures in these areas overall.

These rough calculations suggest that even generous assumptions of enhanced efforts during the last two decades do not compensate blacks for the damages of discrimination and slavery that existed at the passage of the Civil Rights Act of 1964. Indeed, it is doubtful whether these efforts were sufficient even to keep the gaps in wealth ownership from growing. Even if we double-count and subtract all of the $150 billion present value of these expenditures from the present value of the current capital gap, there would still be a social debt of $500 billion.

WOULD ADEQUATE REPARATIONS PRODUCE PARITY?

As the model makes evident, reparations that produced parity in capital ownership would be sufficient as well as necessary to produce racial equality. This is evident from Eq. (5), where we see that, under the assumptions of the model, equality in black and white ownership of capital implies equality in black and white incomes.

The model makes several assumptions that we need to examine in order to have confidence in the conclusion. The model assumes that there will be no discrimination, that blacks and whites will have equivalent productivity, and that blacks and whites will have equal savings and investment propensities. The last two assumptions imply that the tastes and preferences of blacks and whites with respect to productive activities will be roughly the same with equalized capital stocks, and also that blacks and whites have equivalent inherent capacities. These seem reasonable assumptions for purposes of the analysis. Most evidence suggests no significant differences in black and white tastes for work and productive activities after we adjust for differences in income and wealth. Indeed, some evidence implies that blacks have higher commitments to education and the work ethic than similarly endowed whites.

In any case, the issue might be moot differences in taste or preferences; inherent abilities might impact the system parameters in the model and thereby generate differences in actual outcomes. However, parity only requires equivalent payoffs to equal resources and efforts. Thus, these differences would be consistent with parity and would not require additional corrective public action.

The stickier question arises with respect to discrimination. Discrimination results in lower payoffs to equivalent productive resources and efforts. Thus, even with parity in capital ownership, discrimination might still generate inequality in outcomes and reproduce inequalities in wealth over time. This implies that it is necessary to prevent current discrimination as well as to repair damages to the capital stock in order to attain and maintain parity.

Preventing current discrimination would be greatly aided by repairing damages to black capital stock. Such reparations would make discrimination less desirable. If whites discriminated against black workers, blacks could effectively retaliate by discriminating against white workers. The net result, *ceteris paribus*, would be not only workforce segregation, but also maintenance of parity. Thus, whites could not gain from discrimination. If discrimination had costs, they would be a disincentive if parity existed in capital stocks.

Similar results would be expected with other forms of discrimination. Thus, establishing parity in capital stock ownership may be the most effective long-term antidiscrimination policy. It would be sufficient to end discrimination, whereas reparations to the capital stock would be sufficient to bring about permanent parity.

CONCLUSIONS

We have discussed inequality and reparations. Reparations sufficient to compensate blacks for the costs of slavery and discrimination are not required to end racial disparities. The analysis suggests that the costs of slavery and discrimination for the living black population are entirely reflected in current disparities in capital stocks. Moreover, under reasonable assumptions, reparations to repair these disparities in capital stocks would be necessary to end racial disparities.

Rough calculations suggest that to repair the damages of slavery and discrimination would require expenditures of $650 billion. Programs of the past two decades to benefit blacks provided no more than $150 billion in current value. Thus, reparations of more than $500 billion would still be required to compensate for the damage slavery and discrimination did to capital stocks owned by the living black population. Furthermore, reparations, which adequately repaired the damage to the capital stocks, would be sufficient to end racial disparities in economic life.

This analysis, together with the numbers used, is a very rough estimate. Nonetheless, it is unlikely that more refined estimating will change the basic conclusions or produce numbers significantly outside a reasonable margin of error for the figures produced here. These results suggest that reparations is a useful concept for analyzing the problem of how to bring about racial equality.

One conclusion that should be stressed is that equality is not likely to be obtained without some form of reparations. The model makes it evident that, all things being equal, in the absence of reparations the existing inequality is unlikely to diminish over time. In fact, convergence under these circumstances within a reasonable time could occur only if the black system parameters were significantly better than the white system parameters. Blacks would have to save at higher rates, be more efficient, and/or work harder than whites, despite the superior circumstances of whites. Those who advocate bootstrap solutions to the problems ought to be fully aware of this implication.

The analysis also suggests that, in order to provide an effective permanent solution, efforts to assist blacks must repair the disparities in ownership of nonhuman and human capital stocks. Programs that merely transfer current consumption will have little long-term effect on inequality. Many programs of the past decade were of limited benefit because they failed to contribute to eliminating capital stock gaps.

Finally, the damages done by slavery and discrimination were tremendously large. Moreover, the current impact of these damages to living blacks is also very large. The programs and policies of the last two decades have been puny compared to what is required to correct the historic wrongs.

11.

An Illustrative Estimate: The Present Value of the Benefits from Racial Discrimination, 1929–1969 (Berkeley Working Paper #1)

Whether anyone gains from discrimination and by how much is an intriguing subject for analysis, as well as an issue long overdue for attention. Some analysts find that certain classes of whites—employers of low skilled and unskilled blacks, and white investors and certain professionals—benefit most.[1] Others find that white workers lose because of discrimination against blacks.[2]

In this chapter we will, first, estimate the present value, and second determine which classes, in fact, benefit, whether or not they unwittingly suffer a loss relative to what they might have gained in the absence of discrimination. This chapter summarizes a 1972 rough estimate of the income benefits produced from 1929 through 1969 from racial discrimination in employment, wage, and occupational distribution. It then updates that present value to 1986.

Our concern is not with determining the extent to which race explains differences in median income. Instead, it accepts David H. Swinton's finding that 40 to 60 percent of racial income inequality is due to discrimination.[3] It then uses Swinton's 40 to 60 percent in estimating the magnitude of the benefits from discrimination. These benefits apparently were large and continuous. In 1969 Lester Thurow estimated that $15 billion plus or minus $5 billion would be about the range of annual white benefits from labor market discrimination (setting aside capital discrimination, monopoly power discrimination against black capital, racial price discrimination in consumer goods, housing, services, insurance, and so on).[4] This chapter assumes that the primary beneficiaries of discrimination are upper middle and upper income white investors and professionals and those who employ large numbers of black unskilled and semiskilled labor. This chapter employs a modified model of income diversion first developed by Thurow. It estimates the 1969 value of income diverted over the period 1929 to 1968. The estimation dealt with a number of serious data limitations, and therefore presents illustrative, rough approximations.

Has discrimination in the earlier part of this century yielded current aggregate class benefits to identifiable groups? In any discussion of social policy and affirmative action, references are often made to the need to "make up for" or "remedy the past." This statement of need suggests that there is a widely shared notion, though only partially conscious and articulated, that exclusionary practices continue to "harm" or "disadvantage" groups of people whose ancestors were denied education, jobs, capital, and housing opportunities because of their race. This chapter takes a different approach. It assumes that past exclusion in effect diverted income and wealth to classes of people who were unjustly favored by those exclusions in the areas of education, housing, capital, and jobs, and that those benefits were at least partially conserved and transferred intergenerationally. Hence, in the late 1980s some classes are receiving a kind of unjust enrichment and their income and wealth are therefore tainted.

This chapter presents rough estimates of gains from certain forms of discrimination that occurred from 1929 through 1969, and finds the present value in 1987 adjusted for current prices. It builds on Lester Thurow's pioneering *Poverty and Discrimination* (1969) and his later work, *Generating Inequality* (1975).[5]

In the past twenty years a number of works have been published on the causes of the consistent disparity between black and white income. Age, occupation, sex, family structure, education, culture, genetics, geographic location, and other factors have been examined as explanatory variables. However, in addition to those factors, racial discrimination, as well as exclusion from training, occupational entry, and advancement, accounts for a large portion of observed differences. There appears to be an emerging consensus that about 50 percent of the difference is caused by discrimination.

Cultural and other factors that explain part of the differences in economic rewards have been taken into account in our acceptance of 50 percent as the residual attributable to discrimination. Actually, it is unlikely that cultural differences in taste for various rewards and for leisure would persist over as many as fifteen generations, or 350 years, in an open-market, equal opportunity environment.

John Kenneth Galbraith first observed, and Daniel P. Moynihan concurred in *Maximum Feasible Misunderstanding* that statisticians are key actors in the process of social change because it is only when we have measured most problems that it then becomes possible to arouse any substantial broad political interest in solving them. Thus it is with race-related policy issues. Many problems heavily weighted by race in the areas of housing, employment, education, business development, capital formation, and health are assumed to be ultimately redistributive, but will be allowed to fester until estimates that measure the injustice are made.

Who benefits from the process of coerced income and wealth diversion inherent in race discrimination? How are those benefits realized, how are they transferred intergenerationally, and to whom?

In 1983 the median income of blacks was $13,000 versus $24,000 for whites. About half of that $11,000 differential could be attributed to present and past racial bias. Three kinds of discrimination are considered in Figure 11.1. First, *wage discrimination* occurs when blacks and whites with the same sex, occupation, and education receive different wages for the same job. We assume that blacks and whites with the same sex, occupation, and education are comparable and should receive the same wages for the same job. Second, *occupational discrimination* systematically channels blacks into lower paid jobs. Given white and black persons who have the same education and experience and who work equally hard, there is a tendency for blacks to have lower paid jobs. Third, *employment discrimination* occurs when blacks are disproportionately and systematically the last hired and first fired—or simply not hired at all. Unions share the responsibility for the differential burden. Union people tend to be the first hired and last fired. The extent to which nonunion status characterizes blacks itself helps produce a greater than average black unemployment rate. In addition, many, if not most, employers and hiring officials were biased to some degree in their hiring practices during the years in question.

The benefit *B* shown in Figure 11.1 is white average income minus what white average income would be if whites were distributed by sex, occupation, and education (as is the total population) rather than skewed (as is the case in reality). This difference is then applied to all whites in the labor force, which yields the net benefit resulting from favorable occupational distribution. The difference between white average income and total average income reflects wage discrimination.[6]

Finally, for purposes of these rough estimates we assume that the average income of the unemployed is approximately the same as the average black income over this historical period. That total unemployment, which is higher than the white rate, is the rate whites would bear if there were no employment discrimination. Given our assumption that 50 percent of the difference between white employment and total employment results from discrimination, this is the benefit derived from employment discrimination.

Figure 11.2 examines how much income would have been lost by whites if they had been employed only at the rate of the total population as against income lost by whites actually unemployed.

Census data on occupation and education by income did not become available until after 1940. As a result, we had to adjust the model for each census to respond to changes in how the data change. The benefits were capitalized to find the present value. The gross national product (GNP) deflator was used to convert the benefits to 1972 prices, then updated to 1984. (See Table 11.1).

The 1984 present value of benefits from occupation, education, employment, and wage discrimination from 1929 to 1969 was roughly $638 million. The interest rate used was the average of long-term government bond yields. The use of long-

Figure 11.1
Estimating Benefits from Race Discrimination

Benefits from wage and occupational discrimination

$$B \;=\; \sum_i \left[\sum_{jk} \frac{P^w_{ijk}}{P^w_i} I^w_{ijk} \;-\; \sum_{jk} \frac{P_{ijk}}{P_i} I_{ijk} \right] P^w_i$$

was used to determine the Benefit where:

P_{ijk} = total employed, sex i, occupation j, and education k

P^w_{ijk} = white employed, sex i, occupation j, and education k

$P^w_{i.}$ = white employed, sex i

P_i = total employed persons, sex i

I_{ijk} = average income, sex i, occupation j, and education k, and

I^w_{ijk} = white employed average income, sex i, occupation j, and education k

Figure 11.2
Benefit from Employment Discrimination

U total unemployment rate

U^w white unemployment rate

LF^w white labor force

I^n black average income

B^u benefit from employment discrimination

$$B^u \;=\; [(U \times LF^w)] \;-\; [(U^w \times LF^w)] \; I^n$$

Table 11.1
Estimated Benefits from Labor Market Discrimination, 1929–1984

	From Wage and Occupation Discrimination	Extrapolated	From Employment Discrimination	Cap Rates	Summed	Present Value
1929		2.508	.086	3.966	6.272	19.0
1930		2.178	.332	3.135	6.227	18.8
1931		1.725	.487	3.239	6.039	18.2
1932		1.236	.519	3.673	6.936	20.9
1933		1.164	.527	3.794	5.132	20.4
1934		1.430	.562	2.843	5.776	23.2
1935		1.653	.611	2.480	6.500	26.0
1936		1.878	.597	2.339	7.089	28.4
1937		2.126	.583	2.313	7.445	29.7
1938		1.947	.708	2.166	7.396	29.6
1939		2.097	.691	1.995	7.767	27.9
1940	2.343		.696	1.870	8.466	29.3
1941		2.991	.439	1.730	6.296	20.3
1942		3.894	.288	1.881	9.650	28.5
1943		4.802	.123	1.841	10.604	29.4
1944		5.113	.065	1.800	10.881	29.5
1945		5.028	.128	1.737	10.562	27.9
1946		5.002	.273	1.611	9.672	22.0
1947		5.433	.317	1.596	9.427	23.7
1948		6.053	.268	1.619	9.712	23.5
1949		5.829	.262	1.543	9.358	24.2
1950	6.401		.397	1.511	10.366	23.0
1951		7.395	.243	1.540	10.913	22.2
1952		7.730	.386	1.527	11.344	22.2
1953		8.044	.274	1.547	11.519	21.9
1954		7.972	.827	1.403	12.010	23.1
1955		8.705	.779	1.439	12.760	22.9
1956		9.191	1.022	1.354	13.288	23.5
1957		9.555	.826	1.440	13.021	22.5
1958		9.600	1.276	1.401	13.301	23.1
1959		10.400	1.381	1.431	14.181	23.3
1960	10.786		1.453	1.360	14.490	23.3
1961		11.08	1.516	1.307	14.727	22.2
1962		11.84	1.626	1.262	15.566	23.1
1963		12.49	1.742	1.217	16.234	23.0
1964		13.41	1.633	1.177	17.313	23.4
1965		14.60	1.208	1.129	17.433	22.1
1966		16.10	1.351	1.081	18.753	22.5
1967		16.92	1.457	1.049	19.160	22.5
1968		18.50	1.620	1.00	20.12	22.4

Table 11.1 (continued)

1969	20.00	18.4
1970	19.75	18.7
1971	19.50	18.5
1972	19.25	19.3
1973	19.00	20.1
1974	18.75	19.7
1975	18.50	19.2
1976	18.25	19.9
1977	18.00	20.1
1978	17.75	21.5
1979	17.50	21.9
1980	17.25	21.4
1981	17.00	21.7
1982	16.75	20.8
1983	16.50	21.4
1984	16.25	22.5

1277.7   – $638.50

1969–1984, assumed annual incremental decline in discrimination for the purpose of these rough
    estimates.

term government bond rates probably underestimates the present value of the
benefits.

Clearly, further research, using Thurow's basic model and more carefully reviewing a longer period, say, 1870 to 1990, would be illuminating.

NOTES

This chapter is a summary of 1972 Working Paper #1, Office of Urban Programs Schools
of Business Administration, University of California, Berkeley. It was prepared originally by
Gerald Udinsky and Bernadette Chachere for the Office of Urban Programs and has been
edited for inclusion in this volume.

1. Michael Reich, *Racial Inequality* (Princeton, N.J.: Princeton University Press, 1981).

2. Albert Szymanski, "Racial Discrimination and White Gain," *American Sociological
Review* 41 (1970): 403–19.

3. Forty percent to 60 percent of the difference in median incomes is due to discrimination (David H. Swinton, "The Limits of Anti-Discrimination Policy," unpublished).

4. Lester Thurow, *Poverty and Discrimination* (Washington, D.C.: Brookings Institution, 1969), p. 134.

5. Lester Thurow, *Generating Inequality* (New York: Basic Books, 1975).

6. All data are from the Census of Population: Occupation by Earnings and Education,
Special Report PC(2)-7B; they allowed us to estimate the average income of all employed
white people I and average income of all employed people.

12.

Income Transfers:
Are They Compensation
for Past Discrimination?

SHELDON DANZIGER AND
PETER GOTTSCHALK

The extensive literature on black-white differentials in income, occupation, education, and other measures of socioeconomic status provides an a priori basis for arguing that whites benefit from past as well as current discrimination. Given existing public attitudes, however, it is highly unlikely that any political body will directly address the question of reparations. The fact that affirmative action policies have been under attack in the 1980s indicates that whites are reluctant to compensate for their possible current benefits from past discrimination.

This chapter addresses a policy-relevant issue related to reparations by analyzing whether current income maintenance transfer programs actually redistribute more to nonwhites than to whites in similar households. If they do, one might make the case that these transfer programs indirectly function as a system of reparations.

The first section explores some conceptual issues related to reparations. The following three sections analyze three questions related to income transfers: How do average transfers differ by race? Do pretransfer–poor nonwhites receive larger transfers than their white counterparts? Have the changes in poverty rates that have occurred in recent years resulted more from transfer growth for nonwhites?

CONCEPTUAL ISSUES

Robert Amdur (1979) examines two aspects of compensatory justice: Who should receive compensation, and who should pay? To achieve justice, one must impose costs on the perpetrators of injustice and make payments to those who suffered. This principle, while simple, presents insurmountable problems of implementation. Given that the most severe injustice—slavery—ended over a century ago, one would need directly to trace the inheritance of costs and benefits in order to determine both the size of the compensatory payment and who should pay. While intergroup gains and losses may be measured, identification of *individuals* now living who gained or lost from the past wrong is hopeless. How does one treat persons who immigrated after the initial act was committed? How are people to be treated who did not commit the wrong but did not stop those who did? Since the initial wrong redistributed income, future generations faced a different set of prices than if the initial act had not taken place. How is the counterfactual to be defined, and how can we identify how individuals benefited (or lost) from these changes in prices and incomes?

An alternative method of measuring the current results of past wrongs, which avoids these seemingly insoluble problems, is to compare the current incomes of broad classes of individuals who may have benefited or lost from previous discrimination. In the case of past racial discrimination, the primary beneficiaries are current-day whites (though some subgroups of whites may have lost), and the primary losers are contemporary nonwhites. By comparing income differences between whites and nonwhites today, one can approximate the total result of past discrimination, even if one cannot apportion the costs and benefits to individuals.

The question that immediately arises is whether the full difference in incomes should be attributed to the past wrong or whether one should take into account observed characteristics, allowing only the unexplained difference in incomes to reflect past discrimination. Conditioning on experience, occupation, or other characteristics that can also be affected by previous discrimination understates the full impact of past acts. If nonwhites do not complete high school because of differences in constraints, then the lower earnings that result from less education are themselves an outgrowth of discrimination.

Glen Cain (1984) suggests that unadjusted money differences in income can be viewed as rough proxies of discrimination. To argue otherwise is to imply that whites and nonwhites have different tastes, for only under such circumstances would they choose different educational levels, occupations, and hours of work while facing the same constraints. The data we review below show that in 1983 the difference in average income of households with white and nonwhite male heads was $7,341. The comparable figure for households headed by women was $3,703. After reviewing household income differences, we present data on differences in transfers received by whites and nonwhites.

DIFFERENCES IN MEAN HOUSEHOLD INCOMES

We have suggested that the existence of an earnings gap provides a priori evidence of current discrimination or of the lingering effects of previous discrimination which may have decreased the human or physical capital of nonwhites. Table 12.1 documents the gap between the earnings of black and white household heads below

Table 12.1
Mean Earnings of Nonaged Household Heads by Sex and Race of Head,
1968 and 1983

(Current dollars)

Household Head	1968 (1)	1983 (2)	Ratio, 1983/1968: (2)/(1) (3)
White male	$8,048	$20,507	2.55
Nonwhite male	$5,121	$14,180	2.77
Ratio nonwhite/white males	.64	.69	—
White females	$3,188	$10,054	3.15
Nonwhite females	$1,788	$ 6,749	3.77
Ratio nonwhite/white females	.56	.67	—

Source: Computations by the authors from March 1969 and 1984 Current Population Survey data tapes.

Note: Amounts are in current dollars; nonaged persons are under sixty-five. All household heads, including those with zero earnings, are included in the calculations in all tables.

age sixty-five in 1968 and 1983. Nonwhite male household heads earned $5,121 in 1968, which was 64 percent of the earnings of their white counterparts. By 1983 the nominal earnings of white males were 2.55 times that of the earlier year, while the earnings of nonwhite males were 2.77 times the earlier figure. The result was a narrowing of the nonwhite/white male earnings ratio from 64 to 69 percent.

Since the lower earnings of female household heads of both races reflect labor supply decisions as well as lower wages, it is harder to draw firm conclusions from the second half of Table 12.1. However, if again we assume that race by itself should have no impact on relative labor supply decisions, we can use these differences in means as rough indicators of discrimination. Nonwhite female household heads earned $1,788 in 1968, 56 percent of the earnings of their white counterparts. By 1983 the nominal earnings of nonwhite females had grown to $6,749, 3.77 times the previous amount. White nominal earnings increased by 3.15 times, so that the nonwhite/white female ratio increased from 56 to 67 percent. Thus, increased relative success in labor markets was about twice as important a factor for nonwhite women who headed households as for nonwhite men.

The racial gap between total household earnings can be further narrowed by adding other sources of private income—such as the earnings of household members other than the head or property income—which gives the total of pretransfer income, or by public transfers. Table 12.2 shows the rough magnitude of the importance of these two other types of income. In 1968 the $7,117 average pretransfer

Table 12.2
Mean Household Pretransfer and Posttransfer Income, by Sex and Race of
Nonaged Head, 1968 and 1983

Household Head	1968 (1)	1983 (2)	Ratio, 1983/1968 (2)/(1) (3)
White males			
Pretransfer	$10,303	$28,853	2.80
Posttransfer	$10,537	$30,197	2.87
Nonwhite males			
Pretransfer	$ 7,117	$21,355	2.98
Posttransfer	$ 7,385	$22,856	3.09
Ratios nonwhite/white males			
Pretransfer	.69	.74	—
Posttransfer	.70	.76	—
White females			
Pretransfer	$ 4,422	$13,157	2.98
Posttransfer	$ 4,936	$14,516	2.94
Nonwhite females			
Pretransfer	$ 2,671	$ 8,873	3.32
Posttransfer	$ 3,483	$10,813	3.10
Ratios nonwhite/white females			
Pretransfer	.60	.67	—
Posttransfer	.71	.74	—

Source: See Table 12.1.

Note: Amounts are in current dollars; nonaged persons are under sixty-five. Pretransfer income includes wages and salaries, net income from self-employment, property income (e.g., interest, dividends, net rental income), and other cash income from private sources (e.g., private pensions, alimony). Posttransfer income, or Census Money Income, includes income from market sources and cash government transfers, but does not account for in-kind income received or for taxes paid.

income of households headed by nonwhite males was 69 percent as large as that of whites, 5 percentage points higher than the ratio computed on the head's earnings alone. Cash transfers further raised household income to $7,385 but increased the ratio by only one percentage point, to 70 percent. By 1983, however, the nonwhite/ white ratio for men had increased to 74 percent for pretransfer income and to 76 percent for posttransfer income. Thus, transfers had a larger, but still very small, impact on raising the relative incomes of households headed by nonwhite males.

For female-headed households in 1968, the pretransfer nonwhite/white ratio was 60 percent and the posttransfer ratio was 71 percent. Transfers were, therefore, an important factor. But the rapid growth of transfers between 1968 and 1983 was relatively more important in raising the average incomes of households headed by white females, since in 1983 the pretransfer ratio was 67 percent while the posttransfer ratio was 74 percent. Transfers thus reduced the gap by 7 percentage points in 1983, down from 11 points in 1968.

In summary, Table 12.2 shows that both the absolute level of transfers and growth in transfers had only a small effect in reducing the white-nonwhite income gap for males. For female-headed households, the level of transfers was more important, but the gap-reducing effect of transfers eroded with time.

DIFFERENCES IN TRANSFERS TO THE POOR

In this section we examine white–nonwhite differences in the proportion of pretransfer–poor households receiving transfers and the average amount received per recipient. Poor nonwhites may receive larger transfers in a system that is *de jure* race neutral if they live in states with higher benefits or have other traits—such as living in female-headed or low-income households—which influence the size of the grant.

Columns 1 and 2 of Table 12.3 show that pretransfer poverty was higher among nonwhite persons for each of the demographic groups in each year. Because nonwhite poverty rates are higher, a race-neutral income-tested transfer system should disproportionately aid nonwhites if one compares transfers received by all nonwhite households to those received by all whites. However, the probability that any pretransfer-poor household receives a cash transfer should vary little by race. In fact, transfer recipiency among pretransfer-poor households shows only small racial differences (cols. 3 and 4). The proportion of male-headed households with children receiving transfers grew rapidly between 1968 and 1983 for both whites and nonwhites. Nonwhites were slightly more likely to receive transfers, but the average transfers they received were somewhat lower in each year than those received by whites (cols. 5 and 6).

For female-headed households with children, pretransfer poverty rates and transfer recipiency were higher than for males. Nonwhite female heads were more likely to receive transfers than white female heads, but they received lower average benefits. The inflation-adjusted benefit (cols. 5 and 6) fell for all of the nonaged groups. The 1983 values for females, nonwhite and white, were only about 70 percent of the 1968 values. (If the value of in-kind transfers such as Food Stamps, public housing, and Medicaid had been added, the real losses in average benefits between 1968 and 1983 would have been smaller for all demographic groups.)

The smaller nonwhite mean transfers for poor recipients reflect several factors. First, the benefit formulas in social insurance programs such as social security and unemployment insurance provide larger payments to recipients who had higher

Table 12.3
The Antipoverty Impact of Cash Transfers, 1968 and 1983

Person Living in Households Headed by:	Percentage Pretransfer Poor[a]		Percentage of Pretransfer Poor Households Receiving a Cash Transfer[a]		Mean Real Transfers Received by Pretransfer Poor Recipients[b]		Percentage Posttransfer Poor[a]	
	1968 (1)	1983 (2)	1968 (3)	1983 (4)	1968 (5)	1983 (6)	1968 (7)	1983 (8)
All persons	18.2%	24.2%	73.6%	77.2%	$5,123	$6,050	12.8%	15.2%
Nonaged males with children								
White	7.9	13.1	37.5	55.2	6,189	5,174	6.6	10.4
Nonwhite	26.4	23.8	38.7	61.5	5,333	4,940	23.4	20.6
Nonaged females with children								
White	51.3	50.1	58.0	71.6	6,542	4,695	39.6	43.2
Nonwhite	77.3	68.8	70.4	80.2	5,808	3,939	65.8	63.3

Source: See Table 12.1.

[a] Percentage of persons. The poverty rates shown in cols. 7 and 8 are the official U.S. poverty.

[b] Constant dollars; the consumer price index was 57.4 in 1968 and 164.4 in 1983.

earnings when they worked. Second, a greater percentage of poor nonwhites than whites resides in Southern states that provide lower than average welfare benefits.

In summary, nonwhites are more likely to be pretransfer poor and hence eligible for income transfers. However, conditional on their demographic group and pretransfer poverty, they are only slightly more likely than whites to receive transfers. Moreover, despite the fact that their pretransfer incomes are further below their poverty line than those of whites (data not shown), they receive smaller amounts of cash transfers on average.

DIFFERENCES IN THE ANTIPOVERTY IMPACTS OF MARKET AND TRANSFER INCOMES

An alternative measure of the extent to which pretransfer-poor nonwhites gained from transfers is the reduction in their poverty rates that can be directly attributed to transfers. Columns 7 and 8 of Table 12.3 show that posttransfer (official) poverty rates among the nonwhite groups declined somewhat between 1968 and 1983, while they increased for the whites.

In 1968 nonwhite persons living with nonwhite men were about four times as likely to be poor as similarly endowed whites; by 1983 the ratio had fallen to two to one. The ratio of poverty rates of nonwhite females with children to that of white females fell only slightly, from 1.7 to 1.5. Nonetheless, the rates for all persons in female-headed households remain strikingly high.

The fact that nonwhites have become increasingly more likely to live in households headed by women with children than have whites means that aggregate comparisons obscure the economic gains of these subgroups. For example, the ratio of poverty rates for all blacks to all whites has remained relatively constant, even though Table 12.3 shows convergence for both male-headed families and female-headed families.

Did this narrowing in poverty rates primarily reflect racial differences in the growth rates of market (pretransfer) or transfer incomes? To answer this question we use a methodology (developed in Peter Gottschalk and Sheldon Danziger, 1985) which focuses directly on the relationship between changes in poverty and changes in the joint distribution of market income and transfer income. Poverty is viewed as changing because of shifts in the *level* and *distribution* of each income source that affects the proportion of households falling below a fixed real poverty line. These shifts can be described by changes in the means, variances, covariances, and higher level moments of the distribution of market and transfer income.

For expositional simplicity, changes in poverty are attributed to three factors: changes in mean market income, changes in mean transfer income, and changes in the shape of the distribution. Computer tapes for the March 1969 through 1984 Current Population Surveys provide the basic data.

Table 12.4 shows the results of breaking down the changes in posttransfer poverty into its three components for nonaged families with children. The first line shows the actual percentage point changes in poverty rates for the four family types. Line

Table 12.4
Decomposition of Poverty for Nonaged White and Nonwhite Heads of
Households with Children, 1968–1983

| | Persons Living in Households Where Head Is: | | | |
| | Nonwhite | | White | |
	Male (1)	Female (2)	Male (3)	Female (4)
Actual percentage-point change in poverty	-2.8	-2.5	3.8	3.6
Percentage-point change in poverty due to change in:				
(a) mean market income	-8.0	-6.7	-1.5	-0.5
(b) mean transfer income	-2.1	2.9	-0.5	2.7
(c) inequality of income	7.3	1.3	5.8	1.4

Sources: Computations by authors. See Gottschalk and Danziger (1985) for a discussion of methodology.

Notes: In each column, the sum of lines (a), (b), and (c) equals the actual percentage point change. The actual percentage point change is the difference between the 1983 and 1968 poverty rate for each demographic group, as shown in cols. 7 and 8 of Table 12.3.

(a) shows the impact of changes in mean market income on the poverty rate of each subgroup. Clearly, increases in mean market income were much more important for nonwhite males and females than for whites. The poverty rates for nonwhite males and females would have decreased by 8.0 and 6.7 points, respectively, as a result of changes in mean market incomes. The corresponding figures for whites are only 1.5 and 0.5 points. Therefore, most of the drop in poverty rates among nonwhites is attributable to increased market income rather than to increased transfers.

Line (b) shows the impact of transfers. For females, the antipoverty effect of transfers is similar for whites and nonwhites. Both would have experienced an almost 3 percentage point increase in poverty solely as a result of their reduced real cash transfers. For males the poverty-reducing impact of increased transfers was considerably higher for nonwhites (-2.1 points) than for whites (-0.5 points).

Line (c) shows the importance of increased inequality of income within each demographic group. Consistent with earlier studies, these data show that increased inequality was important for all groups, especially among both nonwhite and white men. This increased inequality has been well documented but has not been well explained.

We also conducted a simulation in which real incomes for all nonwhite families were increased from current levels for five consecutive years at 3 percent per year.

Poverty rates fell by about 3 percentage points for male-headed families and by about 6 percentage points for female-headed families. But in 1983, as Table 12.3 shows, the differences between white and nonwhite poverty rates were about 10 percentage points for persons living in male-headed families and 20 percentage points for those living in female-headed families. This suggests that it would take about fifteen years in which nonwhite incomes increased steadily and white incomes remained constant for nonwhite and white poverty rates to equalize. Obviously, racial parity is decades away under "reasonable" forecasts of income growth for whites and nonwhites.

CONCLUSIONS

A distribution of reparations is neither conceptually possible to specify nor politically feasible to deliver. We found that the recent decrease in poverty among nonaged nonwhites is primarily a result of increased market income. Indeed, over the 1968–1983 period real declines in transfers were poverty-increasing for nonwhite and white female household heads. Thus, transfer programs are not reallocating resources disproportionately to the nonwhite poor.

NOTE

This research was supported in part by a grant from the Alfred P. Sloan Foundation. Steven Berry, Karen Fuller, and Christine Ross provided computational assistance.

REFERENCES

Amdur, Robert. "Compensatory Justice: The Question of Costs." *Political Theory* 7(1979):229–44.
Cain, Glen. "The Economics of Discrimination: Part 1." *Focus* 7(1984):2. (Newsletter of the Institute for Research on Poverty, University of Wisconsin-Madison.)
Gottschalk, Peter, and Danziger, Sheldon. "A Framework for Evaluating the Effects of Economic Growth and Transfers on Poverty." *American Economic Review* 74 (March 1985):153–61.

13.

The Social Debt to Blacks: A Case for Affirmative Action

Stanley H. Masters

Blacks and whites have lived together in this country for over 300 years. Through-out this period, the white community has dominated the black community econom-ically. To what extent have whites profited from the inferior economic position of blacks? To what extent do whites owe blacks reparations for white gains that have come at the expense of blacks? As used here reparations refer to actions that favor blacks over whites, actions that create greater opportunities for blacks than will be available through either market competition or through those government policies such as Title VII of the Civil Rights Act of 1969, designed to make the labor market color-blind.

The first section of this chapter summarizes the economic history of race rela-tions in the United States. The second section discusses the nature of racial dis-crimination under capitalism, emphasizing mechanisms that will perpetuate discrimination even in a competitive economy. On the basis of these considerations, the third section develops an argument for reparations from whites to blacks. In the final section affirmative action is analyzed as an example of such reparations.

HISTORICAL OVERVIEW

Let us begin with how blacks and whites first arrived in this country. The ances-tors of most whites came to the United States voluntarily. Initially, the main impetus was religious freedom, but soon the motivation of most immigrants was economic opportunity for themselves and their children. The ancestors of most blacks did not come here voluntarily but were brought forcibly by whites. The slave trade would not have originated and continued if it were not profitable for white shipowners.

Although the slave trade was abolished in the early nineteenth century, the institution of slavery continued and prospered. The slave population continued to increase, with some whites in the business of breeding blacks. Many white planters made great fortunes, based partly on their ownership of slaves. In the long run, however, it is doubtful that either the planter class or the South as a whole benefited from slavery. The costs of the Civil War most likely outweighed the previous gains.

After the Civil War, blacks provided a cheap form of wage labor. The presence of many blacks with relatively little skill and almost no physical capital hurt poor whites by providing competition for their labor, thus reducing wage rates. The existence of such cheap labor, however, aided those whites with greater skill and physical capital. While blacks made some gains in schooling and occupational status in the generation after the Civil War, Jim Crow laws soon reversed this trend.[1] As a result of increasing racial barriers to occupations and declining relative quality of black schooling, less skilled whites gained at the expense of blacks in the late nineteenth century.

Opportunities for blacks increased in the twentieth century, especially during periods of high labor demand, such as World War I and World War II. During and after World War II, a significant proportion of blacks left the South for Northern cities. This migration occurred partly because of the declining demand for unskilled labor in Southern agriculture and partly because of the demand of Northern employers for cheap labor to replace the previous stream of European immigrants.

In the 1960s federal legislation outlawed discrimination in employment and many other areas. Partly for this reason, there was some improvement in the relative economic position of blacks in the late sixties and early seventies. These gains did not continue during the eighties, however. In fact, there has been a decline in the relative family income of blacks. In part, this decline in the relative income of black families has occurred because of the large increase in low-income single-parent families. Blacks have also been hurt disproportionately by the low aggregate demand for labor in the economy over most of the past ten years and by the economic decline of the large Northern cities where many blacks live.

For the past decade there has been relatively little racial differential in the average earnings of women. Among men, however, the average black earns only about two-thirds as much as the average white. Although the earnings rate is somewhat higher for young men who are employed, unemployment is very high among young blacks, about 50 percent for teenagers.

This history, though admittedly very brief and sketchy, highlights several periods when whites have profited at the expense of the elementary human rights of blacks. The most dramatic examples of exploitation are the slave trade bringing blacks to this country, the slave economy of the antebellum South, and the suppression of the economic and political rights of blacks in the period after Reconstruction. Unless it can be shown that the effects of such exploitation have been largely eliminated in subsequent years, there is a strong moral argument for some kind of reparation from whites to blacks.

Reparations from all whites to all blacks for the current effects of previous exploitation runs counter to other equity considerations, however. First, the most flagrant abuses against blacks occurred many years ago. Most people do not wish to be held accountable for the sins of their distant ancestors. Second, not all whites in this country are descended from exploiters and not all blacks are descended from slaves. Most of us see ethical issues primarily in individualistic terms rather than in terms of groups, at least among most white males.

THE NATURE OF DISCRIMINATION UNDER CAPITALISM

With this background in mind, let us now focus on the nature of discrimination in a capitalistic economy. Is it appropriate to view discrimination primarily in individualistic terms, with competitive forces acting to reduce discrimination over time? If one accepts this view of discrimination, originally developed by Gary S. Becker, then there is little argument for reparations from whites to blacks.[2] Indeed, in Becker's theory, discrimination is defined in terms of whether one is willing to pay a price to avoid contact with members of a group. If this theory is correct, then, at least since slavery, whites as well as blacks have been hurt by discrimination. Unless there are productivity differences between blacks and whites, racial earnings differentials will be reduced over time as the least discriminatory firms profit and expand at the expense of firms that are not willing to employ the cheaper labor of blacks. To eliminate racial inequality, reparations are not necessary. Competition is all that is required to eliminate labor market discrimination. Once competition eliminates such discrimination, other forms of inequality, including the handicap of growing up in a poor family, should gradually diminish.

Alternatively, capitalism can be seen as leading to competition between groups as well as individuals. According to this view, advanced among others by Michael Reich, whites (or at least the dominant class of white capitalists) can benefit from discrimination.[3] Racial antagonism between black and white workers not only leads to discrimination against blacks, but also reduces the power of the working class in its struggle against the capitalists. Consequently, it is in the interests of white capitalists to encourage such racial antagonism, antagonism that may be very harmful to blacks. According to this theory, reparations to blacks from white capitalists are appropriate but are not likely to be forthcoming since it is not apparent how such reparations would advance the interests of the dominant white capitalists. The most blacks can expect from the white capitalist class is tokenism to buy off potential black leaders who threaten the establishment.

The two views outlined above are widely known, but both are quite misleading. The radical view, as represented by Reich, does not explain why individuals act in the interest of their group (class) rather than in terms of their individual self-interest.

In our apparently individualistic society, some enforcement mechanism is necessary. Such a mechanism can exist in the form of social pressures, government policies, or the policies of unions or other interest groups. Nevertheless, it is doubtful that such enforcement mechanisms are the primary mechanisms perpetuating racial discrimination today in the United States.

The Becker approach to discrimination is more consistent with standard economic assumptions and thus has received much more attention from mainstream economists. Nevertheless, it is not likely that market competition is effectively eliminating racial discrimination in the United States. Since the Becker model has received much attention in the profession and is consistent with the conservative opposition to government policies such as affirmative action, it is important to examine the validity of this approach. In the remainder of this section, we will outline two models that show how, contrary to the implications of the Becker model, racial inequality can be perpetuated undiminished from generation to generation, even in a competitive economy with no inherent differences between blacks and whites. To the extent that either of these models captures important aspects of our economy, some kind of reparations is necessary if we are ever to achieve an economy in which blacks have the same opportunities as whites.

A Human Capital Approach to Racial Inequalities

In a competitive economy, a worker's income will depend on his or her productivity. According to human capital theory, a worker's productivity is closely related to skills learned at home, at school, and on the job. Children whose parents have little education or income generally will be at a disadvantage.

During slavery, blacks were not allowed to read or write. After slavery, most blacks began with very little capital, either human or physical. In much of the South, only the most rudimentary public education was available to blacks, even in the early twentieth century. As James P. Smith has recently shown, the poor educational opportunities available to blacks in the early twentieth century directly affected the average earnings of blacks until the last few years.[4] Yet the indirect effects continue today and will continue for many years in the future since the educational opportunities of parents also affect those of their children.

Several writers, including Anthony Downs, Glenn C. Loury, and Linda Datcher, have emphasized that education and other forms of human capital developed by children depend not only on their family background, but also on the community.[5] If income and educational levels are low, and if family discipline is weak, perhaps because of overcrowding or the prevalence of single-parent families, then it will be difficult to operate schools effectively. Children may also develop bad work habits and hostile attitudes toward authority.

Loury has shown that, even if there are no differences in preferences or abilities between two racial groups, if one group starts out with lower income and if individuals prefer to live in a community with a disproportionate number of their race, then competitive economic forces will never eliminate racial inequality. Differences in neighborhood preferences by race lead to racial segregation and those growing up in the poorer communities are at a disadvantage, thus perpetuating the initial racial inequality from generation to generation. In the absence of some special efforts to assist blacks, sizable racial differences in economic opportunity will remain, even if the economy were entirely competitive.

Statistical Discrimination

Education and training are not the only dimensions of human capital. Information in the labor market is imperfect, which leads to investment in better information by both workers and firms. Since many kinds of information can be quite costly, however, inaccurate, inexpensive proxies often are used in favor of more accurate data. Race, for example, may be used as a proxy for ability, motivation, or reliability. Using race (or sex) as a proxy for productivity characteristics is called statistical discrimination.[6]

In a competitive economy, statistical discrimination by race will occur only to the extent that race provides employers with useful information. Therefore, in the long run, statistical discrimination will exist only if the average black is a less effective worker than the average white, holding constant any other proxies for ability that the employer has available. Consequently, it might appear that statistical discrimination should not hurt blacks as a group. Such discrimination would only reflect racial differences in productivity, resulting from differences in schooling, family background, and neighborhood, as discussed in the previous section. As we will see, however, this is not necessarily the case.

Under some circumstances, statistical discrimination can cause, or at least reinforce, productivity differences by race.[7] As we have seen, education was forbidden to slaves, and educational opportunities were very limited for blacks as recently as the early twentieth century. Since very few blacks would have the educational background for top positions, it would not be very costly for employers to exclude blacks from such positions. As Lester G. Thurow has emphasized, tastes for discrimination appear to be based on whites' desires to maintain social distance (or status differentials) from blacks, not physical distance.[8] Thus, for top jobs, white tastes for discrimination are greatest and the costs of exercising such tastes are lowest (or at least were so in the past). Consequently, considerable discrimination has existed against blacks with regard to high-paying jobs. Such discrimination, focused on the top jobs that require the most education, can be expected to have reduced the incentive of blacks to achieve higher levels and quality of schooling. If, on average, blacks do perform worse in school, which in turn leads to reduced productivity on the job, then any initial prejudice of employers against blacks will be confirmed, thus leading to statistical discrimination against blacks for jobs requiring a good education. This statistical discrimination will reduce the incentive of blacks to strive hard in school, thereby reinforcing such discrimination. Since it never costs firms much (if anything) to discriminate against blacks for the top positions, this discrimination can continue for many generations even in a competitive economy.

Although statistical discrimination can occur when wage rates are flexible, such discrimination is likely to be much more severe when wage rates are rigid. Thus, let us now turn to a brief discussion of wage rigidity and its effect on statistical discrimination.

Competitive theory assumes flexible wage rates that will adjust to reflect productivity differences. Yet, there are many factors that make wage rates relatively inflexible. One simple example is government regulations, such as minimum wage legislation. In considering discrimination, however, possibly the most important cause of wage rigidities is the principle of equal pay for equal work. This principle is basic in the labor movement.[9] It increases worker solidarity and reduces the ability of employers to lower wage rates by giving more work to the lowest paid employees. Together with seniority for promotion and layoff, equal pay for equal work even has some advantages for employers since it may facilitate on-the-job training of new hires by the firm's present workforce.

For blacks who gain access to desirable jobs, equal pay for equal work eliminates one form of discrimination. Blacks are also likely to gain from the worker solidarity that this principle reflects and encourages. On the other hand, equal pay for equal work is likely to reduce job opportunities for blacks. As long as there are several equally qualified applicants for each job opening, an employer incurs no cost if he or she hires (or promotes) the white instead of the black applicant. If the employer believes that, on average, whites will be better workers than blacks, then the employer has every incentive to hire the white. In this context, note that employers may prefer to hire whites simply because they believe whites will work together better with present workers, who may be white workers who are prejudiced against or at least uncomfortable with blacks.[10]

If wage rates were flexible, the black could offer to start at a lower wage and prove his (or her) ability to do the job, including fitting in as part of a productive team of workers where necessary. The principle of equal pay for equal work can stand in the way of this opportunity, however. Thus, as Thurow has emphasized, rigid wage rates and statistical discrimination can interact to create serious problems for minority groups.[11]

AN ARGUMENT FOR REPARATIONS

Thus far, this chapter has focused on the conservative argument that reparations to blacks are not appropriate since market competition reduces discrimination against any group. In this view, any effort to tamper with competitive forces to favor one group will simply lead to discrimination against other groups. In other words, efforts to assist blacks will lead to reverse discrimination against whites.

We have tried to show that market competition is not likely to end discrimination against blacks. To the extent that the arguments in the second section are important, they weaken the conservative position. Still we have not made a direct case for reparations. To do so, let us consider briefly how whites can gain from the handicaps facing blacks.

In the section on human capital, we saw that community factors are likely to affect the socialization of children, both within and outside of school. If, for whatever reason, poor families have more disruptive children than middle or upper income families, then clearly it is in the interest of nonpoor families to have housing segregation by income and wealth. In our society, race is even more important than income in defining group membership, with race serving as an easily visible proxy for economic status. Thus, it is not surprising that there is great housing segregation by race. Since there does appear to be at least a moderate correlation in our society among race, income, and socially disruptive behavior, it is likely that housing segregation by race has benefited middle and upper class whites.

Statistical discrimination against blacks makes it more difficult for blacks to compete for top jobs. Conversely, such discrimination increases the availability of top jobs for whites. Therefore, upper income whites benefit from statistical discrimination. Given rigidity in wage rates and high levels of unemployment, statistical discrimination probably benefits most whites.

These arguments are based on the assumption that housing segregation and statistical discrimination have not affected the total economic pie that can be divided up among the races. By underutilizing black abilities and increasing racial conflict, discrimination probably reduces the size of the pie. Thus, it is not clear whether, on balance, whites have gained from discrimination. If some kind of reparations can reduce future discrimination against blacks, however, then any positive effect of reduced discrimination on total income strengthens the case for reparations.

We have seen why market forces are not likely to eliminate discrimination and racial inequality. Since the 1960s, however, we have had important federal legislation outlawing many kinds of discrimination. In particular, Title VII of the Civil Rights Act of 1964 prohibits employment discrimination by race. Given this legislation, is there still need for reparations?

Although Title VII has surely helped reduce labor market discrimination, there is considerable controversy concerning empirical estimates of the effects of this legislation.[12] On a priori grounds, there are several reasons to be pessimistic that such legislation can effectively eliminate discrimination, however. First, litigation is very expensive and time consuming. Thus, many likely victims of discrimination do not seek redress in the courts. Second, it is often difficult to prove discrimination, especially statistical discrimination. For example, just how far does an employer have to go in justifying the job relevance of tests or other screening devices that give an advantage to whites relative to blacks? Finally, not all racial inequality results from labor market discrimination. For example, Loury's model, discussed above, places considerable emphasis on the role of housing segregation by race.

In conclusion, whites appear to have benefited from the inferior opportunities of blacks, at least in terms of greater relative opportunities. Neither market forces nor antidiscrimination legislation can be expected to eliminate discrimination or economic inequality by race. Consequently, we need to consider some form of reparations from whites to blacks. Such reparations might compensate for the effects of past discrimination against blacks and thus also eliminate some of the mechanisms that continue to perpetuate such discrimination.

AFFIRMATIVE ACTION

Many kinds of reparation might be considered. Since incomes are determined primarily in the labor market, we should focus on policies in this area. Affirmative action policies can be viewed as reparations since such policies give preference to blacks for jobs where blacks are currently underrepresented.

In contrast to Title VII of the Civil Rights Act of 1964, which seeks to make the employment process color-blind (and gender neutral), affirmative action focuses on outcomes rather than on process. If blacks or other minorities are underrepresented in certain jobs, relative to their availability in the employer's labor market, then an affirmative action employer is under an obligation to make an extra effort to increase their representation in such jobs. This extra effort is one form of reparation, at least as far as the term is defined here. Affirmative action is required of most government contractors, it is often required by the courts when an employer has been found guilty of discrimination; and it also has been chosen voluntarily by many employers. In recent years, however, affirmative action has been criticized increasingly as a form of reverse discrimination against white males. Partly for this reason, the Reagan administration generally opposed affirmative action requirements and reduced enforcement efforts in this area.[13]

If affirmative action is vigorously pursued (and does not degenerate into a bureaucratic exercise in paperwork), it can redress some of the problems we have discussed above. First, affirmative action directly increases employment opportunities for blacks in many high-paying jobs. Second, if affirmative action is handled wisely, it can help break down the racial stereotypes that underlie statistical discrimination. In this way affirmative action today can increase the employment opportunities of blacks in the future, even if affirmative action is no longer practiced at that time.

Given these advantages of affirmative action, why is this concept under so much attack today? First, some believe that labor market discrimination has largely disappeared so that affirmative action is unnecessary. As we have seen, however, there is little reason to believe that either market competition or government antidiscrimination policies, such as Title VII, have eliminated such discrimination. While, in theory, affirmative action could do so, empirical studies suggest that government affirmative action policies have not had large effects.[14]

Second, closely related to this first criticism is the view that affirmative action represents reverse discrimination against white males. Even if racial inequality today does result from past discrimination, opponents of affirmative action believe it is unfair to penalize present white workers for the sins of their fathers. In part, this is a value judgment. In part, however, it depends on assumptions about the opportunities available to blacks in the absence of affirmative action, an issue addressed above.

Third, opponents of affirmative action argue that it reduces economic efficiency by requiring firms to hire unqualified workers. Rigid quotas may have this effect. Yet affirmative action requirements are couched in terms of good faith efforts by employers. If the employer can show that he or she has made a reasonable effort to recruit, select, and train minorities, but still has not been able to employ many minority workers, then employers will have met affirmative action requirements. Clearly, employers must undertake some extra costs to make a good faith effort. But these costs need not be excessive and may be more than counterbalanced by the increase in qualified workers available to the firm—workers of whom the employer might never have been aware in the absence of affirmative action.

Fourth, if affirmative action does lead to the employment of unqualified minorities, the failure of such workers to succeed in their jobs may reinforce rather than reduce the racial stereotypes that underlie statistical discrimination. More generally, whites may believe that most blacks in top jobs received their position only through affirmative action and not on merit. While this danger is real, it can be reduced by trying to recruit and promote blacks that do appear likely to succeed and by giving them whatever training and support are necessary as they take over on the job.

Finally, some have argued that, while affirmative action may have helped increase the job opportunities of well-educated blacks, it has done little to help lower class blacks, a group that has been especially hard hit by reduced job opportunities and less generous welfare benefits in recent years. As William J. Wilson argues, for example, the problem of disadvantaged workers may have been more one of class, or of class and race together, rather than just a racial problem.[15] Moreover, along the lines of Loury's argument, the labor market problem of blacks appears to be compounded by segregation and discrimination in housing, together with schools that are frequently inferior in black neighborhoods.

The criticism of affirmative action as not doing very much for lower class blacks appears to be largely valid. The problem lies not in the theory of affirmative action but in its application. Affirmative action is considered appropriate when blacks are underrepresented relative to their availability in the workforce. This formulation leads to the question of how to measure the available workforce for any position, a complex issue that has received considerable attention.[16] Yet there is a tendency, especially on the part of advocates of affirmative action, to use a very simple measure: the percentage of the labor force in the particular city or metropolitan area that is black. Since average educational levels are lower for blacks than for whites, this approach leads to a disproportionate emphasis on improving job opportunities for blacks in occupations that require considerable education and skill.

Focusing affirmative action on top jobs where blacks are underrepresented has helped overcome the particularly high levels of discrimination that do exist for such positions and does increase the incentive for blacks to achieve high levels of education. Nevertheless, in my view, some preference in recruiting, hiring, training, and promoting blacks is necessary at all occupational levels, not just those that require the most human capital.

In addition to affirmative action, a reasonably high aggregate demand for labor is also essential. High demand for labor can break down racial barriers directly, as we saw during World War II. Conversely, affirmative action policies do little good if employers are not hiring or promoting owing to slack demand. Moreover, opposition to affirmative action by whites is likely to be greatest when there are few job opportunities available for anyone. While high aggregate demand for labor is of great importance in increasing the relative employment opportunities of blacks, the issue of how to achieve such high demand without serious side effects, including an increasing rate of inflation, is very difficult and well beyond the scope of this chapter.

CONCLUSIONS

Neither market competition nor legislation to try to make the employment process color-blind is likely to eliminate labor market discrimination against blacks. More is needed, not only to compensate blacks for the effects of past discrimination, but also to reduce present and future discrimination. The principle of affirmative action, though currently under considerable attack, is well suited for dealing with these problems.

NOTES

1. For example, see James P. Smith, "Race and Human Capital," *The American Economic Review* (September 1984): 685–99 for a recent discussion of changes in the educational opportunities of blacks and the effects of these changes on their relative income and occupational levels.

2. See Gary S. Becker, *The Economics of Discrimination*, 2d ed. (Chicago: University of Chicago Press, 1971).

3. For example, see Michael Reich, *Racial Inequality* (Princeton, N.J.: Princeton University Press, 1981). Also see Paul A. Baran and Paul M. Sweezy, *Monopoly Capital* (New York: Monthly Review Press, 1966).

4. See Smith, "Race and Human Capital."

5. See Glenn C. Loury, "A Dynamic Theory of Racial Income Difference," in Phyllis A. Wallace, ed., *Women, Minorities, and Employment Discrimination* (Lexington, Mass.: Heath-Lexington, 1977); Glenn C. Loury, "Is Equal Opportunity Enough?" *American Economic Review* (May 1981): 122–26; Linda Datcher, "Effects of Community and Family Background on Achievement," *Review of Economics and Statistics* (1982): 32–41; and Anthony Downs, *Opening Up the Suburbs* (New Haven, Conn.: Yale University Press, 1971).

6. For a discussion of statistical discrimination, see A. Michael Spence, *Market Signaling* (Cambridge, Mass.: Harvard University Press, 1977); Edmund Phelps, "The Statistical Theory of Racism and Sexism," *American Economic Review* (1972): 659–61; and Dennis J. Aigner and Glen G. Cain, "Statistical Theories of Discrimination in Labor Markets," *Industrial and Labor Relations Review* (April 1977): 175–87.

7. Statistical discrimination can also hurt blacks if employers are risk averse and if the variance of expected productivity, conditional on other productivity proxies such as years of school or test scores, is greater for blacks than for whites.

8. See Lester G. Thurow, *Poverty and Discrimination* (Washington, D.C.: Brookings Institution, 1969).

9. For example, see Sidney and Beatrice Webb, *Industrial Democracy* (London: published by the authors, 1897).

10. For an analysis of the role of group conflict between black and white workers, see David Swinton, "A Labor Force Competitive Model of Racial Discrimination in the Labor Market," *Review of Black Political Economy* (Fall 1978).

11. See Lester G. Thurow, *Generating Inequality* (New York: Basic Books, 1975).

12. For contrasting views of the effectiveness of government antidiscrimination policies, see Richard B. Freeman, "Black Economic Progress After 1964: Who Has Gained and Why?" in Sherwin Rosen, ed., *Studies in Labor Markets* (Chicago: University of Chicago Press, 1981), and Richard Butler and James J. Heckman, "The Government Impact on the Labor Market Status of Black Americans: A Critical Review," in Leonard J. Hausman et al., eds., *Equal Rights and Industrial Relations* (Madison, Wis.: Industrial Relations Research Association, 1977). Also see Charles Brown, "Black-White Earnings Ratios Since the Civil Rights Act of 1964: The Importance of Labor Market Dropouts," *Quarterly Journal of Economics* (February 1984): 31–47.

13. For a discussion of Reagan policies in this area, see D. Lee Bawden and John L. Palmer, "Social Policy," in John L. Palmer and Isabel V. Sawhill, eds., *The Reagan Record* (Washington, D.C.: Urban Institute, 1984).

14. See Butler and Heckman, "The Government Impact on the Labor Market Status" and the studies they summarize.

15. See William Julius Wilson, *The Declining Significance of Race*, 2d ed. (Chicago: University of Chicago Press, 1980).

16. For example, see Ronald G. Ehrenberg and Robert S. Smith, "Economic and Statistical Analysis of Discrimination in Hiring," *Proceedings of the Industrial Relations Research Association* (1983): 22–33.

14.

What Was Lost: The Cost of Slavery and Discrimination for Blacks

Lynn C. Burbridge

INTRODUCTION

Blacks are not the only ethnic group that has periodically demanded recompense for inequities resulting from historical racism and discrimination. American Indians have demanded that lands that were illegally stolen be returned. Japanese Americans have demanded that property and forgone income lost while they were "relocated" during World War II also be returned. While claims made by Afro-Americans, American Indians, and Japanese Americans are similar, each results from unique events that make treatment of each claim an individual problem. For example, American Indians—by and large—seek compensation for treaties illegally broken. Probably the main reason why they have been more successful than Afro-Americans and Japanese Americans in having their arguments recognized is that they have shown that U.S. citizens and the U.S. government broke their own laws in taking Indian lands. Blacks and the Japanese, on the other hand, were "legally" deprived of wealth and rightful income.

Both Afro-Americans and Japanese Americans, however, make a compelling argument that their disenfranchisement was immoral, regardless of legality. Laws, after all, are only as good as those who make them. Furthermore, it can be claimed that these laws ran counter to the spirit, if not the intent, of the U.S. Constitution.

Further problems arise. Even if an argument can be made for reparations, can the extent of damage be measured? In the case of Japanese Americans, measurement is much easier. First, because most of the injury was committed during a distinct epoch in recent history, more reliable data are available. Second, since we can get reasonable estimates of what the Japanese had been able to acquire up to the time they were relocated, the calculation involves simply measuring what they had and making imputations of what they would have acquired in addition during their relatively brief incarceration. Third, the relocation of the Japanese took place on a smaller scale and for a shorter period compared to the enslavement and economic segregation of blacks.[1] It is likely that fewer distortions occurred in the overall economy as a result of the Japanese relocation. Therefore, measurements of damages to the Japanese—using prevailing wage and interest rates, and other relevant data— are more likely to reflect what was really lost by this group. Given the length, breadth, and intensity of inequities experienced by blacks—so that even the "initial condition" is essentially one of enslavement—it is more difficult to accurately portray "what was lost" by blacks.

This comparison of the experience of blacks to that of other ethnic groups highlights the unique issues involved in measuring injuries done to blacks. Leaving aside questions of political feasibility or the ramifications of reparations, measurement presents obvious practical and methodological problems. Hence, the next section discusses how to measure "what was lost" and comments on the attempts of others to do so. Then problems in implementing reparations as public policy will be discussed.

WHAT WAS LOST

The difficulties in measuring injuries from slavery and discrimination are not unknown. Economic historians have debated the validity of measures used and assumptions made in trying to calculate the impact of racism.[2] Most studies focus narrowly on benefits to whites rather than on costs to blacks (although these benefits are often defined as "expropriated" from blacks). For example, studies on slavery have measured—for both slaveholders and nonslaveowning whites—the benefits derived from this institution minus the costs of maintaining it, rather than calculating the losses to blacks of being enslaved. Similarly, analyses of the post–Civil War period measure gains to whites from discrimination rather than losses to blacks.[3]

There are good reasons for this approach. First, the benefit to whites is in itself an interesting question. Second, measurement of losses to blacks requires a counterfactual question: what would have happened if blacks were not enslaved or discriminated against? An answer to this question requires assumptions about what might have happened rather than an analysis based on what actually did occur. However, there are indications of choices blacks may have made if, for example, slavery had ended earlier. They probably would have been similar to those actually made in the post–Civil War period. According to Roger L. Ransom and Richard Sutch, blacks chose more leisure time; black women in particular did less fieldwork.[4] Blacks did *not* choose to be wage laborers. Sharecropping was a kind of "compromise" between blacks who wanted their "own" land and former slaveowners who wanted blacks to work as wage laborers. There is no reason to assume, therefore, that blacks would have been different from whites who rejected farm (wage) labor. According to Gavin Wright, during slavery wage labor was scarce because of the abundance of land; since farmers "owned more land than they could cultivate efficiently themselves . . . they had little reason to hire themselves out to others parttime."[5] However, Wright also cautions that "free family farms" were not governed by the same economic principles as slavery or wage labor, making comparisons difficult, if not impossible. He writes that the family farm provided security against starvation and unemployment as well as possibilities for capital gains from rising land prices, in contrast to wage labor. While economic differences between slavery, wage labor, and family farming can be—and have been—debated, for purposes of analyzing what was lost by slavery and discrimination, the differences pointed out by Wright are relevant. Blacks have lost not only earnings but also the opportunity to invest in a wealth-augmenting commodity—land. (It is safe to assume that in the absence of slavery, blacks would have chosen the family farm over wage labor (or sharecropping), as long as family farming was thriving.)

In the twentieth century, when the family farm has declined, blacks have still faced barriers to wealth accumulation. Credit restrictions and segregation have limited their ability to purchase property. Business development has been restricted for similar reasons. Lack of access to "old boy networks" has also affected the choices available.

With these considerations in mind, it is important to analyze how useful calculations of the economic benefits of slavery and discrimination are in assessing what was lost. Estimates of gains from slavery to slaveholders have been calculated as the difference between the marginal product of blacks and the "slave wage," the slave wage being the amount spent for the upkeep of slaves. We know, or at least we have estimates of, slave productivity, maintenance costs, cotton profits, and so on. If we assume that slavery did not distort what these values would have been under a "true" market system, then these data can be used to measure the "wages," productivity, and economic benefits of slavery to slaveholders.

To measure benefits from postslavery economic discrimination, it is also assumed that economic segregation did not distort wages and prices. Economic benefits are then measured by the difference between what whites have earned and what they would have earned if they were distributed as the total population in terms of sex, occupation, and education.

The assumption that wages and prices were not distorted is necessary since we do not know what distortions might have occurred. Furthermore, while other forms of discrimination are acknowledged, most calculations are of wage income alone, again because less is known about other variables. However, if we are concerned with the legacy of discrimination intergenerationally, it is important to focus more broadly on barriers to the accumulation of wealth. Although wage income is a source of wealth accumulation, focusing on wage income lost does not convey the extent to which blacks were deprived of choices with respect to the use of this income.

What do blacks pass on to later generations compared to whites? Studies on relative black-white wealth help answer this question. A recent study has found that the median net worth of white households is twelve times the median net worth of black households.[6] This is much larger than the white-black ratio of median earnings, which is about two. White wealth is greater than black wealth in all income classes, although the difference is greater at lower incomes.[7] Furthermore, blacks are more likely to hold consumption-oriented assets (houses, vehicles) than financial assets.[8] However, blacks are no less likely to accumulate wealth than are whites, when controlling for socioeconomic and environmental factors.[9] All this suggests that blacks face limitations on investment greater (although not necessarily more important) than limitations on consumption. In a capitalist economy, such restrictions can significantly determine the economic vulnerability of a group.

How important are these considerations? Webster's defines reparations as a "making of amends; making up for a wrong or injury."[10] If reparations are to provide a "once and for all" payback for injuries, any measurement must be as true and accurate an assessment of what was lost as possible. Focusing on "benefits" to whites will not do this, nor will a measurement that focuses primarily on lost wage income alone. Such a focus may seriously underestimate the "wrong or injury."

To get a sense of the extent to which such calculations may underestimate the loss, it would be useful to identify what information would be needed to get a true estimate of the damages suffered by blacks. In other words, how would we measure "what was lost," if we could? The following accounting framework may be useful.

The loss (L) experienced by cohort j as a result of racism (racism standing for slavery or discrimination) would be measured as follows: $L_j = (C_j^n - C_j^b) + (W_j^n - W_j^b)$; total consumption of j in the absence of racism minus actual consumption $(C_j^n - C_j^b)$, plus total wealth (inherited plus accumulated) in the absence of racism minus actual $(W_j^n - W_j^b)$, where n represents the value in the absence of racism and b represents the real value of the variable. For a cohort, j, wealth (W_j) and consumption (C_j) are:

$$W_j = w_{o,j} + \sum_{t=1}^{T} w_{t,j} \text{ and } C_j = \sum_{t=1}^{T} c_{t,j}.$$

The w_o is wealth inherited from the previous cohort which is added to the wealth accumulated by cohort j, in each year t, during its life (T years). Total consumption is simply that consumed by cohort j, in each year t. Accumulated wealth can be decomposed as follows:

$$w_t = s_t + a_t$$

$$= y_t - c_t + a_t$$

$$= i_t + e_t + t_t - c_t + a_t$$

Accumulated wealth in a given year t equals savings (s_t) plus net appreciation of currently held wealth. Savings equals income (y_t) minus consumption (c_t). Income equals property income (interest, rent, dividends, and profits), earnings, and net transfers (taxes minus transfers); or i_t, e_t, and t_t, respectively.

Substituting for W_j and C_j:

$$L_j = \sum_{t=1}^{T} (c_{t,j}^n - c_{t,j}^b) + (w_{0,j}^n - w_{0,j}^b) + \sum_{t=1}^{T} [(i_{t,j}^n - i_{t,j}^b) + (e_{t,j}^n - e_{t,j}^b)$$
$$+ (t_{t,j}^n - t_{t,j}^b) - (c_{t,j}^n - c_{t,j}^b) + (a_{t,j}^n - a_{t,j}^b)]$$

Since inherited wealth depends on the wealth accumulated by a previous cohort, further substitutions can be made to obtain the following:

$$L_j = \sum_{j=1}^{j-1} \sum_{t=1}^{T} [(i_{t,j}^n - i_{t,j}^b) + (e_{t,j}^n - e_{t,j}^b) + (t_{t,j}^n - t_{t,j}^b) + (a_{t,j}^n -$$
$$a_{t,j}^b)] + \sum_{t=1}^{T} [(i_{t,j}^n - i_{t,j}^b) + (e_{t,j}^n - e_{t,j}^b) + (t_{t,j}^n - t_{t,j}^b) + (a_{t,j}^n - a_{t,j}^b)].$$

The first term is the accumulated losses of each generation prior to cohort j. The second term is the accumulated losses of cohort j.

It appears that income data alone go a long way in explaining what was lost by blacks, if the data include earnings, interest, rent, profits, and dividends. The value of home-produced consumption would be an important component of earnings until the early twentieth century. It must still be assumed, however, that we can estimate income in the absence of racism using available data for whites—in other words, assuming no distortions. Furthermore, estimates of net transfers (taxes minus transfers) and net appreciation—actual and in the absence of racism—would have to be made. The net transfers will be easier to impute—given current data availability—than the net appreciation. (Only the "net transfers" term may possibly be negative. However, it is unlikely to come close to canceling the other terms.) Estimates on net appreciation will depend on estimates of the amount and quality of property that would have been held and that has been held by blacks. Again, this brings us into unknown territory unless it is assumed that blacks would have been similar to whites in the absence of racism.

Whether data are available to make this calculation is another issue. The appeal of the "benefits" calculations is that reasonable estimates can be made with available data. Even if no distortions are assumed, and the earnings of whites are used as a benchmark for what blacks would have had in the absence of discrimination, estimates of nonwage income—particularly capital gains—are very scarce. The further back in time one goes, the more difficult it is to find reliable data.[11]

In sum, the discussion suggests that calculations of the benefits of slavery and discrimination severely underestimate the costs to blacks of these historical patterns. Blacks have lived on the margins of the American economy, not only as workers but also as businessmen and wealth holders. While the authors of papers on benefits acknowledge they are not measuring total costs to blacks, in a discussion of reparations exclusion of these costs can be problematic. Losses of nonwage income and capital gains, for example, have been significant contributors to black-white inequities; it is these inequities that such a policy is meant to address.

REPARATIONS AS PUBLIC POLICY

If a measurement of what was lost were made, how would it be implemented as public policy? Probably the most common implementation problem with regard to reparations is selling the concept. The American public is not going to buy it, particularly in a time of high budget deficits and neoconservatism. That does not mean the argument should not be made, however. It could refute conservative arguments that blacks have "taken" too much in welfare and social programs. A calculation of what was lost could show that blacks have been "net givers" rather than "net takers." But there are other questions that must be addressed.

First, seen as a way of recompensing blacks for the legacy of slavery and discrimination, should reparations be divided equally among blacks or should they go to those who have suffered most from this legacy? For what was lost not only resulted in inequities between blacks and whites, but also greater inequality among blacks. Improvement of the blacks' position relative to that of the whites would involve raising blacks on the bottom.

There have been other costs to blacks as a result of racism, but since they are hard to measure they are often not considered—for example, low education levels, high substance abuse, and incarcerations. "Reparations" for these problems, while requiring money, also require well-designed programs to provide services for those involved.

Finally, it is important to consider the extent to which debate on this issue focuses attention on the unique history of an ethnic group and away from systemic factors in the overall economy that produce poverty. A debate on reparations can easily degenerate into a discussion of who is "truly needy" and ascribing one man's poverty as more worthy than another's. This pitfall can splinter efforts to implement programs that serve the needs of the poor, regardless of how they got there.

CONCLUSIONS

This chapter raises more questions than answers. It highlights important issues with respect to the reparations concept that have not been adequately stated. It focuses on measurement but also questions implementation. It is difficult to measure what blacks lost because it requires answering a counterfactual question. Furthermore, within-group inequities, nonpecuniary costs, and systemic explanations for inequality would complicate implementation of reparations as public policy. Consideration of reparations, therefore, demands more than the mere assertion that it is just; it requires answers to these troubling issues.

NOTES

1. This is not to suggest that Japanese Americans were not discriminated against either before or after the relocation, but the thrust of their claims focuses on what occurred during the war years.

2. A good example of this is in Paul David et al., *Reckoning with Slavery* (New York: Oxford University Press, 1976).

3. The methodology used for the slave period is primarily derived from that developed by Robert Fogel and Stanley Engerman in *Time on the Cross* (Boston: Little, Brown & Co., 1974); for the postslave period the methodology of Lester Thurow in *Poverty and Discrimination* (Washington, D.C.: Brookings Institution, 1969) is used.

4. Roger L. Ransom and Richard Sutch, *One Kind of Freedom: The Economic Consequences of Emancipation* (Cambridge, Eng.: Cambridge University Press, 1977).

5. Gavin Wright, *The Political Economy of the Cotton South: Households, Markets and Wealth in the Nineteenth Century* (New York: W. W. Norton & Co., 1978), p. 45.

6. U.S. Department of Commerce, Bureau of Census, *Household Wealth and Asset Ownership: 1984*, Current Population Reports, Household Economic Studies, Series P-70, No. 7.

7. Henry S. Terrell, "Wealth Accumulation of Black and White Families: The Empirical Evidence," *The Journal of Finance* 26, no. 2 (May 1971).

8. William P. O'Hare, *Wealth and Economic Status: A Perspective on Racial Inequity* (Washington, D.C.: Joint Center for Political Studies, 1983).

9. Terrell, "Wealth Accumulation."

10. *Webster's New World Dictionary of the American Language, Second College Edition* (New York: World Publishing Co., 1970), p. 1204.

11. The method proposed by Robert S. Browne ("Wealth Distribution and Its Impact on Minorities," *Review of Black Political Economy* 4, no.4 [1974]) may be the most logical one for estimating reparations: The difference between the current wealth of blacks and 12 percent of total U.S. wealth. It is assumed that blacks would own wealth in the same proportion as their percentage of the total population, if there had been no discrimination.

15.

Achieving Parity through Reparations

ROBERT S. BROWNE

One hundred and twenty-five years after emancipation, the black community still suffers the ill effects of bondage. Most indices of social welfare show black Americans concentrated in the lowest percentiles, generally with immigrant Hispanics. Blacks, however, are not immigrants, most having been brought here prior to the nineteenth century well before the ancestors of most other Americans.

A quantum improvement in these social indices occurred during the years 1965–1975 under the dual pressures of black militancy and government and corporate commitment. Employment, educational, social, housing, and voting opportunities, previously closed, were partially opened, and limited numbers took advantage. But even with affirmative action and similar programs, the white-black median ratio remained in a range of 57 percent to 61 percent. However, there appeared to be no measurable change in the far more significant gap in wealth. That the gap has not closed more noticeably reflects the meagerness of the resources committed to rectifying this inequity and the thinness of the commitment.

In the 1980s deterioration continued in the bottom third of the black population. The black prison population overtaxed correctional facilities and created gender imbalance in the free black community. Chronic unemployment and burgeoning numbers of female-headed families were reflected in antisocial behavior and other social pathologies.

Although money alone is not a panacea, it helped produce progress for many during 1965–1975, and that demonstrates what can be achieved with commitment, backed by resources. Inequities were only partially corrected, because funds were siphoned off into the Vietnam War, and ultimately the commitment faded. But we glimpsed what could be achieved. Not surprisingly, commitment never faded within the black community; only funds disappeared as political interests shifted. These factors, a glimpse of what is achievable, the observation that substantial resources were required, and the realization that national commitments were shaky, encouraged the black community to look for ways to obtain control over resources it could administer. From where could sufficient resources come? Clearly, only from government. Yet, reliance on government has disappointed, leading increasingly to a focus on "self-help." It is not difficult to see how the reparations concept could easily emerge as a sound and reasonable rationale for a massive transfer of public funds to the black community, whether on a collective basis or to individuals.

What should reparations accomplish? There are a number of possibilities.

1. To provide restitution for the unpaid labor of slave ancestors
2. To redirect to blacks that portion of national income which has been diverted from blacks to whites by slavery and discrimination
3. To provide the black community with the wealth and income it would by now have had if it had been treated as other immigrants after importation ceased

This list is illustrative rather than exhaustive. The rest of the discussion that follows first offers comments on the basis for restitution claims; second, explores an example of one of the approaches to computing the magnitude of the claim; and third, suggests policy implications which an effort to pay this debt might have for the U.S. economy.

THE BASIS FOR REPARATIONS

Although modern history offers examples of war reparations, World War II witnessed a reversal of this type of retributional justice. The victorious United States *dispensed* rather than exacted substantial goods and services. Perhaps the disastrous effects of the heavy reparational demands on Germany after World War I contributed to this 180 degree reversal. Indeed, the principal use of the term *reparations* after World War II centered around claims made on the Federal Republic of Germany by the state of Israel. The operative agreement reads in part:

> Whereas unspeakable criminal acts were perpetrated against the Jewish people during the National Socialist regime of terror. And whereas by a declaration in the Bundestag on 27th of September 1951, the Government of the Federal Republic of Germany made known their determination to make good the material damage. And whereas the State of Israel has assumed the heavy burden of resettling so great a number of uprooted and destitute Jewish refugees from Germany and from territories formerly under German rule and has on this basis advanced a claim against the Federal Republic of Germany for global recompense for the cost of the integration of these refugees . . .

The indemnification agreed to was about $821 million. In addition, Germany was to make certain commodities and services available to Israel.

In the United States, a federal act (of August 13, 1946, Ch. 959, Sec. 1, 60 Stat. 1049) set up an Indian Claims Commission with jurisdiction to hear and resolve claims arising from seizure of Indian property and breaches by the United States of treaties with Indian tribes and nations. Since passage, there has been interest, within and without government, to consider restitution or indemnification for a portion of land taken.

In contrast, slaves "had no rights which the white man was bound to respect." No action was taken at emancipation to provide for retroactive claims by freedmen. Rather, 4 million illiterate, unorganized ex-slaves were precipitously set adrift in a war-ravaged and economically battered region. It was an area already engulfed in hostility, and it was inevitable that they would be heavily dependent for survival on the same repressive forces that had previously held them in bondage. No effort was made at restitution, nor was an effort extended to make the minimal capital investment that could have enabled them to win an equitable place in society. As Gunnar Myrdal observed, "An economic reconstruction of the South which would have succeeded in opening the road to economic independence for the ex slaves would have had to include, besides Emancipation, suffrage and full civil liberties: rapid education of the freedmen, abandonment of discrimination, land reform."

During the century following emancipation, little effort was made to rectify these failures. The 1963 centennial anniversary of the Emancipation Proclamation found the economic status of Afro-Americans, though dramatically improved from a century earlier, nevertheless so seriously lagging behind that of white Americans as to constitute an ominous and growing threat to the security of the society. The 1960s witnessed the first sustained effort to address the issues of black suffrage and civil liberties, of education and racial discrimination. However, the land reform that Myrdal referred to, and that can be interpreted as a proxy for a redistribution of wealth, has not yet been seriously confronted with respect to the ex-slaves and their descendants. It is this deficiency above all which the reparations concept would address.

Although the claims of Native Americans are unique, there is also a powerful "specialness" to the black claim for reparations. It derives from the distinctiveness of the black role in society. Alone of all the immigrants, the African came involuntarily. All other immigrants came to improve their lives. But enslavement was a boon to the American economy without which it seems unlikely that the United States would have emerged as the preeminent industrial power of the twentieth century. Throughout most of the nineteenth century, labor was the vital factor of production. Labor scarcity impeded economic development. Slave labor not only removed this scarcity, but also made possible the development of the industry that spurred economic growth.

Although cotton is generally credited as the basis for the South's economy, it was a major contributor to the North's growth as well. The South's cotton, largely exported in the early years, emerged as the vital element in the industrialization of New England. By 1860 cotton manufactures ranked first in value added and second in total employment. For much of the century, cotton sustained the economy and slave labor was the sine qua non of the cotton economy. Black labor then provided perhaps the integral input into America's first industrial mainstay and, thus, indirectly made possible its transformation from an agricultural to an industrial economy.

African slaves also proved useful in a full range of skills. Their role in railroad building, which Walter Rostow in the *Stages of Economic Growth* identifies as the leading sector in development from 1840 to 1860, was substantial. The Southern Pacific Railroad, for example, was largely constructed with slave labor. Indeed, by the 1850s, growing pressure to reopen the slave trade stemmed from the South's wish to industrialize using slave labor. Robert S. Starobin (1970) has documented the broad use of slave labor in Southern industry and in the building of the infrastructure, as well as by state and federal agencies. Any effort to assess the contribution of slaves to the economy at the time (and to present economic shares) must conclude that the United States' emergence as an industrial nation was possible only because of the massive input provided by slave labor at a time when labor was the scarce factor in the production function.

COMPUTING THE CLAIM

There has been growing interest in the economics of slavery. To earlier interest in whether slavery was profitable to owners or to the South generally has been added an interest in measuring its impact on the total economy and its effects on the economic position of slaves and their descendants, and of direct and indirect beneficiaries and their descendants as a class. One interesting approach, for example, is James Marketti's in Chapter 7 of this volume. He uses capital theory and historical data on slave population and prices to estimate the present value of the benefits of slavery. He computes the income stream that slaves produced and the compound interest on this income to the present. In his chapter slave prices serve as proxies for the "present value of the exploited net income stream" returned on slave capital at several points during 1790 to 1860. Then he derives an implicit net income flow, on which he compounds interest. By refining crude decennial census figures to allow for variable income-generating capacities among slaves, Marketti estimates the current, compounded value of labor exploited. His estimates range from $2.1 to $4.7 trillion in current dollars. His lower estimate was based on compound interest at a 5 percent pre-emancipation rate of return and a 4 percent postemancipation rate of return. The higher estimate used 6 percent pre- and 3 percent postemancipation. The 3 percent rate approximates GNP growth between 1869 and 1967. A case could, of course, be made for using the prime rate of interest instead, which averaged over 4 percent during this period and would have yielded a higher estimate.

Another approach would be to estimate the income flow due slaves based on pre-emancipation wage rates for labor comparable to the slaves' work and, after deducting for maintenance costs, to find the value of this aggregate wage bill presently. Such an approach might produce lower estimates than Marketti's.

Alfred H. Conrad and John R. Meyer (1958) demonstrated that the value of the slave system to owners depended both on returns derived from breeding as well as from labor output. Marketti's method would capture those values by using slave prices, whereas the alternative procedure would include no specific allowance for income from breeding. We should note here the objection that is frequently made in these matters: namely, that these estimates take no account of the loss of freedom from the slaves' perspective. If the estimates used prices that considered what slaves might have been willing to pay for their freedom, instead of merely market prices, the estimates might turn out to be higher.

Implicit in the restitution concept is not only the unpaid wage bill from slavery but also the underpayment of the freedmen and their descendants since emancipation. This estimate is more complicated because at least three practices contributed (as Chapter 11 noted).

1. Lower pay for identical work
2. Exclusion from jobs for which they were qualified
3. Exclusion from jobs because they lacked the necessary qualifications

To arrive at a crude estimate of the cost to black people of discrimination, we could compile the annual per capita earned income differential between black and white over the period 1863–1988 and then find the sum of those differentials at a conservative rate of interest. This procedure, by not distinguishing among several causes for the lower black income, would raise the obvious objection that the former slaves had lower productivity than whites, were less educated, were concentrated in low-wage areas and occupations, and, for other reasons, could not be expected to deserve pay comparable to whites. The objection may have merit for the first generation of freed slaves, but looses force thereafter. If they had been provided facilities to bring themselves into competitive equality, they would surely have done so. The record shows many examples of black individuals who had a white sponsor and who acquired education, property, and status.

On closer examination, even the first generation was entitled to income parity. Gary Becker, Theodore W. Schultz, and others have demonstrated the generous returns from investment in human capital. It might smack of double-counting to estimate both unpaid wages up to emancipation and then to assume instant equality the day following, thereby ignoring the need for a period for the investment in human capital to ripen. But investment in human capital before the Civil War was largely informal, requiring little funds. Slaves were generally prohibited by law from learning to read, so the constraint on their literacy was not a monetary but a legislative one. Hence, it is not double-counting, and a compensatory payment to equalize black and white incomes retroactive to emancipation would equitably counteract the handicaps on freedmen from:

1. Policies that prevented them from a virtually costless investment in themselves
2. Policies that denied them the resources to remedy this deficiency after emancipation
3. Discriminatory treatment of black workers even when their productivity was equal to that of whites

Another handicap which the foregoing estimates do not include arose from the slaves' legal exclusion from acquiring millions of acres that were made available at low prices to settlers and that provided the basis for much white nonwage income. The frontier was virtually closed by emancipation, and in the following decades real and intangible values were capitalized into real estate prices. Thus, the opportunity to share equitably in the ownership of natural resources has been lost unless extremely high cash payments or radical land reforms are used to undo this inequity. This inequity is reflected not only in the racial income differential, but also in wealth disparities.

A reparations formula, then, must encompass at least three elements:

1. Payment for unpaid slave labor before 1863
2. Payment for underpayment since 1863
3. Payment to compensate for denial of opportunity to acquire land and natural resources when they were widely available to white settlers and investors

The first and second elements, together with the interest compounded on them, would compensate for chronic nonpayment and underpayment for labor and for the stock of income earning capital that would have been accumulated over the years had labor been compensated at market prices and had opportunities been provided for investment in the human resources comparable to opportunities available to whites. The third element would compensate for one specific advantage available to early immigrants but from which blacks were specifically excluded.

It should be pointed out again that the reparations concept focuses on compensation to cover costs bequeathed by slavery to persons who are now alive. The objective is to restore the black community to the economic position it would have had if it had not been subjected to slavery and discrimination. No effort is made to compensate for costs borne by slaves in reduced consumption, loss of freedom, brutality, and so on.

IMPLEMENTING REPARATIONS

What are the policy implications of all this? How should the payments be made? The range of possibilities is reflected in the following:

1. A per capita cash payment to each African American on a designated date, based on a pro rata share of the finally agreed on reparations debt

2. Investment of the reparations payments in income-earning assets, with the income allocated annually on a per capita basis

3. Use of the payment to fund massive government-sponsored programs to raise educational and skill levels, provide housing, and generally improve overall economic status

4. A collective payment to the "community" to create conditions necessary for "takeoff" in the Rostovian sense

The list is not exhaustive. Opportunities exist for variations on these proposals as well as for totally different concepts. Some of the proposals have already been at least partially adopted but without the explicit reparations rationale. Proposal 3, for example, suggests the 1960s poverty programs as well as various Freedom Budgets offered in those days, although the sums were well shy of the range envisioned in these reparations estimates.

IMPACT OF THESE PROPOSALS ON THE ECONOMY

The internal capital transfers suggested in these proposals involve no loss of resources to the economy, but rather a redistribution away from heretofore favored classes. To the extent that it is necessary to disguise the redistributive effects, reparations would likely have inflationary effects. If we face the issue squarely, however, and agree to pay through taxation, budgets, and measures amounting to land reform or a kind of democratically agreed to expropriation, then an internal capital transfer need not seriously affect the state of the economy negatively at all. Indeed, to the extent that there are macroeconomic effects they may well be positive.

REFERENCES

America, Richard F. "A New Rationale for Income Redistribution." *Review of Black Political Economy* (Winter 1972).

Becker, Gary S. "Investments in Human Capital: A Theoretical Analysis." *Journal of Political Economy*, Supplement 70 (October 1962): 9–49.

Collins, Daisy. "The United States Owes Reparations to Its Black Citizens." *Howard Law Journal* 16 (Fall 1970): 82–114.

Conrad, Alfred H., and Meyer, John R. "The Economics of Slavery in the Ante Bellum South." *Journal of Political Economy* 66 (April 1958): 95–130.

Hughes, Graham. "Reparations for Blacks?" *New York University Law Review* 43 (December 1968): 1063–74.

Main, Brian. "Toward the Measurement of Historic Data." *Review of Black Political Economy* (Winter 1972).

Moes, J. "The Economics of Slavery in the Ante Bellum South; Another Comment." *Journal of Political Economy* 68 (April 1960): 183–87.

Myrdal, Gunnar. *An American Dilemma*. New York: Harper, 1944.

Schultz, Theodore W. "Investment in Human Capital." *American Economic Review* 51 (March 1961): 1–17.

Starobin, Robert S. *Industrial Slavery in the Old South*. New York: Oxford University Press, 1970.

State of Israel Documents relating to the agreement between the government of Israel and the government of the Federal Republic of Germany, signed on September 10, 1952, at Luxembourg. Published by the Government Printer, for the Ministry of Foreign Affairs, Hakirya, 1953.

Thurow, Lester C. *Poverty and Discrimination*. Washington, D.C.: Brookings Institution, 1969.

16.

Conclusions

Discussion of race-related public and corporate policy problems seems to have lost a constructive focus. Liberals and conservatives, blacks and whites, seem about equally at a loss for ideas. But many vexing problems remain.

It has been asserted that race has declined in significance, and in some social and professional worlds that is so. But the central policy issues that are race related involve redistributing scarce resources, and those issues remain important and unresolved. Moreover, they are still inadequately understood.

We may be avoiding facing some obvious consequences of our economic history. We are not accustomed to talking directly, objectively, and practically about economic injustice and exploitation, but our social and economic problems currently derive in part from patterns of past injustices. Economic injustice, in this case racial discrimination in employment, education, housing, and business development appears to produce benefits to large classes of beneficiaries. This process occurs directly and indirectly, but we have not understood it. They benefit by having a stream of income diverted to them that would have flowed to other recipients if instead of racially exclusionary practices there had been fair competition and fair investment in education and training.

Socially, important pockets of distress apparently exist in which there are unarticulated grievances based on a sense of economic injustice. If this is indeed so, it may help to explain some economic dysfunction. If people feel that economic arrangements are unfair and that they are victims of gross historic injustice, they may perform suboptimally and behave antisocially and self-destructively. If their resentments are well founded, we should try to understand them and make remedies available. If there is such an injustice, and if it is possible to measure it in a way that can remove the doubts, both technical and philosophical about the resulting estimates, then we should do that. Information on this problem can be gradually refined, and it can help steer policy debate and formulation in more useful directions. This volume has been a first step in that direction. Economic health and efficiency require that we try to moderate whatever tendencies exist toward injustice in economic life.

What portion, if any, of the income and wealth presently enjoyed by the upper income and wealth classes derives from those injustices? If that amount can be satisfactorily determined, then are there practical redistributive remedies? This project began with an assumption that measurement would contribute to correction. As time goes on, better technique will provide better, more reliable, and more illuminating numbers and clearer policy guidance.

Over the past twenty years, policy analysis on domestic issues has been stifled by a kind of taboo surrounding the word "exploitation." The broad center of political and policy debate never utters the word. We pretend there is no such thing, and we therefore consign it to the fringes, the extreme ideologues. This avoidance should stop, and this volume is intended to help accelerate that change. It presents disparate views on the notion of current benefits from past exploitation. Attention to what happens to the fruits of exploitation may help minimize the practice in the first place, as well as correct its adverse consequences, heretofore unrecognized.

Obviously, the questions addressed here require that we stretch ourselves both technically and conceptually. The contributors to this book do not agree on the central questions of whether real current unjust enrichments result from the historical discriminatory market process. Nor do they agree on technical approaches to estimation. At this stage of interest, however, they achieve the primary purpose: They outline the technical and philosophical obstacles to understanding. Taken as a whole, they may open a window of analytical and policy opportunity.

The concept of social debt (or reparations or restitution) may help us organize our thinking more effectively. We often hear how leaders are "grasping for ideas." Often this really refers to political leaders' fear of redistributive issues, especially if a racial dimension exists. The reparations concept may offer a basis for overcoming those fears. If the idea of restitution, and the associated estimates can be refined through further work and can stand scrutiny, the time may come when policy debate will be incomplete and defective without reference to this concept. Economic policy should be framed around overriding principles. We consider preservation of market processes, competition, and private property among such principles. Some day we may add the recognition and remedy of exploitation and social debts to that body of principles.

Selected Bibliography

Aitken, Hugh G. *Did Slavery Pay?* New York: John Wiley & Sons, 1971.

America, Richard F. *Developing the Afro-American Economy.* Lexington, Mass.: D. C. Heath, 1977.

Amin, S. *Unequal Development.* New York: Monthly Review Press, 1977.

Auletta, Ken. *The Underclass.* New York: Vintage, 1983.

Becker, Gary S. *Human Capital.* New York: Columbia University Press, 1964.

————. *The Economics of Discrimination,* 2d ed. Chicago: University of Chicago Press, 1971.

Boston, Thomas D. *Races, Class and Conservatism.* Boston, Mass.: Unwin-Hyman, 1988.

Bowser, Benjamin R., and Hunt, Raymond G., eds. *Impacts of Racism on White America.* Beverly Hills, Calif.: Sage, 1981.

Campbell, Colin D., ed. *Income Distribution.* Washington, D.C.: American Enterprise Institute, 1977.

Conrad, Alfred H., and Meyer, John R. *The Economics of Slavery.* Chicago: Aldine Publishing Co., 1964.

Cox, Oliver. *Caste, Class, and Race.* New York: Monthly Review Press, 1970.

David, Paul A., et al. *Reckoning with Slavery.* New York: Oxford University Press, 1976.

Davis, David Brion. *Slavery and Human Progress.* New York: Oxford University Press, 1984.

Davis, Lance E., and North, Douglas C. *Institutional Change and American Economic Growth.* New York: Cambridge University Press, 1971.

Engerman, Stanley L., and Genovese, Eugene E., eds. *Race and Slavery in the Western Hemisphere.* Princeton, N.J.: Princeton University Press, 1975.

Fogel, Robert William, and Engerman, Stanley L. *Time on the Cross.* 2 vols. Boston: Little, Brown, 1974.

Fredrickson, George M. *White Supremacy*. New York: Oxford University Press, 1981.

Glascow, Douglas G. *The Black Underclass*. New York: Vintage, 1981.

Glazer, Nathan. *Affirmative Discrimination: Ethnic Inequality and Public Policy*. New York: Basic Books, 1978.

Goldman, Alan H. *Justice and Reverse Discrimination*. Princeton, N.J.: Princeton University Press, 1979.

Gross, Barry R., ed. *Reverse Discrimination*. Buffalo, N.Y.: Prometheus, 1977.

Higgs, Robert. *Competition and Coercion: Blacks in the American Economy, 1865–1914*. Cambridge, Eng.: Cambridge University Press, 1977.

Hochschild, Jennifer L. *What's Fair?: American Beliefs About Distributive Justice*. Cambridge, Mass.: Harvard University Press, 1981.

Lee, Susan P., and Passell, Peter. *A New Economic View of American History*. New York: W. W. Norton, 1979.

Litwack, Leon F. *Been in the Storm So Long*. New York: Alfred A. Knopf, 1976.

Mandle, Jay R. *The Roots of Black Poverty: The Southern Plantation Economy After the Civil War*. Durham, N.C.: Duke University Press, 1978.

Marable, Manning. *How Capitalism Underdeveloped Black America*. Boston: South End Press, 1983.

Pascal, Anthony, ed. *Racial Discrimination in Economic Life*. Lexington, Mass.: D. C. Heath, 1972.

Pleck, Elizabeth. *Black Migration and Poverty*. New York: Academic Press, 1979.

Rae, Douglas. *Equalities*. Cambridge, Mass.: Harvard University Press, 1981.

Ransom, Roger L., and Sutch, Richard. *One Kind of Freedom: The Economic Consequences of Emancipation*. Cambridge, Eng.: Cambridge University Press, 1977.

Reich, Michael. *Racial Inequality*. Princeton, N.J.: Princeton University Press, 1981.

Schiller, Bradley R. *The Economics of Poverty and Discrimination*. Englewood Cliffs, N.J.: Prentice-Hall, 1980.

Schuchter, Arnold. *Reparations*. Philadelphia: Lippincott, 1970.

Starobin, Robert S. *Industrial Slavery in the Old South*. New York: Oxford University Press, 1970.

Stasz, Clarice. *The American Nightmare: Why Inequality Persists*. New York: Schocken Books, 1981.

Thurow, Lester C. *Poverty and Discrimination*. Washington, D.C.: Brookings Institution, 1969.

————. *Generating Inequality*. New York: Basic Books, 1975.

Webb, John. *Capital and Exploitation*. Princeton, N.J.: Princeton University Press, 1981.

Wright, Gavin. *The Political Economy of the Cotton South: Households, Markets, and Wealth in the Nineteenth Century*. New York: W. W. Norton, 1978.

Index

About the Editor and Contributors

RICHARD F. AMERICA is a policy analyst in Washington, D.C. He has worked as a Development Economist at Stanford Research Institute and lectured at the Stanford Business School and at the University of California, Berkeley. He is co-author of *Moving Ahead: Black Managers in American Business* and author of *Developing the Afro-American Economy*. He has written numerous articles for *Harvard Business Review*, *The Bankers Magazine*, the *Journal of Economic Issues* and other journals.

SHERYL BAILEY-WILLIAMS is Founder and President of S. D. Bailey & Associates, Inc., a management consulting and market research firm. She served formerly on the faculties of The College of William & Mary, Old Dominion University, and Hampton University. Bailey-Williams has also worked as a Visiting Economist at the Board of Governors of the Federal Reserve System and has been a consultant to numerous businesses on both the East and West Coasts. Her research interests include competitive strategy, consumer behavior, and strategic marketing.

ROBERT S. BROWNE is currently the Staff Director of the Subcommittee on International Development, Finance, Trade and Monetary Policy of the House Committee on Banking, Finance and Urban Affairs. He was previously Executive Director at the African Development Fund, where he represented the United States, the United Kingdom, and Yugoslavia. He has served on the faculties of Howard, Fairleigh-Dickinson, and Dillard universities. For the decade of the seventies he headed the Black Economic Research Center, and he was founder and first editor of the *Review of Black Political Economy*. He coauthored *The Lagos Plan vs. the Berg Report* and has published numerous articles on domestic and international economic issues.

LYNN C. BURBRIDGE is Associate Director of the Center for Research on Women at Wellesley College. She has been Senior Associate at the Urban Institute and Research Associate at the Joint Center for Political Studies. She has published on employment and training, labor and welfare policy.

SHELDON DANZIGER is Professor of Social Work and Public Policy and Faculty Associate at the Population Studies Center at the University of Michigan. Until July 1988, he was Director of the Institute for Research on Poverty, Professor of Social Work, and Romnes Faculty Fellow at the University of Wisconsin-Madison. Danziger is a member of the Committee on Child Development Research and Public Policy, National Research Council, and the Social Science Research Council Committee for Research on the Urban Underclass. He is the coeditor of *Fighting Poverty: What Works and What Doesn't* (1986), *The Distributional Impacts of Public Policies* (1988), *State Policy Choices: The Wisconsin Experience* (1988), and the author of numerous scholarly articles on poverty, income inequality, and social welfare programs and policies. He is currently working on a book, *Macroeconomic Conditions, Public Policy and Poverty*.

WILLIAM DARITY, JR., is Professor of Economics at the University of North Carolina at Chapel Hill. During the 1989–90 academic year he has been a fellow at the National Humanities Center. He has published more than sixty articles and book reviews, including papers in the *American Economic Review*, *Southern Economic Journal*, *Journal of Economic History*, *Journal of Macroeconomics*, and the *Journal of Development Economics*. His most recent books include *The Loan Pushers*, coauthored with Bobbie L. Horn, and *The Question of Discrimination*, coedited with Steve Shulman.

STANLEY L. ENGERMAN is John H. Munro Professor of Economics and Professor of History at the University of Rochester. He is coauthor of *Time on the Cross: The Economics of American Negro Slavery* and coeditor of several books on slavery, emancipation, and American economic development.

SUSAN F. FEINER is an Associate Professor of Economics at Hampton University. Her research on the political economy of slavery has appeared in the *Journal of Economic History* and *Rethinking Marxism*. Her research on the textbook treatment of race and gender has appeared in the *Journal of Economic Education* and *Gender & Society*. She chairs the Committee for Race and Gender Balance in the Economics Curriculum and, with Bruce Roberts, is currently coediting a volume titled *Radical Economics*.

LOWELL GALLAWAY is Distinguished Professor of Economics and Faculty Associate of the Contemporary History Institute at Ohio University. His books include *Poverty in America* and *Manpower Economics*. He is also coauthor of *Poverty, Income Distribution, the Family and Public Policy*, a study for the Joint Economic Committee of Congress. His articles and essays have been concerned with topics such as poverty, labor mobility, immigration, the economics of slavery, taxation, and macroeconomic topics.

PETER GOTTSCHALK is Professor of Economics at Boston College and Research Affiliate at the Institute for Research on Poverty, University of Wisconsin-Madison. He has written numerous articles on poverty, income inequality, and welfare dynamics. He is currently writing a book with Sheldon Danziger on the causes of changes in poverty during the 1980s.

DAVID C. KLINGAMAN is Professor of Economics at Ohio University. His principal writing has been in the area of American economic history. He is coeditor with Richard Vedder of *Essays in Nineteenth Century Economic History* and *Essays on the Economy of the Old Northwest*.

JAMES MARKETTI is the Grievance Administrator at the Rutgers University Council of American Association of University Professors Chapters. Since leaving the University of Wisconsin in 1969, he has been a labor union activist at many levels of engagement: rank-and-file coal miner, driver, shop steward, local officer, teamster business agent, and organizer for the International Union of United Mine Workers of America.

STANLEY H. MASTERS is Professor of Economics and Chair of the economics department at the State University of New York, Binghamton. His books include *Black-White Income Differentials*. His main field of interest is labor economics, especially topics related to discrimination and poverty.

LARRY NEAL is Professor of Economics at the University of Illinois, Urbana-Champaign and Editor of *Explorations in Economic History* since 1982. Neal is author of *The Rise of Financial Capitalism* (1990) dealing with international capital markets in the eighteenth century and many articles on American and European economic history. He continues research on the functioning of international capital markets in the nineteenth century.

ROGER L. RANSOM is Professor of History, University of California, Riverside. He and Richard Sutch wrote *One Kind of Freedom*. He is the author of *Coping with Capitalism, The Academic Scribblers*, and other books and articles.

BRUCE B. ROBERTS is an Associate Professor of Economics at The College of William & Mary. His published articles concern principally the theory of value and distribution and the history of economic thought. He serves on the editorial board of the journal *Rethinking Marxism* and is currently editing a volume titled *Radical Economics*, an assessment of current debates in the field.

RICHARD SUTCH is Professor of Economics, Professor of History, and Director of the Institute of Business and Economics at the University of California, Berkeley. He received the Distinguished Teaching Award of the University in 1980 and was a Guggenheim Fellow in 1984–85. He is a Research Associate of the National Bureau of Economic Research. He is an Associate Editor of *Research in Economic History* and has served on the editorial boards of the *Journal of Economic History* and *Explorations in Economic History*. He is a Trustee of the Cliometrics Society and President of the Economic History Association. He is the coauthor of *Reckoning with Slavery: A Critical Study in the Quantitative History of American Negro Slavery*, with Paul A. David, Herbert G. Gutman, Peter Temin, and Gavin Wright (1976), and *One Kind of Freedom: The Economic Consequences of Emancipation*, with Roger L. Ransom (1977). He has had numerous articles published in scholarly journals.

DAVID H. SWINTON is Dean of the School of Business at Jackson State University and has written for national publications, including the National Urban League's *The State of Black America* and the *Urban League Review*. Swinton has held positions as Director, Southern Center for Studies in Public Policy at Clark College; Assistant Director for Research, Black Economic Research Center; and as Senior Research Associate and Director of Minorities and Social Policy Programs at the Urban Institute. He has also served as a Teaching Fellow at Harvard and a Lecturer at City College of New York.

RICHARD VEDDER is Distinguished Professor of Economics and Faculty Associate of the Institute of Contemporary History at Ohio University. He has authored or coedited five books and monographs, including *The American Economy in Historical Perspective*. His articles dealing with American labor in historical perspective have appeared in the *Journal of Economic History*, *Explorations in Economic History*, *Agricultural History*, *Business History Review*, *Research in Economic History*, as well as general economics journals.

WARREN C. WHATLEY is an Associate Professor of Economics at the University of Michigan. He has been a Visiting Professor at the University of North Carolina at Chapel Hill, a Ford Foundation Fellow, and a Rockefeller Fellow. He is co-director of the NSF-sponsored project entitled "Black Workers and Northern Industries before 1950" (with Gavin Wright). His research has dealt primarily with the economics of race, labor markets, and institutions in the rural South and industrial North in the twentieth century. His latest article is "Getting a Foot in the Door: 'Learning,' State Dependence and the Racial Integration of Firms," in the *Journal of Economic History*.

GAVIN WRIGHT is Professor of Economics, Stanford University. He is the author of two books on the economic history of the U.S. South: *The Political Economy of the Cotton South* (1978) and *Old South New South: Revolutions in the Southern Economy Since the Civil War* (1986). He is presently at work, in collaboration with Warren C. Whatley on a study of black workers in Northern labor markets, 1900 to 1950.